Book of Marks

on Antiques & Collectibles

Compiled by
Peter and Barbara Sutton-Smith

Fitzhenry & Whiteside

Unitt's Book of Marks on Antiques & Collectables Copyright
© 2008 Fitzhenry & Whiteside Ltd.

All rights reserved. No part of this book may be reproduced in any manner without the express written consent of the publisher, except in the case of brief excerpts in critical reviews and articles. All inquiries should be addressed to:

Fitzhenry and Whiteside Limited
195 Allstate Parkway
Markham, Ontario L3R 4T8

In the United States:
311 Washington Street,
Brighton, Massachusetts 02135

www.fitzhenry.ca   godwit@fitzhenry.ca

Fitzhenry & Whiteside acknowledges with thanks the Canada Council for the Arts, and the Ontario Arts Council for their support of our publishing program. We acknowledge the financial support of the Government of Canada through the Book Publishing Industry Development Program (BPIDP) for our publishing activities.

Canada Council   Conseil des Arts
for the Arts   du Canada

Library and Archives Canada Cataloguing in Publication

Sutton-Smith, Peter
Unitt's book of marks on antiques & collectables / compiled by Peter Sutton-Smith. — New & enl. ed. with added categories

Includes index.
ISBN 1-55041-866-1

1. Hallmarks. 2. Pottery—Marks. 3. Glassware—Trade marks.
I. Title. II. Title: Book of marks on antiques & collectables.

NK1125.U48 2004   745.1'02'78   C2004-906991-8

Cover and interior design by J & S Graphic Design
Printed and bound in Canada

1 3 5 7 9 10 8 6 4 2

Contents

4 INTRODUCTION

5 SILVER
- Canadian Silver and Silver Plate Marks ... 6
- Silver Standards and Marks ... 69
- George V and Queen Mary Silver Jubilee 1935 ... 74
- Georg Jensen ... 89
- Bibliography - Silver ... 92

93 DOLLS
- Bibliography - Dolls ... 111

112 GLASS
- Art Glass ... 117
- Bohemian Glass ... 120
- Cameo Glass ... 122
- French Marks ... 122
- English Marks (late 19th century) ... 124
- Carnival Glass ... 124
- Mary Gregory ... 126
- Cut Glass Manufacturers ... 131
- Canadian Factories ... 136
- Trade Marks on Glass ... 141
- Bibliography - Glass ... 173

174 CERAMICS, CHINA, PORCELAIN, and POTTERY
- Style of Marks ... 175
- Dating Clues ... 176
- Glossary - Ceramics ... 177
- Marks - Ceramics ... 181
- Bohemian Porcelain ... 189
- Manufacturers - "Dresden" ... 206
- Foreign Backstamps ... 207
- Importer's Marks ... 218
- Bibliography - Ceramics ... 286

287 MAJOLICA

292 CANADIAN POTTERS

303 AMERICAN POTTERS

319 BRITISH DESIGNED ART and STUDIO POTTERY

324 THE POTTER'S ART IN CHINA
- Principal Periods of Chinese Art ... 326
- Period Marks ... 327
- Periods Classified by Dynasties and Emperors ... 329
- Seal Characters ... 330

331 THE BRITISH REGISTRY MARK
- British Monarchy Accession and Coronation dates ... 334

335 U.S. PATENT NUMBER REFERENCE TABLE

336 INDEX
- Ceramics ... 336
- Dolls ... 341
- Glass ... 342
- Silver ... 346

Introduction

Unitt's Book of Marks on Antiques and Collectibles was first published in August 1973.

Since then there has been several revisions and reprintings, this one being the fourth expanded and enlarged edition and the 13th printing.

Throughout the 28 years, Unitt's Book of Marks has fulfilled the expectation that it would prove useful and informative. But as the population of Canada has become progressively more cosmopolitan, so have the collecting choices of its people, hence several categories have been broadened to include marks from overseas hither to not familiar in this country.

We trust therefore that this latest endeavour will continue to meet the current needs of our readers.

Manufacturers names normally run alphabetically but on occasion a better recognized trade name is used, causing the alphabetical order to appear irregular. Please refer to the Index for further help and guidance.

We gratefully acknowledge the assistance of Collin O'Leary who corrected and updated the silver section of this revised edition.

Collin is manager of Donohue and Bousquet, Antique Silver Specialists in Ottawa.

Peter & Barbara Sutton-Smith are the editors of the canadian Handbook of Pressed Glass, Unitt's Canadian Price Guide to Antiques & Collectables Book 16 & 17, Unitt's Identification & Price Guide to Home & Country Collectables, and have been full-time antique dealers for over 30 years. Both have held the position of Editorial Director of Antique Showcase, Canada's only national antiques magazine, now in its 42nd year of publication. Peter also publishes the Antique Showcase Guide to the antique shops of Ontario and is the Vice-President of the Associated Antique Dealers of America.

The Sutton-Smiths are residents of Ontario.

Key to Silver Section Abbreviations

b = date of birth
d = date of death
b 1815 - 1875 - = known 1875 date of death unknown
- 1815 - d 1875 = known 1815 date of birth unknown
1785 - 1850 = known date of work
- 1785 - 1850 or 1785 - 1850 -
(dash before or after) = approximate date
information often gained from advertisements and/or property ownership records.

Silver

One of several trophies illustrated in the Toronto Silver Company Catalogue of 1888.

CANADIAN SILVER and SILVER PLATE MARKS

Arranged alphabetically in order of province, town, and maker's name.

NEW BRUNSWICK

FREDERICTON

SPAHNN, JUSTIN (b 1803 - 1856 -)
Born in Fredericton, established himself as working silversmith. Spahnn with Pseudo hallmarks used identical to those of Josiah Allen, Halifax, NS.

WOLHAUPTER, BENJAMIN (b 1800 - d 1857)
Refused a land grant in 1821, was granted Block 2 on Regent Street in 1826. Became Sheriff of Fredericton 1847. Gold and silversmith. Teaspoon on display Fredericton Museum.

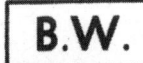

MILLTOWN

Y.S. & CO. (- 1815 -)
Table fork on display in Fredericton Museum.

SAINT JOHN

AGNEW, JAMES (- 1834 - 1850)
Situated on Dock Street. Lost business through fire 1837. Last heard of in Eastport, Maine. Understood to have disappeared whilst on a visit there in 1850.

BARRY, JOHN (b 1815 - 1875 -)
Working silversmith, purchased stock from John Munro. Situated on Germain Street, later on King and then Prince William Street 1865. Also used BARRY with Leopard Head and Anchor & Lion.

BOOTH, JOHN (- 1785 - 1813)

Working gold and silversmith from Scotland. Known to have repaired jewellery. Teaspoon with his mark on display in Fredericton Museum.

BROTHERS, WILLIAM (1785)

BURNS, JAMES (- 1813 - 1876)

From England, worked for a time in Halifax then settled in Saint John.

FAIRBANKS, WHITCOMB (1851 - 1876 -)

Dessert spoon on display at the Fredericton Museum.

W.F. with pseudo hallmarks

GARD, THOMAS DAPLETON (1856 - 1877)

Working silversmith situated at 25 Germain Street. Also used pseudo hallmarks similar to those of James Burns and John Barry. Moved 1860-65 to Worcester, Mass.

HARWOOD, ARTHUR (- 1871 - 1879)

Was successor to William Norris Venning when he retired in 1871.

HAY, A. & J. (kn 1839 - 1923)

Partnership of Albert Stephen Hay and John Hay. Albert in business on own account 1859-1869. Joined John Hay that year and continued in business as active partner until shortly before his death in 1923.

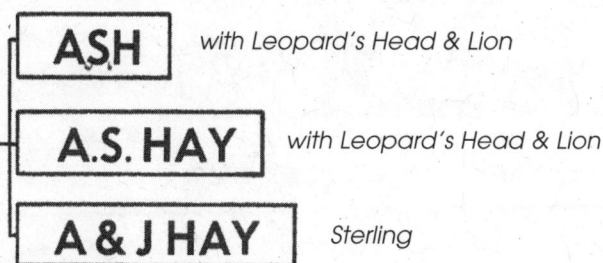

ASH	with Leopard's Head & Lion
A.S. HAY	with Leopard's Head & Lion
A & J HAY	Sterling

HERSEY, JOHN A. (1823 - 1830 -)

Working silversmith advertised extensively. Newcastle, NB.

| J.A.H |

HUTCHINSON, GEORGE G. (b 1825 - 1877 -)

Born in Saint John in 1825. In 1840 he entered the business with his father. Burnt out in the great fire of 1877.

| HUTCHINSON ST. JOHN N.B. |
| GH |

KERR & THORNE (- 1870 - 1886)

The late Senator W.H. Thorne refers to Kerr & Thorne as hardware merchants in an article written in 1917 for the magazine *Hardware & Metal*. The partnership was dissolved in 1885. Believed to have had silver made for them by Hendery & Leslie. Spoons found bearing their name Kerr & Thorne, also some with K&T.

KERR & THORNE

K.T

LORD, DANIEL (- 1840 - 1852 -)

Silversmith, pieces bearing his mark have been found in New Brunswick.

MELICK, JAMES GODFREY (b 1802 - d 1885)

Long established watchmaker, jeweller & silversmith. Prince William Street, 1845. Had premises in Market Square, 1828.

MUNRO, ALEX (b 1754 - d 1828)

Advertised extensively as working jeweller & silversmith. Also advertised engraving service. Bought old gold and silver.

MUNRO, JOHN (b 1791 - d 1874)

According to Professor Traquair the mark of John Munro was almost certainly "JM" "NB" in separate cartouches, with a lion passant, anchor and sovereign's head which might face either way. The marks shown may be those of James Munro, who was working in New Glasgow in the '60s.

PAGE BROS. (1850 - 1870)

Sons of Amos Page of Amherst, NS., Richard and Clement Page partners. When Clement retired in 1870 the firm became PAGE, SMALLEY & FERGUSON. Richard's son Henry Page, and Ferguson (brother-in-law of Richard and Clement) in business together with another silversmith, Smalley. Continued business till 1880, then Ferguson retired and name of firm again changed. This time it became FERGUSON & PAGE.

PAGE, SMALLEY & FERGUSON (1870 - 1880)

See remarks above.

THOMPSON, RICHARD (b 1809 - d 1890)

VENNING, J.H. (1850 - 1877)
Was an apprentice of John Munroe and became his successor. Silversmith and engraver. Mark small J.H.V. with lion.

VENNING, WILLIAM NORRIS (b 1795 - d 1877)
Silversmith and jeweller.

WARLOCK, DANIEL O'LEARY (b 1819 - d 1901)
Irish silversmith born in Killarney. Was situated on King Street, Saint John, 1858, corner of King and Charlotte 1880.

D.W. NB *with lion*

NOVA SCOTIA

AMHERST

PAGE, AMOS (b 1803 - d 1895)
Born August 4, 1803 in Onslow NS. Son of David Page and Jean Fraser Page, natives of Haverhill, Mass. Silversmith. Brothers David, John and Thomas all silversmiths. His brother Benjamin became a doctor with a practice in Truro. Listed in the 1864 Nova Scotia Directory. He and his brother Thomas were partners for a brief period. Died on December 4, 1895 in Amherst.

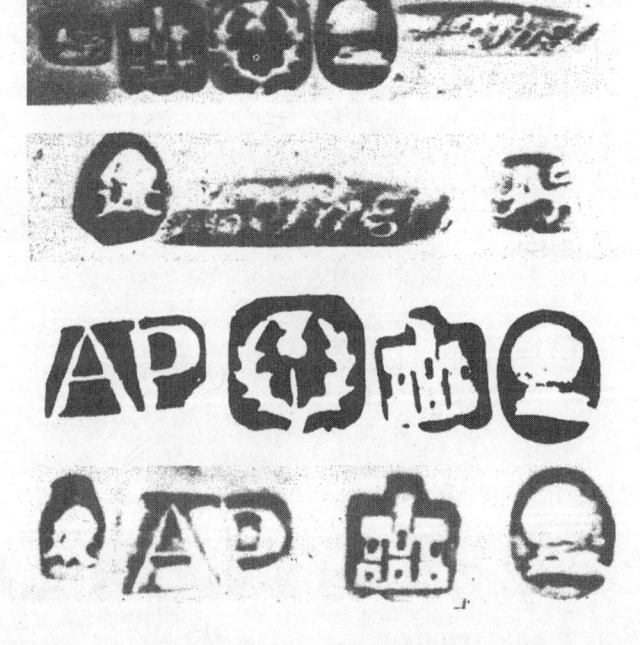

PAGE, THOMAS (b 1801 - d 1879)
Brother of Amos Page, known to have been a partner of Amos for brief period. Moved to Pugwash.

HALIFAX

ALLEN, JOSIAH (- 1753 -)
Was acquitted of counterfeiting silver coins in Halifax 1786. Occupation given as silversmith. Used pseudo hallmarks.

BAUME, GUSTAVE LA (- 1835 - d 1838)
Advertised himself as maker of silver and jewellery in the *Acadian Recorder* (1853). Address Granville Street, Halifax. His tools were auctioned by Deblois & Merkel, October 30, 1838. Gustave La Baume drowned September 30, 1838.

BECKER & CORNELIUS (1869 - 1870)
John Becker and Robert Cornelius partners at 81 Granville Street. Silversmiths and jewellers.

BENNETT, JOHN B. (- 1877 -)
65 Barrington Street.

BESSONETT, J.S.B. (1827 - 1837 -)
Believed to have been partner in BESSONETT & BROWN in 1834. November 1834 *Acadian Recorder*.

J.B. with pseudo hallmarks.

BLACK, WM. A. & S. (1812 - 1826)
William and Samuel advertised their business 1814 through 1826. Wm. A. was well known as the Hon. W.A. Black in the legislative council.

BLACK & PARKER (- 1809 -)
Recorded as Engravers; also advertised themselves as working silversmiths.

BLACK, PARKER & BLACK (1810 - 1812)
Halifax Chronicle of June 30, 1811 carried advertisement. Silversmiths. Manufacturing jewellers. Partnership dissolved in April, 1812.

BOLTON, THOMAS (- 1808 - d 1846)
With F. Meyer as partner. Firm known as Meyer & Bolton. Silversmiths and Jewellers.

BRAUN, F.B. (- 1857 - 1859 -)
46 Hollis Street.

BROWN, GEORGE STAIRS (b 1815 - d 1889)
Working silversmith, Halifax & Yarmouth.

BROWN, MICHAEL SEPTIMUS (b 1818 - d 1886)
Son of William Brown. Apprenticed to Peter Nordbeck. Established himself in business in 1840 at 3 Granville Street. Moved to 106-108 Granville. Did not marry, was succeeded by his nephew Thomas Brown whom he had taken as an apprentice in 1851. Also apprenticed to M.S. Brown, David Hudson, Whiston and Henry Wentworth Tully. Died November 28, 1886.

BROWN & CO., M.S. (1872 - 1919)
This was the name given to the firm by Thomas Brown when he succeeded to the business of his uncle Michael Septimus Brown in 1886.

BROWN, THOMAS (b 1837 - d 1920)
Nephew of Michael Septimus Brown. Established M.S. Brown & Co. which was taken over by William J. Stewart on the retirement of Thomas. In 1919 the business was in the hands of Col. I.W. Vidito who sold it to Henry Birks & Sons. Col. Isaac Vidito is listed as a director of Birks, Halifax, January 11, 1920 to May 1920.

BROWN, T. B. (- 1800 -)
Four marks ascribed. One having T.B. intertwined.

BUTLER, JAMES (b 1713 - d 1776)
Working silversmith. Was born in 1713 in Boston, Mass. Came to Halifax in 1750-52 with Jacob Hurd, after an appeal for rangers to combat hostile Indians by Gov. Edward Cornwallis. Died in Boston, Mass. in 1776.

CORNELIUS, JULIUS (b 1825 - d 1916)

Born July 4, 1825 in Prenzlau, Brandenburg, Prussia. Won prize for design at Berlin Art school. Served apprenticeship under manufacturing jeweller named Rhode. Travelled extensively. Worked for Tiffany & Co., NY between 1853-54. Settled in Halifax in 1855. Married in 1856 to his wife Henrietta Blackader of Pictou, her father was Henry Blackader, member of the Provincial Legislature. Store at 97 Barrington Street 1864, situated at 99 Granville Street during 1870 to 1878. He was one of the finest craftsmen in Canada. He and his highly trained workmen designed and made exquisite jewellery from Nova Scotia gold delicately set with precious gems. He applied his very special skill and artistic talent to the making of gold brooches with applied mayflowers and foliage — hairwork jewellery was made by him with meticulous care. Handed business over to Herman Cornelius in 1905 on retirement. Died September 20, 1916.

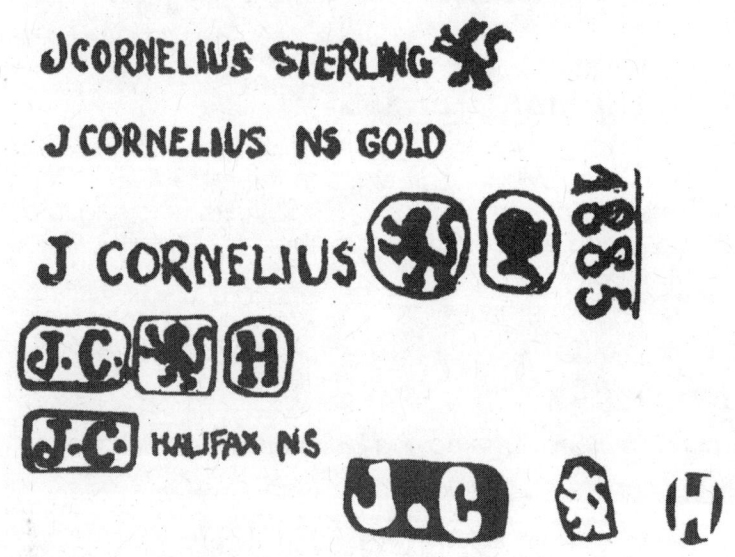

CORNELIUS & CO. (- 1905 -)

Herman Cornelius succeeded to his father's business and established the firm of Cornelius & Co.

CRAWFORD, WILLIAM (1816 - 1865)

1827-47 member of North British Society. 1831, advertised as silversmith and watchmaker. 1841, his advertisement says jeweller and watchmaker. 1863-64 situated at 153-5 Barrington Street.

ETTER, BENJAMIN (b 1763 - d 1827)

Born in Braintree (Quincy) Mass. Apprenticed in Berne, Switzerland. 1783 arrived in Halifax. 1787 took over store of Peter Etter (brother). 1813 business taken over by son-in-law Thomas Hosterman and B.B. Etter (son). During the interim period he had James Tidmarsh (1789-1799), then Thomas Hosterman (1806-1813) as partners. He died on September 28, 1827.

ETTER, B. B. (- 1813 - d 1838)

Son of Benjamin Etter. 1813 was partner of Thomas Hosterman. 1815 the partnershp dissolved. 1816 situated at 26 George Street. He died on April 21, 1823 at Margaret, Cape Breton.

GRIGG, WILLIAM (1765 - 1797)

1765 worked in Albany, NY. Advertised in *Nova Scotia Gazette* September 30, 1783. Believed to have arrived in Halifax around 1787. Returned to New York in 1796 and died the following year in 1797. Serving spoon with his mark on display at the Nova Scotia Museum in Halifax.

HALL, GEORGE A. (- 1830 - 1831 -)

Situated at 6 Granville Street. Advertisement *Acadian Recorder*. Working silversmith. Sugar tongs bearing mark on display at the Nova Scotia Museum in Halifax.

HAMMAN, THOMAS (- 1793 - 1798 -)

Sugar tongs bright cut on display at the Nova Scotia Museum in Halifax.

HOSTERMAN & PARKER (- 1813 -)
Partnership dissolved December 11, 1813. Hosterman joined B.B. Etter that year.

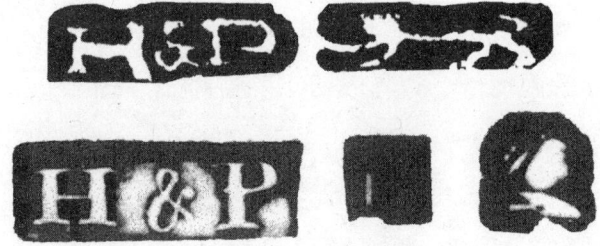

HOSTERMAN, THOMAS (b 1790 - d 1863 / w 1812 - 1820)
See B.B. Etter.

HULSMAN, LEWIS (- 1784 - d 1815)
Served apprenticeship in Europe. 1799 situated on Duke Street according to advertisement in *Royal Gazette* February 26. Death reported in *Acadian Recorder* December, 1815.

HUNT, WILLIAM (- 1806 - 1810 -)
Teaspoon on display at the Nova Scotia Museum in Halifax.

HURD, BENJAMIN (b 1739 -)
Church silver marked B. Hurd (name engraved) in collection of Church Silver, Public Archives, Halifax. Date inscribed on bowl October 25, 1769. He was the younger son of Jacob Hurd, brother of Nathaniel Hurd. Hurd family listed as American Silversmiths by G. S. C. Ensko. Nathaniel believed to have worked in Canada around 1777. It is possible some of the silver bearing the Hurd marks was brought into Canada by Loyalist families.

Mark of Jacob Hurd.

HURD, NATHANIEL (- 1777 -)
Teaspoon on display at the Nova Scotia Museum in Halifax. N Hurd in oblong or M. Hurd very small in cartouche.

JOHNSON, THOMAS CHARLES (1853 - 1923)

Apprenticed to John McCulloch. Working silversmith, situated at Duke and Barrington Streets. Two sons, Charles E. and Albert G. became partners in February 1890, firm became JOHNSON & SONS LTD., T. C., Silversmiths and Jewellers.

TCJ&S STERLING

T·C JOHNSON & SONS

[TCJ] [H]

T·C JOHNSON & SON · HALIFAX N.S.

LANGFORD, JAS. I. (b 1815 - d 1847)

Originally from London, 1841, entered into partnership with Franz F. Meyer whom he had trained. Gold and silversmiths. Died in Halifax on February 6, 1847. The business of Langford & Meyer was acquired by William James Veith and George Witham. VEITH & WITHAM advertised that they had taken over the business as of March 20, 1847. In 1848 the partnership dissolved.

NOTE: All silver marks are greatly enlarged - see below.

The actual mark.

Above: photographic enlargement. Below: artist's impression

MARSTERS, R.U. (b 1787 - d 1845)

Teaspoon on display at the Nova Scotia Museum in Halifax. Also made medals and insignia for militia.

| R·U·MARSTERS | + LION

MCCULLOCH, JOHN (b 1821 - d 1875)

Originally from Scotland. Learned his skill from Peter Nordbeck. Started business in 1844. Clockmaker, jeweller, silversmith. Made lovely jewellery in gold. Thomas C. Johnson one of his apprentices. Married Mary Jane Kerr in 1858. A prominent citizen, alderman, and school commissioner. Continued in business until death. Believed to have been connected with Arthur W. Carten of Liverpool, N.S.

MCDONALD, DANIEL (- 1817 - 1828)

Dissolved partnership with David Ross June 5, 1822. Working Silversmith.

MELROSE. GEORGE (- 1837 - 1838 -)

Teaspoon on display at the Nova Scotia Museum in Halifax.

MEYER, FRANZ F. (b 1809 - d 1847)

1841, partner of Jas I. Langford, partnership dissolved in 1843, joined Thomas Bolton as partner. Died on December 11, 1847.

MIGNOWITZ, HENRY (- 1824 - 1835 -)

Situated at 234 Water Street, goldsmith, also importer of jewellery and silver gilt from England. Offered new silver in exchange for old gold and silver.

NEWMAN, WILLIAM HERMAN (b 1826 - d 1894)

1863, situated 92 Granville Street. 1873, corner of George and Granville. Working silversmith, clock and watchmaker, and jeweller. Made fine jewellery and Masonic jewels. Died in 1894. Business continued by son until 1905.

NORDBECK, PETER (b 1789 - d 1861)

1789, born in Germany, received his training there as gilder, jeweller, and silversmith. Known to have used the mark N.S. for Nova Scotia. 1815, was in the West Indies. 1819, situated at 40 Duke Street. Entered into partnership with Henry Mignowitz and a Mr. Clark, this partnership was dissolved in 1827. Established Nordbeck & Co. in that year. 1832, wife Caroline died at age 37. 1833, moved to 4 Granville Street. Michael Septimus Brown was apprenticed to Nordbeck. Married widow of Jas. I. Langford sometime after 1847. Had three daughters and a stepdaughter. Died 1861.

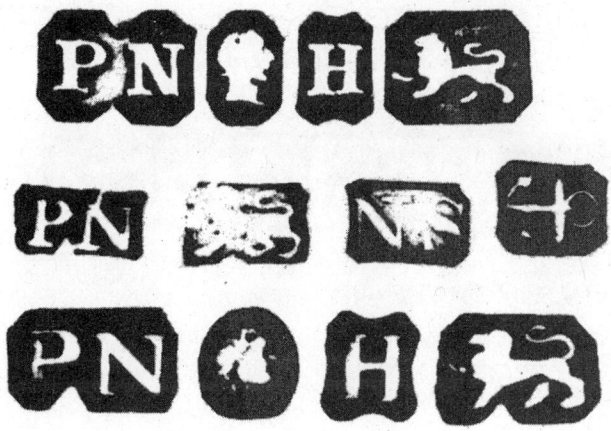

ROSS, ADAM (- 1813 - d 1843)

1818, had shop adjoining gunmaker Henry Watkey. 1822, partnership of Ross & McDonald dissolved. June 5, 1826 advertised that he had restarted business, situated on Granville Street. 1828, offered a saving of 10 per cent in manufacturing for those supplying their own silver. 1828, announced the discovery of molasses. 1840, umbrella repairing service advertised. 1841, situated second corner above Northrup's Country Market. Died 1843.

ROSS, J. (- 1818 -)

Listed as silversmith.

SPIKE, EDMUND LLOYD (b 1837 - 1870 -)

1863, situated 78 Granville Street, moved to 102 Granville Street, there from 1864 to 1867. 1868, was proprietor of "Ophir House." Made jewellery from Nova Scotia gold. Also made emblems for various organizations. He and his brother Thomas Daniel Spike were both apprenticed to J. Cornelius, silversmith. The brothers were partners about 1867. Moved to New York area. Died in 1927 in Maplewood, NJ at the age of 90.

SPIKE, THOMAS DANIEL (b 1840 - d 1922)

Carried on business after his brother Edmund Lloyd Spike had decided to move to New York area. He died in 1922.

STEPHANIS, GOTHELF (- 1784 - 1790 -)

Advertised in the Nova Scotia Gazette on November 12, 1787 as Silversmith and engraver. 1791. (Okie) New York City. 1793-1795 located in New York (Ensko).

STERNS, EDWIN (b 1807 - d 1856))

1832 situated at 12 Barrington Street. In 1839 was situated at Barrington and Buck Street. Gold and silversmith.

TOLER, JOSEPH (- 1831 - 1842 -)
Sugar tongs located at the Nova Scotia Museum in Halifax.

TROUP, ALEXANDER (b 1776 - d 1856)
In 1843 was situated on Argyle Street. Silversmith and watchmaker. Died December 30, 1856.

TROUP, JR. ALEXANDER (b 1806 - d 1873)
Situated at 45 Duke Street in 1868-69, business taken over by James Carr. Died in Halifax on October 8, 1873

TULLY, HENRY WENTWORTH (b 1863 - d 1944)
1880, apprenticed to D.H. Whiston. Trained as silversmith and jeweller. Foreman of the jewellery manufacturing department for M.S. Brown and Co. In 1894 he went into partnership with his brother Thomas, firm name, Tully Bros. Manufacturing and repairing jewellery. Died April 14, 1944.

Tully Bros. trade mark, used principally on gold work.

VEITH, WILLIAM JAMES (b 1827 - d 1900)
Born in Halifax on February 3, 1827. In 1847 he aquired business of Jas. I. Langford with a partner George Witham. Gold and silversmiths. Partnership dissolved on November 11, 1848. He continued the business at 10 Granville Street. Lost the store in Granville Street fire in 1854 and retired. Started entirely different type of business, stage coach and stables, but gave it up in 1863 and became a farmer. Died on August 8, 1900.

VEITH & WITHAM (1847 - 1849)
Mustard spoon on display at the Nova Scotia Museum in Halifax.

WALLACE & BALCOM (- 1865 -)
Teaspoon on display at the Nova Scotia Museum in Halifax.

WHISTON, DAVID HUDSON (b 1834 - d 1917)

Born in Halifax on April 23, 1834. He was apprenticed to Michael Septimus Brown. Foreman of silversmithing department for many years. Between 1864 and 1868, he was situated at 26 Buckingham Street before moving to 149 Granville Street between 1870 and 1877. In 1884 he shared a store with R.T. LePine at 181 Barrington Street. Made silverware for T.C. Johnson. Marked it TCJ-H. Killed in Halifax explosion on December 6, 1917.

WITHAM, GEORGE (b 1825 - d 1875)

Partner of William James Veith in 1847. His father was a general merchant. George became a stage coach operator after 1848.

NEW GLASGOW

EASTWOOD, JAMES (b 1848 - d 1920)

In 1900 he advertised as manufacturer of jewellery and rolled plate in *The Trader*. Large manufacturing firm. Introduced rolled gold plate into Canada. The firm employed about 50 men and women in the factory. Gold and silversmiths included HILTZ, a native of Nova Scotia, who left and started CRESCENT JEWELLERY; GRIMNER (German); PARSONS (English); DES JARDINS (American) and OLAF LARSEN who worked in Halifax after 1904. Larsen used this mark.

Olaf Larsen

James Eastwood

NEW MINAS

BISHOP, HENRY (- 1864 - 1871 -)
Mark H.G.B. in oblong pseudo English hallmark.

HGB WITH LION

PICTOU

FLETCHER, W.S. (- 1839 - 1852 -)

GEDDIE, JOHN (b 1778 - d 1841)

SHELBURNE

BRUFF, CHARLES OLIVER (b 1735 - d 1817)
Recorded as having come from New York with other Loyalists. Jeweller, goldsmith and silversmith. Moved to Liverpool in 1793 where he later died in 1817.

C.O.B

GANO, DAVID (- 1756 - 1786 -)
Spoon on display at the Nova Scotia Museum in Halifax.

DG

TRURO

MORGAN, CHARLES P. (- 1870 - 1907 -)
Was listed in 1891 as silversmith and engraver in the Nova Scotia Directory. Situated on Prince Street.

SILVER **C.P.M.**

PAGE, DAVID (b 1770 - d 1840)
Originally from Haverhill, Massachusetts. In 1793 he settled in Onslow, NS, but later made his home in Truro. Sons David Jr., Thomas, John and Amos were trained as watchmakers and silversmiths. He died on June 22, 1840.

WINDSOR

ANDERSON, ROBERT (- 1816 -)

WOLFVILLE

HERBIN, JOHN FREDERIC (b 1860 - d 1923)
Mark was a fleur de lis. Fine goldsmith, no silver work traced. Situated at 191 Hollis Street in 1871.

The fleur de lis of Herbin is on a number of historic pieces.
(see Nova Scotia Gold & Silversmiths, by Harry Piers and D. McKay.)

23

TWEEDELL, RICHARD HENRY (b 1843 - d 1906)

R.H. TWEEDELL

NOVA SCOTIA SILVER C. B. & CO. (- 1883 -)

Location not known. Several spoons found bearing trade mark. M.S. Brown was believed to have manufactured for the trade but B.M. Co. might be his choice of mark.

(CORNELIUS BECKER & CO. another possibility.)

MERIDEN BRITANNIA CO. LTD. (1879 - 1912)

It was in 1879, the year Sir. John A. MacDonald with the National Policy came into power that 1847 Rogers Bros. made its debut before the Canadian public, in the city of Hamilton, as the Canadian branch of the Meriden Britannia Co. of Meriden, Conn. The first Canadian manager was John E. Parker, with James A Watts as sales manager. Mr. Watts remained only a short time. The business progressed steadily, additional factory space was added from time to time, and in 1900 the original branch was incorporated as the Meriden Britannia Co., Ltd.

It was in 1880 that J.W. Millard came to Hamilton as assistant to Mr. Parker. These positions were held respectively by the two senior officers until June 1907 when Mr. Parker – a man of sound judgement, sterling integrity and a progressive citizen – passed away. He was succeeded as manager by Mr. Millard.

In December 1924 the International Silver Co. of Canada, Ltd. was incorporated to further the best interests of three firms – Meriden Britannia Co.; Standard Silver Co.; and Wm. Rogers & Son. George Wilcox was the first president. These three companies operated as separate units in the company as 1847 Rogers Bros.; Factory E.C. Hamilton, makers of silverplated nickel silver and white metal holloware, 1847 Rogers Bros. silverplate and sterling silver flatware; Wm. Rogers & Son, Factory H.C. Niagara Falls; and Standard Silver Co., Factory S.C. Toronto.

Copy from *The Trader & Canadian Jeweller* - 1929.

Written by Mr. J.W. Millard

Pages 25 to 30 show marks of these various companies.

Organized in 1894 as part of Meriden Britannia Company.

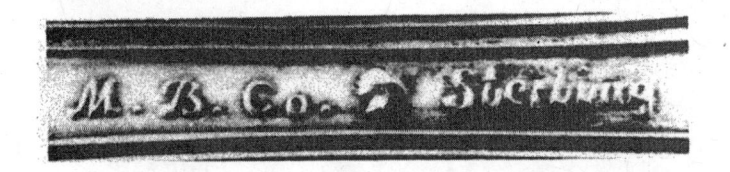

...Sections 8 and 10 of "The Trade Mark and Design Act" of 1879 which they verily believe is theirs on account of having been the first to make use of the same.

The said Specific Trade Mark consists of, a Conventional Bird with neck, head and wings pointing upwards mounted on a bar over the word "Sterling," the letter "M" (in old English) immediately over the Bird's head, as fully and clearly shown in the accompanying wood cut illustration; and we hereby request the said Specific Trade Mark to be registered in accordance with the law.

MERIDEN S.P. CO.
INTERNATIONAL S. CO.

The HIGHLAND Brand
WARRANTED 8 DWT.

STANDARD "S" CO.
INTERNATIONAL 'S' CO.

MERIDEN B. CO.
INTERNATIONAL S. CO.

SIMPSON, HALL, MILLER CO
INTERNATIONAL 'S' CO

SIMPSON, HALL, MILLER & CO.
QUADRUPLE
PLATE

WATROUS MFG CO.
W

TRADE MARK
Sterling

INSICO

I S

INTERNATIONAL S STERLING

INTERNATIONAL STERLING

INTERNATIONAL W STERLING

INTERNATIONAL STERLING

IS
INTERNATIONAL
SILVER COMPANY

Wilcox IS   I S

VIANDE

INTERNATIONAL SILVER CO.

I.S. CO.

"HOLMES & EDWARDS"

STERLING INLAID

"HOLMES & EDWARDS"

HOLMES & EDWARDS SILVER – INLAID

HOLMES & EDWARDS STERLING INLAID

(E. P. on Copper.)
MONARCH SILVER CO.

An International Silver Company Product

SOLE MAKERS OF THE
GENUINE
ORIGINAL
ROGERS
SILVERPLATE

MADE IN CANADA

E.G. Webster & Son bought by International Silver Co. 1928.

WHAT WE HAVE WE'LL HOLD

BULL DOG BRAND

SILVER-PLATE ON
SHEFFIELD
REPRODUCTION

"R & B"

W

PINE TREE

VICTOR · SILVER · COMPANY

Pieces of 8

A promotional trade mark for chest containing eight place settings – a best-selling idea.

DSCo.
DERBY SILVER CO.

W STERLING.

ONTARIO

BELLEVILLE

DINGMAN, JAMES F. (- 1894 -)
Situated at 1 Front Street.

With Pseudo Hall Marks

CARLETON PLACE

BREADNER, S. (b 1870 - d 1948) *see page 48.
Advertised in The Trader as manufacturing jewellers. Moved to Hull Quebec in 1956.

GUELPH

SAVAGE, DAVID (- 1851 - 1869 -)
Situated on Market Square. Worked in Montreal in 1847.

MARKS – Leopard Head in Shield and Uncrowned Head in Octangle

GUELPH

SMITH, S.W. (- 1885 -)
Advertised as silversmith, jeweller in *The Trader*. Worked for Savage, father and son for 17 years.

JUDGE, MICHAEL (- 1850 - 1857 -)
Gunsmith, engraver, working in Market Square. Worked in gold and silver.

MALONE, WILLIAM (- 1851 -)
Watchmaker and jeweller.

HAMILTON

BEEMER & NEWBURY (- 1851 -)
Clocks, gold and silver jewelry and watches – watches, clocks and jewelry repaired.

CAMPBELL, A. (- 1875 - 1880)
Entry in *The Trader* August 1880, Davis & McCollough practical workmen have bought out A. Campbell, jeweller.

CARTER, J.F. (- 1851 -)
Jeweller, King St.

With pseudo Hall Marks.

31

CLARINGBOWL, FRED (- 1880 - 1890)
Situated at 140 King Street E. Advertised in *The Trader*, January 1890. Jeweller.

LEES, GEORGE H. (- 1885 - 1900)
Situated at 47 Main St. Advertised in *The Trader* as gold and silver refiners and jewelry manufacturers.

OSBORNE, ROBERT (- 1851 - 1869)
Situated on James St. Watchmaker, jeweller.

R. OSBORNE or **R.O**   With pseudo Hall Marks including beaver.

RUSSELL, RICHARD (- 1851 - 1885)
Situated at 15 King St. W. Later at James St. opposite Fountain in 1869.

WARE, T.P. & CO. (- 1851 - 1853)
Clocks, watches, jewelry, fancy goods, temperance regalia and emblems. Situated on King St.

KINGSTON

RAMAGE, JOHN (- 1851 - 1869)
Situated on Brock St. Listed 1853-1854 Canadian Directory

J. RAMAGE

SPANENBERG, GEORGE (- 1845 - 1870)
Situated at 30 King St in 1857, sold business to Frederick Spanenberg in 1870.

S or *S*   Sometimes with pseudo Hall Marks, sometimes with **KINGSTON**

SPANENBERG, FREDERICK W. (- 1870 - 1887)
(See above.) Situated at 347 King St. E. 1885-1887.

F.W.S

SPANENBERG, S.A. (- 1885 -)
Pieces found bearing mark S.A.S. and pseudo halmarks.

STENNET, WM. (1822 - 1847)
Watchmaker, jeweller and silversmith. Known to have been in Kingston in 1822. Later moved to Toronto (York) and was there from 1832 through 1847. Believed to have come from London via Bermuda.

LONDON

BAKER, T.H. (1881 - 1970)
Manufacturing jewellers established in 1881. Now owned by T.W. Baker & W.S. Brown.

DAVIS, HENRY (- 1851 - 1883)
Watchmaker, Ridout Street.

DEWEY, WILLIAM (- 1853 - 1854)
Working gold and silversmith. Jeweller from London, England, six doors east of Robinson Hall – "all kinds of repairs neatly executed."

JEANNERET, ROBERT J. (- 1852 - 1869 -)
Watchmaker, Dundas St.

WARE, D.T. & CO. (- 1853 - 1869 -)
Watchmaker and jewellers, 31 Dundas St. – wholesale and retail, watches clocks, jewelry and silver plate.

NIAGARA FALLS

NIAGARA SILVER CO.
See Wm. A. Rogers

NIAGARA FALLS SILVER CO.
Wm. A. Rogers Mark.

ROGERS, WM. A. (1899 - 1929)
According to the history of the Oneida Silversmiths, the Wm. A. Rogers Ltd. had originated in Ontario, Canada and had factories in Niagara Falls, Ontario, New York and North Hampton, Massachusetts. Wm. A. Rogers had taken over the Niagara Silver Company around 1903, Simeon L. & Geo. H. Rogers Co. in 1918 and the Toronto Silver Plate Co. in the 1920s. The (R) ROGERS (R) trade mark was first used in 1900, the 1881 (R) ROGERS (R) in 1910. There ae many variations of the Rogers mark and Wm. A. Rogers Ltd. added their share. When the Wm. Rogers Manufacturing Co. of Meriden, Connecticut decided to open a Canadian branch Wm. A. Rogers already owned the Niagara Silver Co. In 1914 the company name was changed to CANADIAN ROGERS COMPANY LIMITED. This was opposed and the name was changed to "CANADIAN WM. A. ROGERS LIMITED. Oneida purchased the business in 1929.

NIAGARA FALLS CO., 1877

N.F. NICKEL SILVER

Marks continued on next page.

33

N.F. SILVER CO. 1877

WM. A. ROGERS A1
WM. A. ROGERS

1881 ROGERS A1

SIMEON L. & GEORGE H. ROGERS COMPANY

ONEIDA LTD. (1847 - 1970)

The founder of the Oneida Community of Perfectionists, John Humphrey Noyes, studied at the Yale Theological Seminary, and many of the early converts were lawyers, doctors, clergymen and teachers and their families. The members of this deeply religious group not only shared work and worldly goods but also practiced a kind of group marriage and mating under the community's direction. Their communal rearing of children prefigured the modern Israeli kibbutzim.

Originally Oneida Community Limited included five manufacturing enterprises. The name first appeared on bottled fruits. The Oneida label being put on 1,000 jars of home preserves and to the "delighted surprise" of the group found a very ready market. The packing of fruit and vegetables continued for 70 years from 1847-1916.

The second enterprise was the manufacturing of traps. Started in 1852, within five years the orders for the Newhouse trap were coming from all over the world including Australia, Canada and Russia. In 1896 a factory was built in Canada to help meet the demand of the Canadians for this highly successful and popular product. The trap business lasted until 1925.

Silk manufacturing was started by three of the "Community" members in 1865, by 1900 the business had an anunal return of $300,000. This business was not as profitable as the Newhouse Trap. It was sold in 1913 to M. Hemingway & Son.

Chain manufacturing was started in 1880 and continued until 1912 then sold to The American Chain Company.

In 1877 the Oneida Community began to manufacture tableware. A branch of the Community had been formed at Wallingford, Connecticut on the farm of Henry Allen. It was there that two iron spoons changed the fortunes of a great many people. *Lily* and *Oval* were the first patterns of what was eventually to become "COMMUNITY PLATE". By 1880, the silver business had grown to such an extent that it was moved to Niagara Falls. In 1895, Dr. Theodore Noyes became president of Oneida Community Ltd. Pierrepont Noyes was appointed superintendent of the company's three departments at Niagara Falls.

In 1901, the first "silver" *Community Plate* pattern was made and shown at the Buffalo Exposition. Designed by Pierrepont Noyes, who took the bowl from one spoon, the top from a second, the side ornaments from a third, the whole adapted to the contours of a fourth and the result *Avalon*.

The next pattern was *Flower De Luce* which was designed by Grosvenor Allen with the help of professional artist Julia Bracken. Other designs which followed were the work of Allen in consultation with artists, who were put on the payroll.

In 1910, "The Coles Phillips Girl" appeared in Oneida advertisements. At the same time International Silver launched their *1847 Girl*. This started the 'pretty girl' trend in advertising.

35

Oneida

**HEIRLOOM
ONEIDA
RELIANCE
SILVER METAL
REX PLATE
TUDOR PLATE
ONEIDA COMMUNITY
COMMUNITY
COMMUNITY SILVER
COMMUNITY PLATE
N. F. NICKEL SILVER 1877**

Trade mark on stainless steel.

BURKE & WALLACE LIMITED
234 BELFIELD ROAD, REXDALE, ONTARIO

Registered Manufacturers and Distributors
WM. A. ROGERS AND 1881 (R) ROGERS (R)

Silverware manufacturers advertised Wm. A. Rogers lines in Canadian Jewellery Directory, 1969.

OTTAWA

ADDISON, CHARLES (1882 - 1892)
Situated at 117 Sparks Street for a period of at least 10 years. Mark used included in the Robert Hendery and Hendery & Leslie punch marks.

LESLIE, JOHN (- 1848 - 1895)
Situated on Rideau Street in 1848. Had a jewelry store and repaired silver. Was on Sparks Street in 1869, moved to 62 Sparks in 1876. He died in Ottawa on November 19, 1895. Two of the punch marks bearing his name are those used by Robert Hendery and Hendery & Leslie on his behalf.

| J.L | OTTAWA with Lion & head |

JOHN LESLEY

NOTE: Examples are known to exist with both the alternative spelling of the name.

MARKS, N.M. (- 1876 -)
Situated at 85 Sparks Street, also had silver marked by Robert Hendery and Hendery & Leslie.

N. M. MARKS

OLMSTED, C.A. (- 1890 - 1903)
Situated at 97 Sparks Street, was joined in partnership by Mr. Hurdman in 1902. Business sold to Henry Birks & Sons in 1903.

C.A.O
O & H

OLMSTEAD
STERLING

ROSENTHAL, A.J. (- 1882 - 1903)
Situated at 87 Sparks Street. Business became part of Henry Birks & Sons in 1903.

ROSENTHAL

TRACY, WILLIAM H. (- 1851 - 1892 -)
Watchmaker, jeweller, Rideau St.

W. H. TRACY

SIMCOE

DARLING, GEORGE (- 1852 - 1899 -)
Had silver made by Hendery & Leslie, Montreal. Clock, watchmaker, jeweller, Rideau St.

G.L.DARLING

TORONTO

ACME SILVER CO. THE (1885-1895)
Situated at 9-11 Church Street. Manufactured quadruple plated ware. Advertised spoons and forks with the G. Rodgers A.1 trade mark and G. Rodgers 12 DWT mark on knives. The firm moved to a new factory 31-41 Hayter Street in 1890. In 1895, sold out to W.K. George and others who formed the Standard Silver Company Toronto Ltd. which later became part of International Silver Company of Canada Ltd.

ARMS & QUIGLEY (- 1879 - 1882 -)
Manufacturing jewellers. Won the award for Gold and Silver watch cases exhibit at the first Toronto Exhibition. Office located at 10 King Street E. Advertised in *The Trader*. December 1879 had moved to factory, 33-35 Adelaide Street. Listed in the February 1882 edition of *The Trader* as manufacturers of cuff buttons and watch cases in gold & silver.

BELL, WM. (- 1841 - 1867)
Situated in Niagara in 1835. Moved to Church Street Toronto around 1841 and then to 172 Yonge Street in 1846. Address given as 123 Yonge St. in 1853. Succeeded by John Wanless Snr.

CANADA MFG. CO (1890)
Known both in Toronto and Montreal.

CANADIAN WM. A. ROGERS LTD. (1914-1929)
This firm came into being after Wm. A. Rogers Co. had purchased The Toronto Silver Plate Co. Wm. A. Rogers later sold out to Oneida, Niagara Falls and Sherrill, New York. Canadian Rogers Company Limited 1914. *See Wm. A. Rogers.*

CROWN SILVER PLATE CO. (1909 - 1920)
Listed in Jewellers' Circular – Keystone. Mark well known in Canada.

DERBY SILVER CO. (1881 - 1884)
Factory at 31 Adelaide Street E. *The Trader* in October 1884 reports Derby Silver Co. closed. Trade Mark advertised March 1900 by Standard Silver Company which at that time had become part of the International Silver Company of Canada.

EAGLE BRAND
Advertised in *The Trader* by Simpson, Hall, Miller & Co., Toronto and Montreal. Made in Montreal factory. *See Simpson, Hall, Miller & Co.*

38

ELLIS & COMPANY. P. W. (- 1876 - 1928)

Situated at 4 Toronto Street in 1879. Awarded first prize Goldsmiths Work at Industrial Exhibition, Toronto. Jewellery manufacturers, also made badges, medals and presentation articles. *The Trader* in September 1879 carried an advertisement which stated "First home made jewellery ever exhibited in this country." 1880, R. Y. Ellis and Brothers Hardware Store, Ingersoll, dissolved partnership. A. H. Ellis continued business independently. P. W. Ellis & Co. admit R. Y. Ellis as partner. The partners were Phillip W. Ellis and Matthew C. Ellis (nephews of James E. Ellis.) A George Ellis joined the firm in 1890. *The Trader in* 1882 (Feb.) lists 8 manufactures, cuff buttons and watch cases in gold and silver. P. W. Ellis & Co. headed the list. In 1918, Matthew C. Ellis became the first president of "The Canadian National Jewellers Association". Company liquidated in 1928. Soverign Plate trade mark for silver plate made by the firm. P. W. Ellis married the daughter of Goodham, manager Toronto Silver Plate Company.

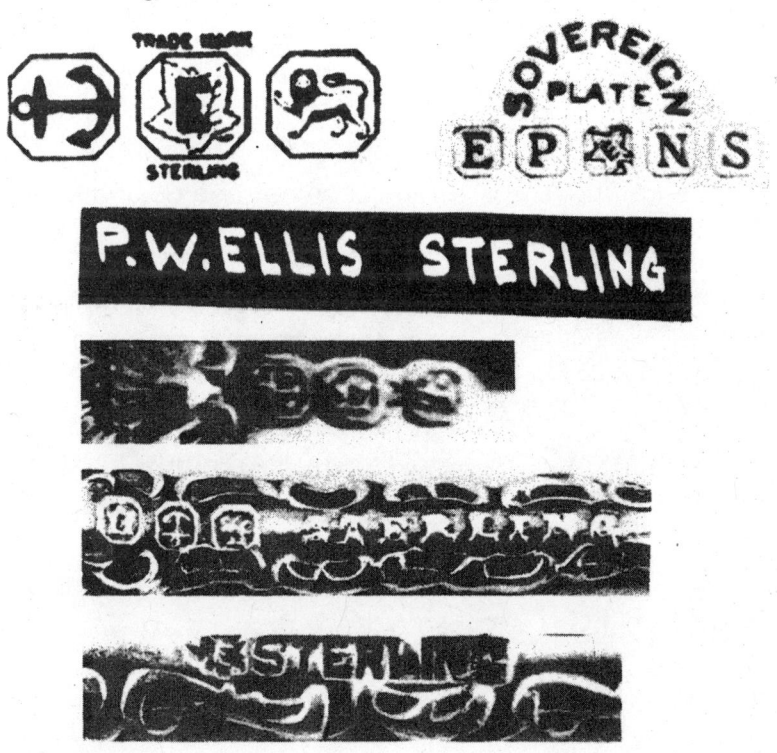

ELLIS, JAMES E. (- 1848 - 1871 -)

Came from England in 1848. Situated at 30 King St. in 1852. Retired in 1871 and son, who had joined the firm in 1862, carried on in partnership with M. T. Cain. Firm became ELLIS & CO. J.E. 1881-1901.

GOLDSMITH'S STOCK COMPANY OF CANADA LTD. (- 1880 - 1897 -)

Partners Henry Smith and Harris Fudger, formerly senior partners in Robert Wilkes &. Co. Situated at 48 Yonge Street in 1890. Advertised in *The Trader* as Manufacturers agents. Acted as agents for Roden Bros. who produced Flatware, Hollowware, Enamelled Souvenir ware, Sterling Silver and Cut Glass. The Goldsmith Company also had silver stamped with their trade mark made for them by Robert Hendery and Hendery and Leslie. Listed in J. C.K 1915-22.

HILL & HOUGHTON. (- 1879 - 1882 -)

Listed as one of 8 manufacturers of cuff buttons and watch cases in gold and silver in *The Trader* Feb. 1882.

HOLMES & EDWARDS

*See International Silver Co. of Canada.

INLAID SILVER CO. (- 1889 - 1890 -)

Advertised in *The Trader*, April edition, that they had purchased the rights to manufacture Inlaid Silver Spoons and Forks. The advertised wares were stamped Inlaid Silver Patd.

JACKSON, HENRY (1837 - 1869)

Situated at several addresses on King St. E., during the 32 years known to be in business. Silversmith, watchmaker and jeweller. Manufacturer of silver plate.

JOSEPH & CO., J.G. (- 1857 - 1877 -)

Situated 56 King Street E. in 1857. 35 Front Street in 1877. Silversmith, watchmaker and jeweller. Had silver made by Robert Hendery and Hendery & Leslie. Used a variety of marks. Some pieces stamped Toronto. Included every type pseudo Hallmark.

KENT BROS. (- 1867 - 1882 -)

Situated at 116 Yonge Street in 1867. 166 Yonge Street in 1878. Indian Clock Palace, 168 Yonge Street in 1887. Issued annual catalogue with "The Sign of the Indian Clock" on cover. Importers and manufacturers. Made fine jewellery and emblems of every kind. Specialized in hand enamelled work of highest quality.

KENT BROS.

KENT & SONS LTD., AMBROSE (1894 - 1946)

Situated at 156 Yonge Street in 1894. Fairweather Ltd. amalgamated in 1946 and firm became KENT-FAIRWEATHER LTD. Kent sold his interest in 1953. Firm now FAIRWEATHER LTD.

STERLING

LASH, J.B. (1865 - 1887 -)

Lash of Lash & Co., King St. in 1865. In business on own account at 13 King St. E. in 1887. Silversmith & jeweller. Listed as Secretary Toronto Silver Plate Company in 1879.

SILVER **LASH & CO.**

LEE & CHILLAS (- 1879 - 1889)

Partnership of Thomas H. Lee and George Chillas. Situated at 4 Wellington Street. The partnership was dissolved and T. H. Lee advertised in *The Trader*, January 1890, from 1 Wellington Street. Was joined in business by son and name changed to T. H. LEE & Son, Wholesale Jewellers.

LOWE, WM. G.H. (- 1879 - 1904)

In 1879 principal in the firm of ZIMMERMAN, McNAUGHT & CO. In 1884, partner in the firm of McNAUGHT & LOWE, other partners were Wm. K. Zimmerman and Wm. G.H. McNaught. This partnership formed after the retirement of Joseph Zimmerman of ZIMMERMAN & McNAUGHT & CO., manufacturers of gold chain, cuff buttons, watch cases. Importers and Jobbing Jewellers. In 1885, formed partnership with A.C. Anderson after a short period of business on own account. Firm then became LOWE & ANDERSON. 16 Wellington St. East. In 1888, partnership dissolved upon the retirement of William Lowe.

Z. McN & Co   with pseudo hallmarks.

LOWE & ANDERSON (1885 - 1888)

*See Wm. G. H. Lowe.

L&A   with pseudo hallmarks.

MCNAUGHT & LOWE (1884 - 1885)

*See Wm. G. H. Lowe.

MERIDEN SILVER PLATE CO. (1881 - 1884)

This branch of the American Company had plating rooms in Toronto which were transferred to Hamilton in 1884, having been taken over by the Meriden Britannia Company.

MONARCH SILVER PLATE CO.

See Standard Silver Company.

MORPHY, EDWARD M. (1847 - 1882)

Situated at 98 Yonge St. in 1847. Morphy Bros. listed at same address 1851-1856 and as Morphy Son & Co. E.M. at 141 Yonge St. in 1897. Morphy Bros. were also listed at 141 Yonge St. in 1859. Also E. Morphy with pseudo hall mark.

OLIVER, RICHARD KESTELL (- 1843 - 1860 -

In 1843, situated on Duchess Street. Moved to Parliament Street in 1847. Had several addresses on King Street being at 213 East in 1853 and at 296 in 1860. Working silversmith.

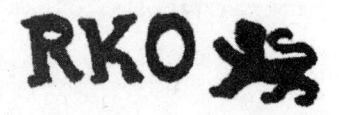

POST, JORDAN (b. 1770 - d. 1853)

The Trader referred to Jordan Post as the pioneer watchmaker of Toronto who advertised that he kept "a complete assortment of watch furniture". It is considered that he was the first silversmith in Toronto having arrived with his father from Connecticut in 1787. He was a prominent figure and two streets were named as a tribute to him and his family, Jordan Street and Melinda (his wife) nee Woodruff. He owned considerable property. He started on the corner of King and Bay Streets. In 1833 he was situated at 221 King Street. C. Clinkunbroomer who died in 1881 at the age of 82 served his apprenticeship with Jordan Post.

ROBINSON & CO., JOSEPH (- 1859 - 1880)

Partner with brother Charles at 15 King Street. Retired in 1880, the firm then became ROBINSON & BRO.

RODEN BROS., LTD. (KN. 1891 - 1922)

In 1900 moved to Royal Opera House Building, King St. Silverware and Cut Glass Manufacturers. Workers for the trade. Goldsmiths Stock Company of Canada were sole selling agents from 1900 to 1922. Thomas Roden was Honorary President of Canadian Jewellers Association. Factory on Carlaw Avenue in 1917. Made silver for other firms putting trade marks as required. Makers of Duchess Plate, Sterling Silver, Cut Glass Signed.

RICH CUT GLASS

RODGERS, G.
See Standard Silver Co.

ROSENTHAL, ABRAHAM (b 1866 - d 1965)
This business started in 1895. Abraham Rosenthal died on February 8, 1965.

RYRIE BIRKS (- 1905 - 1925)
Henry Birks & Sons consolidated with Ryrie Bros. in Toronto in the year 1905, name of business not changed until 1924.

RYRIE, JAMES (b 1854 - d 1933)
Ryrie Brothers contributed a great deal to the growth of the jewelry business in Canada. James had a business at 113 Yonge Street from 1879. Joined Harry in 1882, the firm became RYRIE BROS. in 1897. Opened a new store on Yonge Street & Adelaide in 1890. where they had six men engaged for repair work in the watchmaking department. J. Ryrie was apprenticed to John Segsworth in 1870. *See Robert Hendery and Hendery & Leslie mark for RYRIE.* Used this plus pseudo hallmarks.

RYRIE BROS.

SARGANT, S.J. (- 1879 -)
"Manufacturer of Masonic and Society Regalia, Jewels, &C., &C., A.O.U.W. Badges. Send for price list. Box 1152. Toronto." Series of advertisements in *The Trader* 1879.

SAUNDERS, LORIE & CO. (- 1897 - 1920 -)
SAUNDERS, LORIE & CO.

Manufacturing jeweller. Situated at 35 Adelaide Street W. in 1897 and at 114 Bay Street in 1900. Still advertising in *The Trader* in 1920 offering platinum and gold jewellery.

SAUNDERS, S. & A. (1848 - 1900 -)
S & A SAUNDERS

Advertised in *The Trader*. January 1900 issue states "established 1848" Silversmiths, jewellers, manufactured all kinds of jewellery. Situated at 20 and 22 Adelaide Street.

SAVAGE, GEORGE (1829 - 1854 -)
G.S.

Son of George Savage, Montreal. Was in business with father 1829-1845. (George Savage & Son). A branch in Toronto at 3 Wellington Buildings, King St. 1853. Listed under Silversmiths (*Canadian Directory*). Importer and manufacturer of watches, clocks, gold and silver ware. Address 57 Victoria Row, King St. E. *See George Savage & Son.*

SAXTON, JOHN (- 1853 - 1854 -)
Situated at 17 Church St. Listed as silversmith in *The Canadian Directory* 1853-1854.

SHEFFIELD HOUSE (- 1882 - 1888)
Situated in Toronto. Actual address not known.

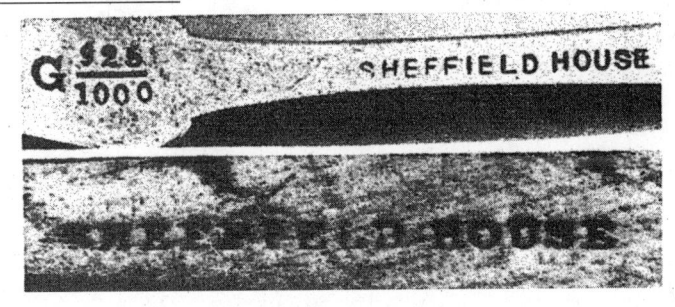

SOVEREIGN PLATE
Trade mark for silver plate made by P. W. Ellis & Co. Ltd.

STANDARD SILVER CO. (1895 - 1925)
Meriden Britannia. One of the companies taken over by Meriden Britannia Company of Hamilton, Ontario and Meriden Connecticut. Name was continued for some years afterwards. Standard used several trade marks, some of which had been acquired in the takeover of the ACME PLATE COMPANY. Monarch being one of the more popular, this mark is found on many of the items in antique stores. They also made the HOLMES & EDWARDS 'inlaid silver flatware' under licence.

INTERNATIONAL SILVER COMPANY OF CANADA
Absorbed Standard Silver Company, Toronto; Simpson, Hall, Miller & Company, Toronto and Montreal; Meriden Britannia Company, Hamilton.

STANLEY & AYLWARD LTD. (- 1920 -)
This company used a trade mark of their own but no known factory. Wholesalers of plated hollow ware.

NORMAN PLATE
*See Stanley, Aylward.

STERLING CRAFT LTD. (- 1920 - 1927 -)
Situated at 107 Richmond St. East in 1927. Working silversmiths and repairers.

STERN, SAMUEL (- 1879 - 1882 -)
Advertised as "The Largest Clock House in Canada" in 1879 *The Trader*. In 1882 listed as one of 14 jobbing jewellers.

TAGGART, FRANK (- 1886 - 1887 -)
Previously general manager for Charles Starke Co. Opened own store at 87-89 King Street, first catalogue offered sterling silver souvenir spoons of Sir John A. MacDonald and Miss Canada. Made gold and silver thimbles.

TORONTO SILVER PLATE COMPANY (1882 - 1914)
Founded in 1882 by J. A. Watts, formerly manager Meriden Britannia Co., Hamilton. All Canadian company. Won awards for silverware. Bought by W. A. Rogers Co. Ltd. (Canada) ca. 1914. The following were directors in 1888: Geo. Gooderham, W.H. Partridge, E.G. Godderham, H.W Beatty, Wm. Thompson, James Webster, Frank Turner C.E.

STERLING

TORSIL E. P.—N. S.

TORSIL METAL

TORSIL STEEL

WANLESS, JOHN (b. 1830- d. 1905)

Born in Scotland John Wanless moved to Canada 1851. Worked with Wm. Bell who had moved from Niagara in 1840. Suceeded to the business in 1861. Joined by his son John Jr. in 1890. Firm became WANLESS & CO. In 1920 John Wanless Jr. was elected Treasurer of The Canadian Jewellers Association. Also had silver made by Roden Bros.

J.W with Lion, Beaver and Crowned Head.

JOHN WANLESS & CO., Established 1840. TORONTO.

Manufacturers of rings, brooches, watch chains, medals, class pins, lockets, cuff links, and fine diamond and pearl jewellery.

VIKING PLATE

- is a registered trade mark of Lipman-Levinter Industries Limited, 41 Peter Street, Toronto.

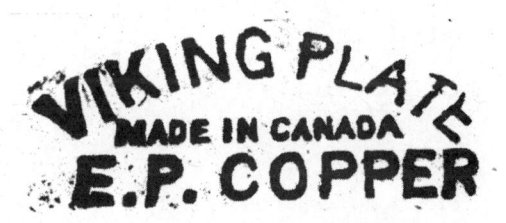

VIKING PLATE MADE IN CANADA E.P. COPPER

WELCH & TROWERN (- 1880 - 1886)

Manufacturing Jewellers. Advertisement in *The Trader*, September 1880, offers Silver lockets, Napkin rings, Masonic Jewels, Trowels, Stick heads, Silver Prize Cups, etc. 1882, mentioned as manufacturers of cuff buttons and watch cases in gold and silver. 1886, A. H. Welch retired.

WELCH & TROWERN

WHITE & SON, T. (- 1879 - 1885 -)

Advertisers in *The Trader* 1879. Manufacturing Jewellers, situated at 12 Melinda Street. Were listed in *The Trader* Feb 1882 edition as one of 8 manufacturers of cuff buttons and watch cases in gold and silver.

TRENTON

BENEDICT PROCTOR MFG. CO. (- 1920 - 1970 -)
Manufacturers of quality plated silverware. Sheffield reproductions.

Trade Mark of Benedict Proctor

BREADNER, S. (b 1870 - d 1948) *see Carlton Place pg. 31*
Samuel Breadner commenced manufacturing silverware in Carlton Place Ca. 1900.

BREADNER MANUFACTURING CO. (- 1900 -)
Mr. Breadner moved to Ottawa in 1904 and formed the Breadner Manufacturing Co. and built a factory in about 1910. The firm specialized in souvenir jewellery for the tourist trade and the business acquired a collection of spoon dies from a Montreal firm that went bankrupt and these spoons became a background of the souvenir line. In 1930 the business was reorganized as the Breadner Company Limited and continued to feature souvenir jewellery along with badges and emblems. During the Second World War the company made insignia for the armed forces and at the end of the war resumed the manufacture of souvenir jewellery. By this time the company had developed their own die making facilities and many new spoons were added to the line. Samuel Breadner died in 1948 and his son Jack Breadner took over the presidency of the company. In 1956 the company moved to Hull, Quebec where they continued to specialize in the production of fine quality souvenir jewellery and sterling spoons.

STERLING *BMCo* MADE IN CANADA

STERLING BMCO

QUEBEC

MONTREAL

ALLAN, THOMAS & CO. (b 1839- d 1899)

1839, born in England. 1857, apprenticed to Savage & Lyman, Henry Birks also entered the firm that year as a junior. Joseph Savage at that time the "Old Man" of the firm, resting much of the time on a sofa in the back office. Thomas Allan was partner with Wood & Wood. 1866-67, operated as Wood & Allen with Wood as partner. Acquired business of W. Learmont, changed business name to T. ALLAN & CO. 1869, situated at 375 Notre Dame Street. 1881, 167 St. James Street. 1888, bought business of T. A. Adkins. 1891-92, situated on St. Catharine Street. Died February 1899.

ARNOLDI, JOHN PETER (1769 - 1808 -)

Son of Peter Arnoldi believed to have settled in Montreal before 1769. Brothers, Charles Arnoldi and Michael Arnoldi. Worked with John Oakes, leased workshop from brother Michael in 1792. Wife, Margaret Cayley. Those known to have served under him as apprentices include John Glatter and H. Morand.

ARNOLDI, CHARLES (b 1779 - d 1817)

1779, born in Montreal, September 23, 1805, married Ann Brown, October 5, 1806, succeeded to the business of John Irish. Benjamen Comins entered into partnership with him at 16 Notre Dame Street. Dissolved 1807. 1810, mentioned in poll book, *Western Ward*, Montreal as silversmith, made silver for Indian trade. 1812, became postmaster at Lavaltrie. Died in Montreal Dec. 17th, 1817.

ARNOLDI, MICHAEL (b 1763 - d 1807)

1763, born in Montreal June 19, 1784, dissolved partnership with Robert Cruickshank November 1, 1792, made agreement with brother Peter and partner John Oakes to lease them his workshop in return for board, lodging, laundry and to provide him with a suit of fine cloth each year for a period of two years. 1793, bought property at Trois Rivieres. 1802, returned to Montreal. took John Justus Diehl, his nephew into apprenticeship. Died at Trois Rivieres August 27, 1807.

BARLOW, EDOUARD (- 1829 - 1837 -)
1829, situated on Craig Street. 1837, listed in Notre Dame Church records.

E{d} Barlow *Leopard's Head & Lion.*

BEAN, JOHN (1819 - 1823 -)
Originally from London, England. 1819, situated at 41 Notre Dame Street. 1820, worked with Alex. McNaughton at 5 St. Joseph Street. 1823-26, working at 13 Mountain Street. Advertisement for Old Gold, Silver and Silver lace appeared in his name in the *Quebec Gazette* of August 25, 1823.

J.B *with pseudo hallmarks.*

BEAUDRY, NARCISSE (- 1862 - 1880 -)
1856-58, partner of E. P. Boivin at 116 Notre Dame St.

N. BEAUDRY *Lion and Head.* **STERLING**

BIRKS, HENRY & SONS
See page 55.

Canada's first silver marks granted to Henry Birks & sons Ltd.

BOHLE, DAVID (- 1831 - d 1870)
Partner with brother Peter Bohle for short period. Partner, George C. Denman 1863-66, employed W. H. Denham at that time. Partnership dissolved. Carried on own business till 1870. Drowned, Montreal Harbour.

DB **MONTREAL**

BOHLE, PETER (b 1786 - d 1865)
1800, apprenticed to Robert Cruickshank till 1807. 1851-56, partner with Robert Hendery. Were silversmiths to the trade. Customers included Savage & Lyman. 1862, worked for Maysenhoelder & Baddley.

PB *with leopard's Head and Lion.*

BOHLE, FRANCIS (- 1843 - 1867 -)
1843, worked independently till 1849. 1849, partner with D. Maysenhoelder. 1859-1868, partner with Albert Desroches. Working silversmiths.

F.B *with repeated Lions.*

BOIVIN, LOUIS PHILLIPE (- 1842 - 1856 -)
1842, situated corner of Notre Dame and St. Vincent Sts.
1844-45, 80 St. Paul Street. 1850-51, 88 Notre Dame St. Working silversmith.

L P B   *with Lion and sometimes with Montreal.*

CAMIRAND J. D. & CO. (- 1920 -)
Manufacturers of silver, also plated silver.

MADE BY J. D. CAMIRAND & CO. MONTREAL

CARON BROS. (- 1920 -)
Manufacturers of silver, silver plate and jewellery. Situated 233-239 Bleury St., Montreal.

CANADIAN JEWELLERS LTD. (- 1920 -)
Manufacturers of Jewellery and silver deposit ware.

CRUICKSHANK, ROBERT (- 1767 - d 1809)

DENMAN & BOHLE (-1863 - 1866 -)
Partnership of George C. Denman and David Bohle. Made silver for Savage & Lyman. Geo. Denman carried on business on own account after partnership dissolved.

DESROCHES, ALFRED. (- 1858 - 1890 -)
1859, partner with Frances Bohle. After partnership dissolved worked independently. 1860, listed at 99 Sanquinet Street.

DWIGHT, JAMES ADAMS (- 1818 - 1847 -)

1818, partner of George Savage. Situated at 56, St. Paul Street. Associated with Martin Cheney and the Twiss Brothers, American Clockmakers who had settled in Montreal. 1844, partner with son at 151 Notre Dame Street.

DWIGHT & SAVAGE (- 1818 - 1819)

Partnership of James Adams Dwight and George Savage. Partnership dissolved in 1819.

HEMMING MANUFACTURING CO. (- 1909 - 1915 -)

Listed in *Jewellers' Circular* as manufacturers of Sterling silverware and jewellery. Also in *Trader* as manufacturers of boxes and jewel cases.

LEARMONT, WILLIAM (- 1841 - 1870)

1843-1854, situated at 147 Notre Dame Street. Moved to several different sites on the street during the following 20 years. Seven marks attributed to this firm. The Learmont Estate managed the business in 1870. Professor Ramsay Traquair refers to him as a jeweller who sold plate "probably not a working silversmith".

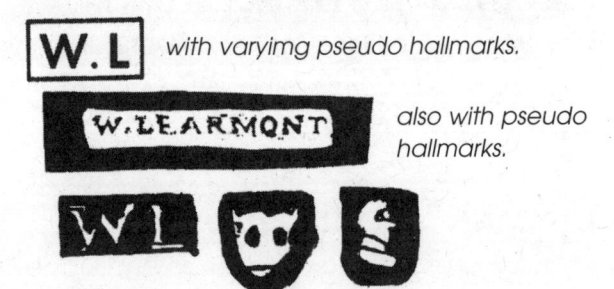

W.L with varyimg pseudo hallmarks.

W.LEARMONT also with pseudo hallmarks.

LIDO JEWELLERS CO. (1867-1970)

Manufacturers of jewellery.

MEVES OTTO (- 1858 - 1871 -)

1860, situated at 10 Lambert Hill. Had been associated with John Maysenholder at 159 Notre Dame Street. 1862, moved to Kingston, Ontario.

O. MEVES with pseudo hallmarks. Sometimes KINGSTON.

MILLER & BREMNER (- 1880 - 1900 -)

1880, situated 191 St. James Street. Partners David Miller and James Bremner. 1890, situated 35 Bleury Street and 2325 St. Catharine Street in 1900.

MILLER BREMNER *With pseudo hallmarks.*

PEACOCK, HENRY (- 1847 - 1890 -)

Advertised in The Canadian Directory 1853-54 from 67 St. Paul Street offering watches, clocks, and jewellery, etc. for sale at a small advance on cost. 1890, situated at 194 St. George Street.

ROGERS SONS & CO., HENRY (- 1909 - 1915)

British company, Sheffield ca. 1897. Usual mark – flag over crown over H.R.S. & Co. Probably had branches in Canada as the firm was listed in Jewellers' Circular under plated silver. Address given as Montreal, Quebec.

H.R.S. & Cº
HENRY ROGERS, SONS & Cº
CUTLERS SHEFFIELD

SAVAGE, GEORGE (b 1767 - d 1845)

Born in Huddersfield, England. Listed in *Watch and Clockmakers of the World* G. H. Baillie. Worked in Huddersfield and London 1808-23, then came to Canada. A very able watchmaker, patented a remontoir in 1808, and gained award of Soc. Arts for a detached escapement for watches, desc, in Trans. Soc. Arts, Vol. 40, 1823.

1818, partner of Adam Dwight at St. Paul Street and St. Diziere Lane. Carried on independently after one year, in business there until 1840. 1823, opened a West End store with Mr. Wood in charge, had a very large stock of English Key Wind Lever Watches. Peter Bohle made silver spoons etc., for him at this time. Robert Hendery joined Bohle in 1840. George Savage was joined by his eldest son in the business. Name changed to George Savage & Son. Uptown store opened at 1612 Notre Dame Street, which later became 40 Notre Dame St. East, due to renumbering. Business carried on at this address till May 1858. In 1850 the name of the firm was changed to Savage & Lyman (Joseph married Abigail Lyman, sister of Major (later Lt. Col.) Theodore Lyman). The partners were Theodore and Joseph.

1857, Henry Birks entered Savage & Lyman, Montreal, as a junior. It was considered the finest retail store in Canada and was lit by three sperm oil lamps. 1867, Henry Birks and Chas. W. Hagar joined Savage & Lyman as partners. Name changed to Savage, Lyman & Co. 1878, depression caused by withdrawal of British troops from Montreal in 1870, seriously affected business and the firm went into bankruptcy. Henry Birks remained on as manager whilst the assets were liquidated. A branch of the business was carried on in Toronto at 3 Wellington Buildings first as George Savage then as Savage and Lyman.

SHARPLEY, RICE (- 1835 - 1880)

Situated at 131 Notre Dame Street, 1851-54. Advertised in *The Trader* and *The Canadian Directory*. Judging by his advertisements Rice Sharpley had an interesting business being an importer, and wholesale and retail dealer of fancy goods, silver, jewellery, guns, rifles, swords, and pistols, etc. Did not claim to make or manufacture any of the lines offered. Two sons carried on the business when he retired. He lived in England in the year 1880.

SHARPLEY & SONS, RICE (- 1870 - 1890 -)
Fred and William Sharpley, sons of Rice. First at 281 Notre Dame St.

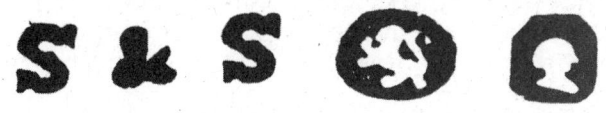

SIMPSON, HALL, MILLER & CO. (- 1879 - 1898)
Canadian branch of Wallingford, Connecticut company. Advertised in *The Trader* November 1879. Zimmerman McNaught their sole agents in Ontario. Manufactured silver plate in the Montreal factory. In September 1882 advertised "The Wm. Rogers goods sold by us are made under the supervision of Mr. Wm. Rogers, formerly of Hartford and West Meriden. Son of the old original Wm. Rogers who died in 1873. Please do not associate us with goods made in Hartford, Connecticut, with which we have no connections. We make all the goods we sell and have our own special patterns. 1896, advertised their address as 50 Bay Street, Toronto. Also advertised Sterling Silverware, Fine Electroplate, Flat & Hollow ware. 1899, became part of The International Silver Co. Canada. Two Canadian patterns, "St. James" and "Geneva".

BIRKS & SONS, HENRY (1840 - 1970)
1832, John Birks and his wife Anne, nee Massey, arrived in Montreal from Barnsley, Yorkshire, England. 1840, Henry Birks born at 84 Little St. James Street on November 30. 1857, Henry Birks becomes Junior in the firm of Savage & Lyman, April 22, 1866, Henry Birks travels to Europe as a Buyer for his Firm. 1868. salary that year $1,000 per annum. Married Harriet Phillips Walker, (born Brantford, Ont., December 5, 1847.) Marriage took place in Toronto on January 16, 1868. 1868, son, William Massey Birks, born on Mansfield Street, October 25. 1870, John Henry Metcalfe Birks born in Metcalfe Cottages, August 31. 1872, Gerald Walter Birks born at 108 University Street. 1877, Henry Birks sells his interest in Savage Lyman & Co. to make good a note for $1,000 (equal to his annual income) which he had endorsed for a brother. (It is understood that members of the family in the business have, since that time, on their 21st birthday signed an agreement not to sign any negotiable paper without the consent of the Directors.) Henry Birks remained with Savage, Lyman & Co. as Store Manager. 1878, Company failed, Henry carried out liquidation of company on behalf of the liquidator. 1879, Henry Birks & Co., established at 222 St. James Street, staff beside himself numbered three – Bertram Cox, watchmaker, George

C. Robinson, bookkeeper/salesman and William H. Lavers, messenger boy. The space rented was 15 ft. x 50 ft. this included a wrapping area at the rear of his store. Capital was $3,000, plus $1,000, which was a gift to his wife from an uncle. He also had an advance shipment of clocks from Germany, to be paid for as they were sold. Various firms with which he had dealt as Store Manager of Savage, Lyman & Co. gave him agencies, Gorham, Nardin Watches, Reed & Barton, etc. His business policies were unusual – cash for all purchases, one price for all and no haggling – He turned over his inventory seven and one-half times in the first year, his sales $30,000. 1885, moved business to 235-7 St. James St. Floor space 1,500 square feet. Staff 10. Added three new departments – china, crystal and leather goods. Son graduated from Montreal High School and enters the business. 1887, first factory opened – jewellery only. James Davidson from Hamilton, manager, seven employees.

RIDEAU PLATE

a Henry Birks & Sons Trade mark.

Canada's first silver marks granted to Henry Birks & Sons Ltd.

1888, Gerald W. Birks starts in business, graduated from Montreal High School. 1890, reported in *The Trader*, that "Henry Birks & Co., one of the leading retail jewellery houses of Montreal have just completed some alterations to their establishment which have improved its appearance very much." 1891, John H. Birks, graduated from Massachusetts Institute of Technology with B.Sc. Enters the family business. 1893, Henry Birks admits his three sons as equal partners – name of the partnership – Henry Birks & Sons. 1894, moved to Phillips Square. New premises had 90 ft. frontage on St. Catharine Street and 55 ft. on Phillips Square, in all 4,950 sq. ft. 1895, staff 56. 1895, Hendery & Leslie dissolve partnership. Mr. Leslie sole owner of the business, Robert Hendery died in 1897 and in 1898 an agreement is made that Hendery & Leslie will confine their Montreal sales to Birks only. 1899, Henry Birks & Sons buy Hendery & Leslie. John Leslie continues as head of the factory until 1925. 1900, factory moved from 134 St. Peter Street to the Birks building, Phillips Square.

Factory staff of Hendery & Leslie, 20. In 1904 the staff of Henry Birks & Sons numbered 221 plus the four seniors. Seniors 4, Glass Cutters 11, Silversmiths 47, Ottawa 13, Watchmakers 13, Goldsmiths 44, Winnipeg 17, Stationery Factory 9, Salesmen 36, Office and Mail Order 31. 1905, Henry Birks & Sons Ltd. incorporated.

The first directors were the four partners and Wm. H. Lavery (the original messenger boy 1879.) 1907, sold Glass Cutting Factory to Phillips Glass Co. Bought the Gorham Co. of Canada Ltd. Acquired dies of Chantilly and Louis XV. Gorhams pledge to remain out of Canada for 10 years. In 1907 staff of 453 increased at Christmas to 793.

Absorbed various businesses right across Canada, opened branches in all major cities, expansion rapid in every direction. 1912, The Birks Chair in Metallurgy at McGill University established by Gift of $100,000 from the four seniors. 1925, registration of Trade Marks (1) Garb of Wheat; (2) Birks' Coat-of-Arms; (3) Canada Lynx Standant. 1926, own date letter on silver started (on London Key) – retarded one year in 1967. April 16, 1928, Henry Birks died. Taken ill in Florida and brought back to Montreal General Hospital. 1935, William M. Birks admitted as liveryman to Goldsmiths Guild, London, England. Henry G. Birks, liveryman, 1949 and Drummond Birks in 1955.

HENDERY, ROBERT (b 1814 - d 1897)

Born in Scotland, Robert Hendery emigrated sometime before 1837. Worked with Peter Bohle, partnership Bohle & Hendery 1837-1840. Worked for the firm of George Savage & Son and Savage & Lyman. Established himself in business on his own account in 1840. 1850, Situated at 62 Lagauchetiere Street. Peter Bohle partner 1850-56. Their customers numbered many watchmaker-jewellers. These had their own initial or names along with the Hendery "hallmarks" punched on the articles ordered. As the demand for electroplated articles grew the work of the skilled silversmith producing quality sterling silver was concentrated in the hands of a few firms. 1864, John Leslie became an apprentice to Hendery. 1867, by this time Robert Hendery had become the leading silversmith in Quebec. Only a few independent silversmiths remained in Montreal. Peter Bohle had died in 1865. Francis Bohle and David Smillie in 1867. Otto Meves had gone to Kingston. William Learmont for whom Hendery was making silver had died. There remained only three firms of note in the city. John Street (known for plated wear bearing the beaver mark). John Wood & Son and Savage & Lyman. In Quebec City there remained only Ambroise LaFrance and Pierre Lesperance as active silversmiths. Robert Hendery had already begun to make silver for Gustavus Seifert of Fabrique Street. In the years following Hendery manufactured for many well known firms adding M. S. Brown & Co. and Julius Cornelius of Halifax to his customers in the late 1870s. 1887, John Leslie became a partner, the name of the firm was changed to Hendery & Leslie. Factory at 134 St. Peter Street, Montreal. 1895, dissolved partnership with John Leslie leaving John sole owner of the business which was sold by him to Birks in 1899. 1897, Robert Hendery died after 67 years in the silver business (Names of firms for whom he made silver and whose touch marks were acquired by Henry Birks & Sons Ltd. in 1899 follow.

R H with pseudo hallmarks.

RH also with pseudo hallmarks.

H & L
with pseudo hallmarks.

Hendery & Leslie used
H & L STERLING

R. HENDERY
MONTREAL

Year	Marks	Year	Marks
1898	a	1901	d
1899	b	1902	d
1900	c	1903	d

1904–1924 BIRKS STERLING

Year	Marks	Year	Marks
1925	🐎 I k	1945	G 🐎 K
1926	🐎 I l	1946	G 🐎 L
1927	🐎 I m	1947	G 🐎 M
1928	🐎 I n	1948	G 🐎 N
1929	🐎 I o	1949	G 🐎 O
1930	🐎 I p	1950	G 🐎 P
1931	🐎 I q	1951	G 🐎 Q
1932	🐎 I r	1952	G 🐎 R
1933	🐎 I s	1953	G 🐎 S
1934	🐎 I t	1954	G 🐎 T
1935	● 🐎 I u	1955	G 🐎 U
1936	🐎 I A	1956	G 🐎 a
1937	G 🐎 B	1957	G 🐎 b
1938	G 🐎 C	1958	G 🐎 c
1939	G 🐎 D	1959	G 🐎 d
1940	G 🐎 E	1960	G 🐎 e
1941	G 🐎 F	1961	G 🐎 f
1942	G 🐎 G	1962	G 🐎 g
1943	G 🐎 H		
1944	G 🐎 I		

Firms Which Became Part of Henry Birks & Sons

- 1899, Hendery & Leslie, situated at 134 St. Peter Street, John Leslie remained as manager until 1925. Director of Henry Birks & Sons Ltd. from March 11, 1925-1939.
- 1903, Olmstead & Hurdman, Ottawa, Charles Olmstead, manager. Replaced by Howard S. Porter in 1914.
- 1905, Ryrie Bros., Toronto. Harry Ryrie Director of Henry Birks & Sons, 1906-1917. James Ryrie elected first Hon. Treasurer of "The Canadian National Jewellers Association" on September 25, 1918. J. H. Birks was elected 1st. Vice-President.
- 1907, George E. Trorey, Vancouver (b. 1861 - d. 1946). Director to 1931.
- 1907, Gorham Co. of Canada Ltd., silver plate factory situated on Vitre Street, west of Beaver Hall Hill.
- 1919, M. S. Brown & Co., Halifax.
- 1920, D. E. Black & Co., Calgary. David E. Black, Director to 1953.
- 1927, D. A. Kirkland, Edmonton.
- 1928, N. C. Maynard, Hamilton. Mr. Maynard resigned his position as Managing Director Birks Toronto in 1923. Started with Ryrie Bros.
- 1929, J. E. Wilmot, Ottawa, closed out this store, 1931.
- 1930, G. Seifert & Co. Gustavus Seifert (b. 1831 d. 1909) Quebec.
- 1931, Firm of Birks-Ellis-Ryrie formed.
- 1933, Firm of Birks-Dingwall formed.

Touch Marks Acquired by Henry Birks & Sons

Name of Firm	Date	Mark
C. & J. Allen, Toronto	1870-1887	C. & J. ALLEN; C. & J. A
Lowe & Anderson, Toronto	1885-1888	L & A
C. Addison, Ottawa	1882-1892	C.A.
T. Allen & Co., Montreal	1862-1900	T A & CO
Messrs. H. Birks & Co., Montreal	1849-1893	BIRKS (five sizes)
Messrs. H. Birks & Co., Montreal	1894-	H. B. & CO
Bilsky & Son, Ottawa	1885	BILSKY & SON
N. Beaudry, Jeweller, Montreal	1880	N. BEAUDRY
W. Bramley, Montreal	1890-1891	~W. BRAMLEY

Name of Firm	Date	Mark
M. S. Brown & Co, Halifax	1886-1919	M. S. B. & CO
A. Beauchamp. Jeweller, Montreal	1865-1880	A. B
Geo. B. Bailey, Montreal	1880	*G. B.
Smith Bros., Kingston	1885	S. Bs
M. Cochenthaler, Jeweller, Montreal	1885-1931	M. COCHENTHALER M.C
Canada Manufacturing Co. Montreal and Toronto	1890	CANADA M'FG. Co STERLING SILVER
J. Cornolius, Halifax	1825-1916	J. CORNELIUS (two sizes)
Lee & Chillas, Toronto	1881-1889	L. & C.
John C. Copp, Montreal	(possibly) 1892	*J. C. C.
G. L. Darling, Simcoe	1852-1899	G. L. DARLING
J.E. Ellis & Co., Toronto	1871-1901	J. E. E. & Co.
J. Froland, Kingston	1865-1885	J. FROLAND J. F.
Matthew Gage, Kingston	1851-1879	M. GAGE
M. L. Gurd, Jeweller, Montreal		M. L. GURD
J..R. Harper & Co., Montreal	1880	J. R. H. & CO
R. Hendery, Montreal	1814-1895	R. HENDERY R. H
Hendery & Leslie, Montreal	1887-1899	HENDERY & LESLIE H&L
Olmstead & Hurdman, Ottawa	1892-1903	O & H
J. G. Joseph & Co., Toronto.	1857.1877	J. G. J. & Co
A.C. Johnson & Bros. Kingston, Montreal Believed sold to Mappin & Webb,	1894-1913	A. C. J. & B.
J. H. Jones & Co. Montreal	1880-1890	*J. H. J. & Co.
W. H. Kearney, Toronto	1880	W. H. KEARNEY
W. H. Kirk, Toronto	1885	W. H. K.
Kent Bros., Toronto	1867-1882	KENT BROS
Ambrose Kent & Son, Toronto	1894-1897	A. K. & S.
John Leslie, Ottawa	1845-1895	J LESLIE (two sizes)
Lowe & Co., Toronto	1885	LOWE & Co.
J. W. Millar & Co., Toronto	1882	J. W. M. & Co.
Simpson Hall Miller & Co, Montreal.	1879-1890	S. H. M. & Co.
N. Marks, Ottawa	1876	N. MARKS
E. M. Morphy, Toronto and London, Ont.	1847-1882 about	E. M. M
Miller & Bremner, Working Jewellers, Montreal	1880-1890	M & B
W. C. Morrison, Toronto	1846-1886	*W. C. M.

61

Maker	Dates	Mark
Zimmerman McNaught & Co. Toronto	1882-1885	Z. McN & CO
Hugh S. Murray, London	1869	*H. S. M.
D. Miller, Montreal		D. MILLER
David McPherson, Montreal	1849-1903	*D. M M
C.A. Olmstead, Ottawa	1890-1903	OLMSTEAD C. A. O.
P.E. Poulin, Quebec, Ottawa	1867-1869	POULIN P. E. P.
Pelton, Montreal	1885	PELTON
George G. Robinson & Co., Montreal	1890	G. G. R. & CO
A.J. Rosenthal, Ottawa	1882-1903	ROSENTHAL A. J. R
C. E. Redfern, Victoria	1874-1900	C. E. R
Ryrie Bros., Toronto	1882-1905	RYRIE
Savage, Montreal		SAVAGE
Savage & Lyman, Montreal		*SAVAGE & LYMAN SAVAGE & LYMAN
Savage & Lyman & Co., Montreal	1767-1885	*S. L. & CO
George Savage, Montreal		GS
W. H. Savage, Montreal		W. H. S
Gustavus Seifert, Quebec Used with Seifert's mark.	1857-1930	G. SEIFERT SEIFERT *QUEBEC
R. Sharpley & Sons, Montreal	1837-1900	R. SHARPLEY & SONS
T.B. Steacy, Brockville	1860-1966	T. B. STEACY
H. & A. Saunders, Jewellers Toronto, Montreal	1869-1885	H & A. S
F.W. Spanenberg, Kingston	1870-1887	F. W. S. *F. W. S.
S.A. Spanenberg, Kingston	1885	S. A. S *S A. S
F.W. Sark & Bros., Napanee	1885	F. W. S & B
Tasker & Sons, Toronto	1882	TASKER & SONS
Toronto Silver Plate Co., Toronto	1882-1920	TORONTO SILVER PLATE Co
W. H. Tracy, Ottawa	1851-1892	W. H. TRACY
Kerr & Thorne, Saint John	1878-1885	K & T
G. Warren, Toronto	1880	G. WARREN
Watson, Montreal	1870	WATSON
Watson & Pelton, Montreal	1880	W. & P. M

W. S. Walker, Montreal	1855-1890	WALKER W. S. W
J. Wanless, Toronto	1865-1905	WANLESS
R. Wilks & Co., Montreal & Toronto	1847-1880	R W & Co.
J.B. Williamson, Montreal	1885	*J. B. W
William Walker, Montreal	1855-1890	W. W
S.B. Windrum, Toronto	1882-1885	S. B. W
W. G. Young, London, Ont.	1890	W. G. YOUNG
J. Zimmerman, Toronto	1882	J. ZIMMERMAN

Most of the marks are incised. Those which have letters in relief on a sunk panel are marked *

Pseudo-English "Hall" and Combined Marks used by Hendery and Leslie

These marks, individually, or in various combinations, were used on silver manufactured for the trade. The date letters conform to the London date letters up to 1903. "a" is 1896-1897 and the others follow in annual succession. These letters serve to date pieces by Hendery & Leslie up to 1903. J.R. & Co. was John Round & Co.

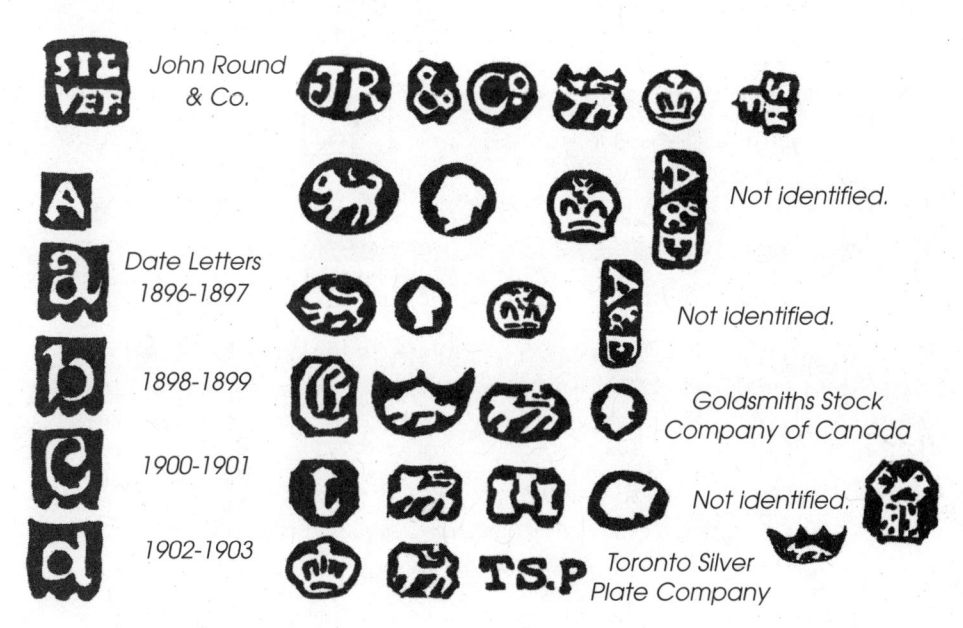

John Round & Co.

Date Letters
1896-1897

1898-1899

1900-1901

1902-1903

Not identified.

Not identified.

Goldsmiths Stock Company of Canada

Not identified.

Toronto Silver Plate Company

QUEBEC CITY

AMIOT, JEAN NICOLAS (- 1750 - d 1821)
Apprenticed to Joseph Schindler 1767. Repaired silver for the Notre Dame de la Victoria Church. Father of Laurent Amiot. Died March, 1821.

AMIOT, LAURENT (b 1764 - d 1838)
Born in Quebec, father of Jean Joseph Amiot, brother of Augustin and Jean Amiot Jr. One of 12 children. Apprenticed to I. F. Ranvoyze. Studied in France. Worked in Quebec for many years. His apprentices included Paul Morin. Made beautiful silver for the church. His punch was later used by Ambroise Lafrance who sometimes added a 'Napoleonic' head.

BEGUAY, JEAN BAPTISTE (- 1786 - 1815 -)
Recorded as working goldsmith.

BEWES, DANIEL (- 1844 - 1852 -)
Watchmaker, Jeweller and Gold and Silversmith. Believed to be the same man as Daniel Bews known in Toronto in 1856.

D.B — *with Lion, Leopard's Head Letter & Fleur de lis.*

BOURÉ, NARCISSE (- 1854 - 1865 -)
Listed at several addresses in Quebec.

N.B — *Lion and Head of Man.*

CHRISTMAS, D. S. (- 1836 - 1854 -)
Listed as Silversmith. Situated at 58½ St. John Street, 1854.

COUTURE, PIERRE (- 1844 - 1854 -)
Listed as silversmith. Situated at 25 Mountain Street. Wife believed to have taken over business at that time.

ELLIS, JAMES (- 1820 - 1822 -)
Working Silversmith situated at 20 St. Ursule Street.

J. ELLIS — *with other marks similar to those used by James Adams Dwight of Montreal.*

GATIEN, M. (- 1762 -)
Made silver for the Church of St. Jean Deschaillons.

GENDRON, P. (- 1852 - 1865 -)
Partner and brother of Hector Gendron. Advertised in Canadian Directory 1853-1854.

GROTHE, Z. (- 1849 - 1850 -)

HANNA, JAMES (- 1763 - 1807)
Believed to be an Irishman, originally from Dublin. In business in Quebec about 40 years. Succeeded by son James Godfrey Hanna.

HANNA, JAMES GODFREY (- 1803 - 1819 -)
Clock and Watchmaker as well as gold and silversmith. Succeeded to his father's business in 1807 having worked with him as partner for the previous four years. F. Delagrave his partner 1816-18.

HANNA & DELAGRAVE (1816 - 1818)
See above. This partnership disolved when Hanna went into bankruptcy.

HARDY, ANSELM (- 1850 - 1856 -)
Situated at 18 St. Peter Street. L.T.

[A.H] with Lion. [A.H]

HARRIS, E. B. (- 1844 - 1857 -)
Situated at 7 Notre Dame Street.

HULL, MRS. E. (- 1852 - 1857 -)
Listed in Canadian Directory at 13 Buade Street U.T.

HUNTER, WILLIAM (- 1805 -)
Partner with brother Francis Hunter 1804. Silver with Laurent Amiot mark plus W.H. would suggest that Amiot made silver for Hunter.

Plus Crown & Lion.

INNES, WILLIAM (- 1848 - 1864)
Situated on St. John Street 1848 - 54. Address 12 Palace Street 1864. Listed in the Directory of 1853 at St. John Street.

[W.I] with Leopard's Head & Man's Head.

65

LAFRANCE, AMBROISE (- 1822 - 1918)
See Laurent Amiot.

LAMBERT, PAUL (b 1691 - 1749 -)
Born in Quebec. Considered one of the more outstanding silversmiths of the French Period.

LAMONTAGNE, MICHAEL (- 1833 - 1871 -)
Silversmith, Jeweller and Watchmaker 3 St John Street 1853 to 1864. Moved to Coulliard St.

LANDRON, JEAN FRANCOIS (- 1686 - 1759 -)
Church silversmith.

LESPERANCE, PIERRE (1819 - 1882)
Trained by his Uncle Francois Sasseville. Became his partner then his successor. Laurent Amiot's tools came to him from his uncle. Made church silver.

LUCAS, JOSEPH (- 1775 -)
Listed as silversmith.

MARTYN, MRS. JOHN (- 1853 - 1854 -)
Situated at 45 St. Peter Street. Specialized in the repairing and regulating of chronometers, listed as silversmith.

MORIN, PAUL (- 1775 - 1805 -)
Church silversmith, apprenticed to Laurent Amiot.   also with pseudo hallmarks.

MCLAUGHLIN, SAMUEL (- 1850 - 1857 -)
Clockmaker and Silversmith. Situated at St. Peters Street.

ORKNEY, JAMES (- 1791 - 1826 -)
Working silversmith. Partner of Joseph Sasseville around 1800. Listed as juryman in 1797.

PAGE, JACQUES (- 1686 - d 1742)
One of the outstanding early silversmiths. Apprenticed to Levasseur. Was in Paris 1713-1715. Returned to Quebec. Died 1742.

PARADIS, ROLAND (- 1696 - 1754 -)
Made a great deal of Church silver.

POULIN & CO., P. E. (- 1888 -)
Situated at 40 Fabrique Street. Silver made for this firm by Hendery & Leslie.

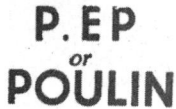

P.EP or **POULIN** with Pseudo Hallmarks.

POWIS, THOMAS (- 1781 -)
English goldsmith and jeweller. Believed in advertising. Made silver for Indian trade, all manner of jewellery and much flatware.

RANVOYZE, IGNACE FRANCOIS (1739 - 1819)
Church silversmith. Served in the Militia. Worked three years as locksmith.

SASSEVILLE, FRANCOIS (- 1797 - d 1864)
Son of Joseph Sasseville, silversmith and brother of Geo. Sasseville, silversmith. Francois succeeded Laurent Amiot. Was in partnership with Pierre Lesperance 1854-56. Situated 17 Mountain Street. 1853-54. Made silver for the church.

SASSEVILLE, JOSEPH (1776 - 1831)
Father of Francois and George Sasseville. Made Indian trade silver and ceremonial pieces as well as other silver items.

SASSEVILLE & ORKNEY (- 1800 -)
Partnership of Joseph Sasseville and James Orkney. [IS] with Lion [IO]

SCHINDLER, JONAS (- 1760 - 1786 -)
Made trade silver.

SEIFERT, GUSTAVUS (b 1831 - d 1909)
A firm of long standing 1857 - 1930 acquired by Henry Birks & Sons, Montreal. Used a variety of marks. Some silver made for him by Hendery & Leslie.

(G.S)　**G. SEIFERT**

Sometimes with STERLING or Pseudo Hallmarks and some pieces marked QUEBEC.

SHEFFIELD, HOUSE (- 1867 -)
Listed in Quebec 1867.

SILVER STANDARDS AND MARKS

The bullion value has traditionally been the most important cost of a silver object. Since pure silver cannot be worked, it is always alloyed with some baser metal. It is possible to add up to one third of some base metal to silver without changing the colour of the finished product.

Therefore, to protect the consumer, and ultimately the State who received silver as tax or duty, governments always and everywhere took steps to regulate the quality of metal both in coinage and in silverware. It was the universal custom that the same standard applied to both, so that private owners, and at times the Kings themselves, could treat their money stocks and their stocks of silverware back and forth as the occasion demanded without going through a reassay and revaluation each time.

From these requirements proceed all the hallmark systems in use throughout the world. Please remember that marks were not placed on a piece of silver to tell you where and by whom the piece was made. They were placed there to tell the owner, and the government, what the exact standard of metal was and who was legally responsible in case of fraud.

Americans tend to think of silver as being either "sterling" or "plate." In fact, many standards are and have been in use. Based on pure silver expressed as 1000/1000 fine, some of the more common are:

950/1000 fine.
Britannia standard, compulsory in England for the years 1697 to 1718, and optional ever since. Also the ancient French Royal standard, in use exclusively till the revolution and optional since.

925/1000
The sterling standard English, from the 13th century. Later adopted by American manufacturers around 1868.

900/1000
A common European standard, also the American coin silver standard after about 1835.

890/1000 through 800/1000 fine.
Various European standards. The 800 standard is the common German standard in use throughout central Europe.

750/1000
About the lowest authorized standard, below which no government would certify the quality of metal.

This decimal system of indicating fineness is universal since about 1885. Before that, you may encounter standard marks based on the ancient Mark of Cologne, which was divided into 16 units, or deniers, from the Roman denarius. Thus, a mark "13" would indicate 13/16ths, or about 800/1000 fine.

In many cases with older silver, there will be no standard stated at all. In these cases, as in England, the mark of the Wardens of the Goldsmiths Guild (a lion passant) indicated that the metal was of standard fineness, whatever the local law declared that to be.

Special Note

Whenever a legal marking of authority, for example a certain town in Germany, went out of existence for legal purposes, there was nothing to prevent the use of that town's mark on illegal work. Thus, a vast quantity of 19th and 20th century European silver is marked with town and standard marks of places which had not assayed silver in years.

Plated Silver

There are three kinds of plated silver. Each is some form of placing a thin surface of silver on a base metal body. There are few rules about the marking of silver plate, since governments usually did not set standards of quality for legal purposes. What marks there are are often meant to deceive. The three types of plate are:

1. **"Silvering"** or **"Close plating."** This is an ancient method, mostly used to coat steel or brass, which consisted of fixing a thin sheet of silver to the base metal using a flux and a hot soldering iron. Not very durable on steel. You will encounter close plating on 19th century steel objects such as snuffers and coffin fixtures, also sometimes on 18th century brass. Most early brass was silvered originally.

2. **Old Sheffield Plate**. These words describe a METHOD of plating which consisted of fusing a sheet or sheets of sterling onto a copper bar under heat and high pressure. The coated bar was then rolled out and made up into objects just as a bar of pure sterling would have been, with special methods used to conceal the copper centre at the edges. This method dates from around 1760, and is marked in various ways. At first, the manufacturers used pseudo-hallmarks, meant to look superficially like London marks. This was forbidden by law after a few years, and for the remainder of the 18th century Old Sheffield Plate NEVER BEARS ANY MARKS AT ALL. Most good Old Sheffield Plate is not marked, and you can only identify it by the method of manufacture. In the 19th century, the law allowed the use of makers names and devices, provided they did not in any way resemble legal hall marks.

3. **Electroplate** First in commercial use about 1840, this method of plating by placing the finished object in a bath containing silver in solution, quickly supplanted Old Sheffield Plating, although many of the same companies continued to use the traditional marks. All American silver plate is electroplate. A large number of "standard" marks appear on electroplate, both in England and in the U.S. For example: A-1, EPNS,

EPBM, EPC, Silver soldered, Quadrupple, etc. None of these "standards" mean anything. The plating is either in good condition, or it is worn off.

SOME WARNINGS: Nothing marked "Sheffield" is Old Sheffield Plate. NO plate marked "ENGLAND" can date before the 1880s. Any mark incorporating the word "silver" such as "Nevada Silver", "German Silver", "Brazil Silver" mean that the piece is nickel silver (which contains NO SILVER) which may or may not be plated.

REPLATING: Old Sheffield Plate is valuable because it is an antique object, by definition. It should not be replated, unless the piece is so worn that its antique value is gone already. In those cases, it might as well be replated. On the other hand, worn electroplate is virtually worthless, so if the piece is worth saving, it should and may be replated, which will only enhance the value.

French and Russian "Old Sheffield Plate Type" silverplate is marked with quality marks, but this sort of work seldom appears and you should only know where to look for the information.

Look for the HALLMARK

A hallmark on a gold or silver article shows that it has been accurately tested or assayed at one of the four official assay offices and that the metal conforms to one of the legal standards of purity. A hallmark consists of several symbols:

| Maker's | Standard | Assay Office | Date Letter |

The **Maker's Mark** nowadays consists of the initials of the person or firm submitting the article to the assay office. It takes the form of the symbol NM in the above example.

The **Date Letter** indicates the year in which the article was hallmarked. It consists of a shield enclosing a letter of the alphabet. The letter is changed in May each year at the London office, in July at Birmingham and Sheffield and in October in Edinburgh. To determine the date of the marking of an article it is necessary first to identify the particular assay office from the assay office mark and then to refer to a published list of date letters. This is because each assay office uses different alphabetical cycles.

| Lion Passant | Lion Passant Guardant | Lion Rampant |

Hallmarked Silver

Standard Mark
Denoting the minimum silver or gold content.

Mark	Standard	Minimum Percentage
🦁	STERLING SILVER MARKED IN ENGLAND	92.5
	Sterling silver Marked in Scotlland	92.5
	Britannia silver	95.84
22	22 carat gold Marked in England	91.66
18	18 carat gold Marked in England	75.0
14 585	14 carat gold	58.5
9 375	9 carat gold	37.5

Assay Office Mark
Showing which assay offices treated the mark.

Mark	Office	Standard
	London	Sterling silver & gold
	London	Britannia silver
⚓	Birmingham	Silver & gold
	Sheffield	Silver
	Sheffield	Gold
	Edinbugh	Silver & Gold

There were formally Assay offices at other towns, each having its own distinctive mark.

800   German Federal mark after 1888.

Typical 18th century European mark. Rotterdam, mid 18th century.

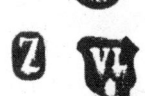

Crowned Lion: Province mark.
Shield: Rotterdam mark.
Z: Date letter.
VL: Maker's mark.

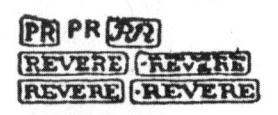

Various marks used by the 18th century American silversmith Paul Revere.

PREMIUM
STANDARD
COIN
FRENCH FRANKS
SP. DOL.
STER. AMER. MFG.

Standard marks used by American silversmiths in the first half of the 19th century.

"11 oz." and "10.15"   Baltimore standard marks. Based on 12 ounce Troy.

Silver Marks - Silver Plate

Mark   Origin

English 18th - 19th century CLOSE PLATE mark. This was a silver-leaf process on steel, for buckles, blades, etc.

English FUSED PLATE mark (Old Sheffiled Plate.) Most Old Sheffield Plate is NOT marked. If marked, either a symbol or full name may occur. The words "Sheffield", "Sheffield Plate", "England", or "Silver on Copper" were NEVER used on Old Sheffield Plate.

English ELECTROPLATE mark. Consists mostly of maker's initials and quality marks such as Al, EPNS, EPC, or BP. Such marks are arranged to look like hallmarks.

American ELECTROPLATE mark. Similar to the English marks.

GEORGE V and QUEEN MARY SILVER JUBILEE 1935

TWENTY-FIVE YEARS

From 1784 to 1890 the Sovereign's head always appeared as part of the legal hall-mark stamped by the Assay Office on silver to denote the payment of duty. Only on one occasion has the Assay Offices ever used the head of the Sovereign and his Queen, this was when it was agreed to commemorate the Silver Jubilee of their Royal Majesties King George V and Queen Mary. This mark was used from 1933/4 to 1935/6.

Arthur Tremayne, the well-known authority on clocks, watches, diamonds and silver was the originator of the idea and went to a great deal of trouble to get it put into effect. In fact before the mark could be used, the laws of England had to be changed and not only did the Goldsmiths' Company, provincial Assay Office, Board of Trade, The Mint and Treasury have to be convinced and give their approval, but the Home Office sanction had to be waited for. The original of the obverse side of the official Jubilee Medal (designed by Mr. Percy Metcalf) was used for the punch.

This was a very exciting event in the history of silver for in more than six centuries of hall-marking it had never been used as anything but a mark of high quality for precious metals; never before had it been linked with events of national importance. Certainly it was the first time two crowned heads appeared on any stamp used for marking silver articles.

This fact alone makes any piece with the Jubilee mark of considerable importance. Samples can be found today, as thousands of sets of spoons, six to the set, each bearing the mark of a different Assay Office, were made and sold. The British Industries Fair sold many pieces to both home and overseas buyers, so you can be certain that Canada received its share. Many items: tea-services, trays, coffee pots, vases, flatware, boxes etc., were so marked and are definitely worth looking for as an addition to a collection of silver or Royal Commemoratives.

Town Marks & Date Letters

Town Mark	1933-4	1934-5	1935-6
🦁 London	S	T	U
⚓ Birmingham	J	K	L
👑 Sheffield	q	r	s
🗡 Chester	h	i	k
🌳 Glasgow	K	L	M
🏰 Edinburgh	C	D	E

75

BIRMINGHAM MARKS 1773-1861

Assay office established in 1773 for the marking of silver. The anchor is the mark of the office. Date letter changed each July. Sovereign's head duty mark 1874 - 1890.

Year	Mark	Year	Mark	Year	Mark	Year	Mark
1773	⚓ 🦁 A	1796	⚓ 🦁 👑 Y	1818	🦁 👑 u	1840	⚓ 🦁 👑 R
1774	B	1797	Z	1819	V	1841	S
1775	C			1820	W	1842	T
1776	D	1798	⚓ 🦁 👑 a	1821	X	1843	U
1777	E	1799	b	1822	y	1844	A
1778	F	1800	c	1823	z	1845	M
1779	G	1801	d			1846	E
1780	H	1802	e	1824	⚓ 👑 A	1847	D
1781	I	1803	f	1825	B	1848	Z
1782	K	1804	g	1826	C		
1783	L	1805	h	1827	D	1849	A
1784	👑 M	1806	i	1828	E	1850	B
1785	N	1807	j	1829	F	1851	C
1786	👑 O	1808	k	1830	G	1852	D
1787	P	1809	l	1831	H	1853	E
1788	Q	1810	m	1832	J	1854	F
1789	R	1811	n	1833	K	1855	G
1790	S	1812	o	1834	L	1856	H
1791	T	1813	p	1835	M	1857	I
1792	U	1814	q	1836	N	1857	J
1793	V	1815	r	1837	O	1859	K
1794	W	1816	s	1838	👑 P	1860	L
1795	X	1817	t	1839	Q	1861	M

BIRMINGHAM MARKS 1862 - 1968

Year	Mark	Year	Mark	Year	Mark	Year	Mark
1862	⚓✠♦N	1884	⚓✠♦k	1906	⚓✠g	1929	⚓✠ E
1863	O	1885	l	1907	h	1930	F
1864	P	1886	m	1908	i	1931	G
1865	Q	1887	n	1909	k	1932	H
1866	R	1888	o	1910	l	1933	✠⚓♦ J
1867	S	1889	p	1911	m	1934	K
1868	T	1890	q	1912	n	1935	L
1869	U	1891	r	1913	o	1936	M
1870	V	1892	s	1914	p	1937	N
1871	W	1893	t	1915	q	1938	O
1872	X	1894	u	1916	r	1939	P
1873	Y	1895	v	1917	s	1940	Q
1874	Z	1896	w	1918	t	1941	R
		1897	x	1919	u	1942	S
		1898	y	1920	v	1943	T
1875	a	1899	z	1921	w	1944	U
1876	b			1922	x	1945	V
1877	c			1923	a	1946	W
1878	d	1900		1924	b	1947	X
1879	e	1901		1925	C	1948	Y
1880	f	1902		1926	d	1949	Z
1881	g	1903		1927	e	1950	A continuing thus
1882	h	1904		1928	f	1952	C continuing thus
1883	t	1905				1968	T

77

CHESTER MARKS 1701 - 1962

Gold and silver was assayed in Chester as early as the 15th century, but the marks were not regulated until about the end of the 17th century. Three wheatsheafs with sword were the assay office mark 1686 - 1700. Three wheatsheafs with sword was used again after 1779.

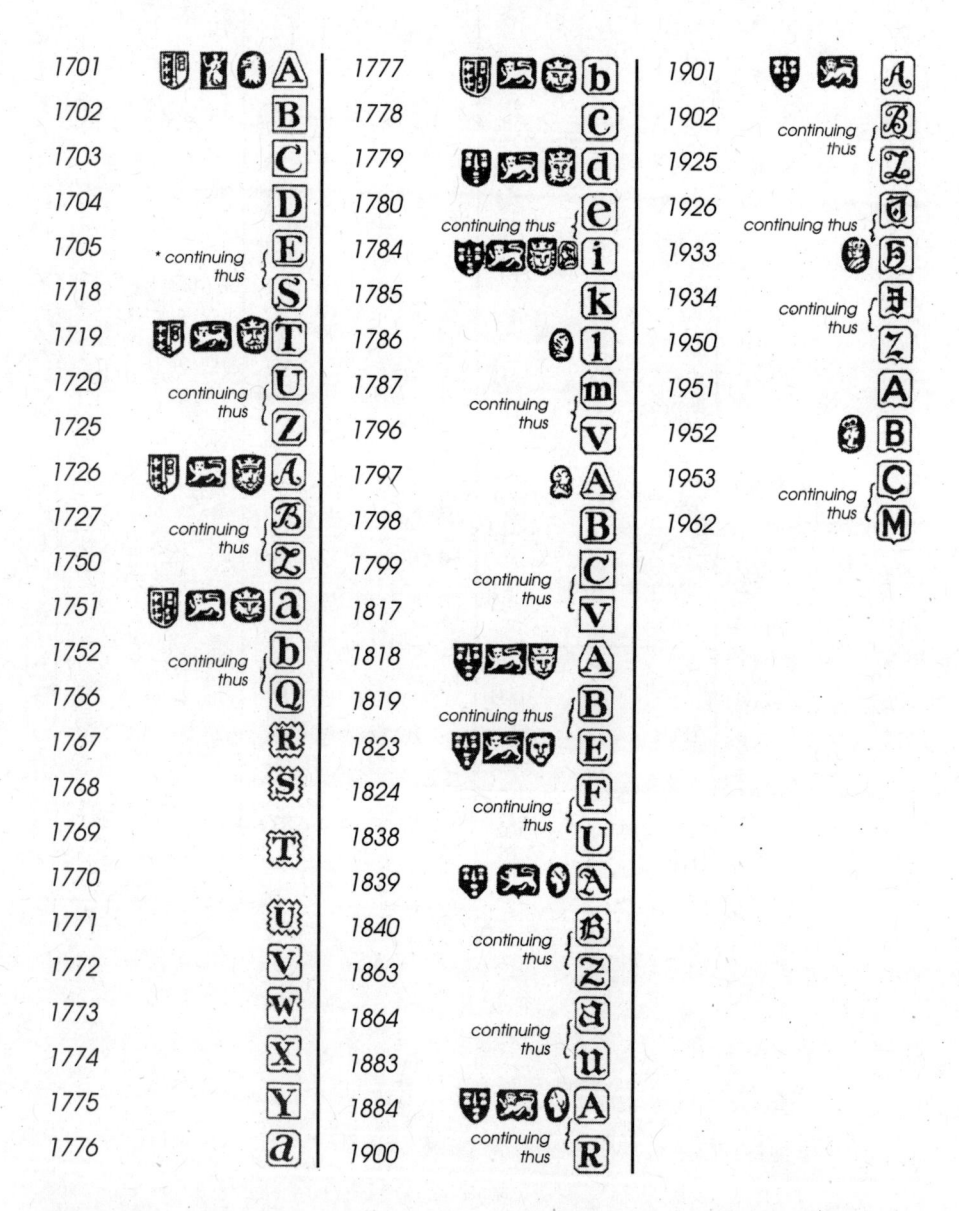

Year	Mark	Year	Mark	Year	Mark
1701		1777		1901	
1702		1778		1902	
1703		1779		1925	continuing thus
1704		1780		1926	
1705	*continuing thus	1784	continuing thus	1933	continuing thus
1718		1785		1934	
1719		1786		1950	
1720	continuing thus	1787		1951	
1725		1796	continuing thus	1952	
1726		1797		1953	continuing thus
1727	continuing thus	1798		1962	
1750		1799	continuing thus		
1751		1817			
1752	continuing thus	1818			
1766		1819	continuing thus		
1767		1823			
1768		1824	continuing thus		
1769		1838			
1770		1839			
1771		1840	continuing thus		
1772		1863			
1773		1864	continuing thus		
1774		1883			
1775		1884			
1776		1900	continuing thus		

NOTE: * "continuing thus" i.e. 1705 - 1718 continued the same style of lettering from E to S on the same shape of shield and with other markings identical to those used 1701 to 1704. The words "continuing thus" have a similar meaning in every instance.

EXETER MARKS 1701 - 1882

Wrought silver was made in Exeter during the middle ages. Roman X is the 16th and 17th century town mark. Three towered castle mark of assay office from 1701. Date letter changed in August each year.

Year	Mark	Year	Mark	Year	Mark
1701	A	1791	f	1830	O
1702	B (continuing thus)	1792	t	1831	P
1720		1793	u	1832	q
1721	W (continuing thus)	1794	w	1833	r
1724	Z	1795	x	1836	u (continuing thus)
1725	a (continuing thus)	1796	y	1837	A
1748	z	1797	A	1838	B
1749	A (continuing thus)	1798	B	1839	C
1759	L	1799	C	1840	D
1760	M (continuing thus)	1800	D (continuing thus)	1841	E
1768	U	1805	I	1842	f
1769	W	1816	U (continuing thus)	1843	G
1770	X	1817	a	1856	(continuing thus)
1771	Y	1818	b	1857	A
1772	Z	1819	c	1858	B
1773	A (continuing thus)	1820	d	1859	C
1778	F	1821	e	1860	D (continuing thus)
1779	G (continuing thus)	1822	f	1876	U
1784	L	1823	g	1877	A (continuing thus)
1785	M	1824	h	1882	F
1786	N	1825	i		
1787	O	1826	k		
1788	P	1827	l		
1789	q	1828	m		
1790	r	1829	n		

LONDON MARKS 1658-1770

Gold and silver assayed and marked since 1327. Various styles of Leopard's head used as office mark, also note changes of lion mask which indicated sterling standard. Date letter changed in May each year.

Year	Year	Year	Year
1658	1687	1715	1743
1659	1688		1744
1660	1689	1716	1745
1661	1690	1717	1746
1662	1691	1718	1747
1663	1692	1719	1748
1664	1693	1720	1749
1665	1694	1721	1750
1666	1695	1722	1751
1667	1696	1723	1752
1668		1724	1753
1669	1697	1725	1754
1670		1726	1755
1671	1698	1727	
1672	1699	1728	1756
1673	1700	1729	1757
1674	1701	1730	1758
1675	1702	1731	1759
1676	1703	1732	1760
1677	1704	1733	1761
	1705	1734	1762
1678	1706	1735	1763
1679	1707		1764
1680	1708	1736	1765
1681	1709	1737	1766
1682	1710	1738	1767
1683	1711	1739	1768
1684	1712	1740	1769
1685	1713	1741	1770
1686	1714	1742	

LONDON MARKS 1771 - 1881

Year	Mark	Year	Mark	Year	Mark	Year	Mark
1771	🦁 👑 O	1799	🦁 👑 D	1827	🦁 👑 m	1855	🦁 👑
1772	R	1800	E	1828	n		
1773	S	1801	F	1829	o	1856	🦁 👑 a
1774	T	1802	G	1830	p	1857	b
1775	U	1803	H	1831	q	1858	c
		1804	I	1832	r	1859	d
1776	a	1805	K	1833	s	1860	e
1777	b	1806	L	1834	t	1861	f
1778	c	1807	M	1835	u	1862	g
1779	d	1808	N			1863	h
1780	e	1809	O	1836	🦁 👑 A	1864	i
1781	f	1810	P	1837	B	1865	j
1782	g	1811	Q	1838	C	1866	k
1783	h	1812	R	1839	D	1867	l
1784	i	1813	S	1840	E	1868	m
1785	k	1814	T	1841	F	1869	n
1786	l	1815	U	1842	G	1870	o
1787	m			1843	H	1871	p
1788	n	1816	🦁 👑 a	1844	J	1872	q
1789	o	1817	b	1845	K	1873	r
1790	p	1818	c	1846	L	1874	s
1791	q	1819	d	1847	M	1875	t
1792	r	1820	e	1848	N		
1793	s	1821	🦁 👑 f	1849	O	1876	🦁 👑 A
1794	t	1822	g	1850	P	1877	B
1795	u	1823	h	1851	Q	1878	C
		1824	i	1852	R	1879	D
1796	🦁 👑 A	1825	k	1853	S	1880	E
1797	B	1826	l	1854	T	1881	F
1798	C						

LONDON MARKS 1883 - 1968

Year	Year	Year	Year
1882	1910	1936	
1883 H	1911 q	1937 B	
1884 I	1912 r	1938 C	
1885 K	1913 s	1939 D	
1886 L	1914 t	1940 E	
1887 M	1915 u	1941 F	
1888 N		1942 G	
1889 O	1916 a	1943 H	
1890 P	1917 b	1944 I	
1891 Q	1918 c	1945 K	
1892 R	1919 d	1946 L	
1893 S	1920 e	1947 M	
1894 T	1921 f	1948 N	
1895 U	1922 g	1949 O	
1896 a	1923 h	1950 P	
1897 b	1924 i	1951 Q	
1898 c	1925 k	1952 R	
1899 d	1926 l	1953 S	
1900 e	1927 m	1954 T	
1901 f	1928 n	1955 U	
1902 g	1929 o	1956 a	
1903 h	1930 p	1968 n	
1904 i	1931 q	*continuing thus*	
1905 k	1932 r		
1906 l	1933 s		
1907 m	1934 t		
1908 n	1935 u		
1909 o			

82

NEWCASTLE MARKS 1702 - 1883

Silver and goldsmiths are recorded as working in Newcastle from the mid-13th century. A single castle with lion passant was used prior to 1670. Three castles were used after that date. The assay office was re-established in 1702.

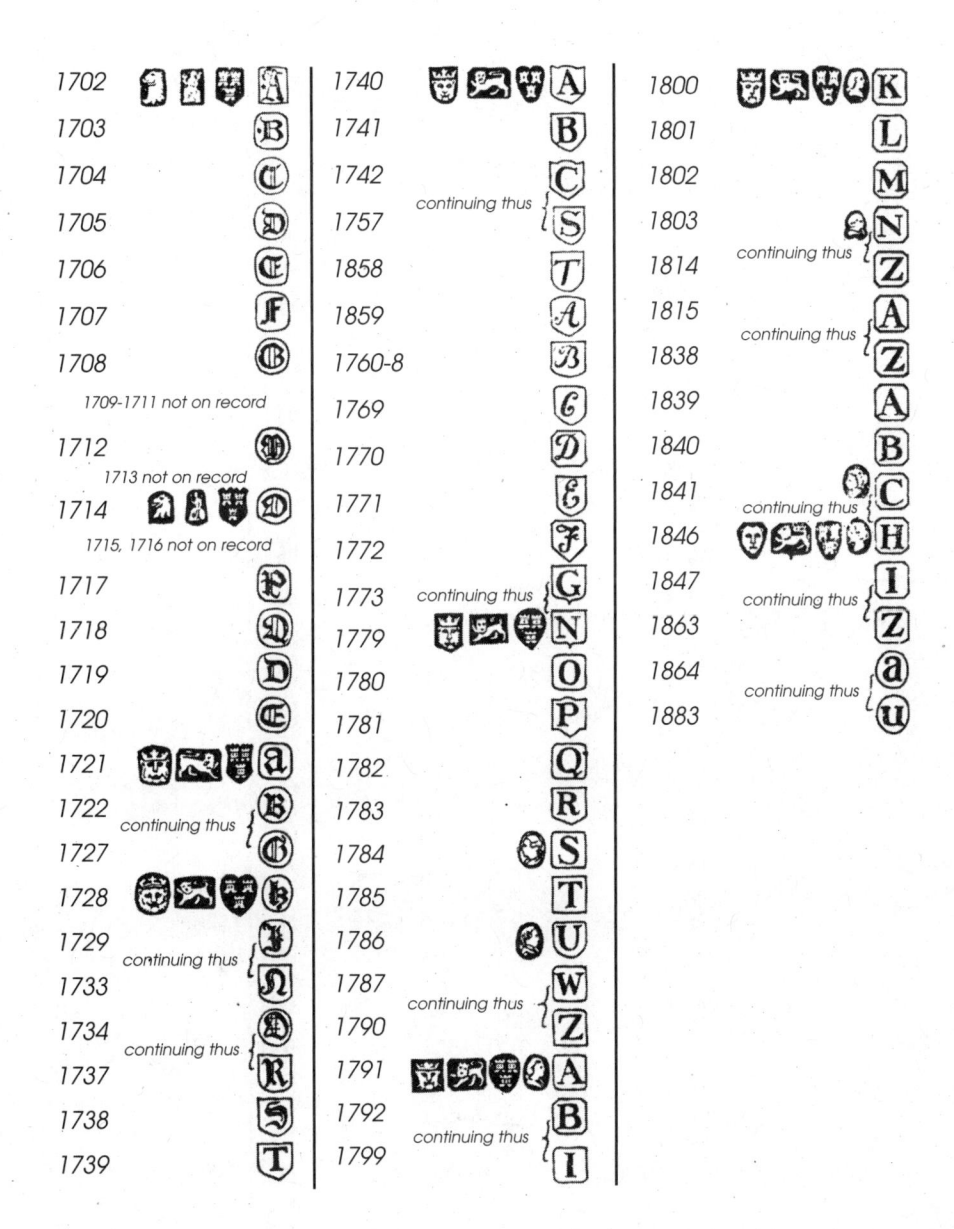

Date	Mark	Date	Mark	Date	Mark
1702		1740		1800	K
1703	B	1741	B	1801	L
1704	C	1742	C	1802	M
1705	D	1757	continuing thus S	1803	N
1706	E	1858	T	1814	continuing thus Z
1707	F	1859	A	1815	A
1708	G	1760-8	B	1838	continuing thus Z
1709-1711 not on record		1769	C	1839	A
1712	M	1770	D	1840	B
1713 not on record		1771	E	1841	continuing thus C
1714		1772	F	1846	H
1715, 1716 not on record		1773	continuing thus G	1847	continuing thus I
1717	P	1779	N	1863	Z
1718	Q	1780	O	1864	continuing thus a
1719	D	1781	P	1883	u
1720	E	1782	Q		
1721	a	1783	R		
1722	continuing thus B	1784	S		
1727	G	1785	T		
1728	b	1786	U		
1729	continuing thus f	1787	continuing thus W		
1733	n	1790	Z		
1734	continuing thus o	1791	A		
1737	R	1792	continuing thus B		
1738	S	1799	I		
1739	T				

83

SHEFFIELD MARKS 1773 - 1883

Assay Office established in 1773 for the marking of silver. The crown is the mark of this office. Date letter changed each July. From 1784 - 1890 a duty was levied on all silver in Britain and the sovereign's head was the duty mark.

Year	Mark	Year	Mark	Year	Mark	Year	Mark
1773	🦁👑 C	1800	🦁👑😊 N	1828	🦁👑😊 e	1856	🦁👑😊 N
1774	👑 F	1801	H	1829	f	1857	O
1775	A	1802	M	1830	g	1858	P
1776	R	1803	F	1831	h	1859	R
1777	h	1804	G	1832	k	1860	S
1778	S	1805	B	1833	l	1861	T
1779	A	1806	A	1834	m	1862	U
1780	C	1807	S	1835	p	1863	V
1781	D	1808	P	1836	q	1864	W
1782	G	1809	K	1837	😊 r	1865	X
1783	B	1810	L	1838	s	1866	Y
1784	😊 J	1811	C	1839	t	1867	Z
1785	U	1812	D	1840	😊 u	1868	A
1786	😊 K	1813	R	1841	v	1869	B
1787	L	1814	😊 W	1842	x	1870	C
1788	M	1815	O	1843	z	1871	D
1789	N	1816	T	1844	🦁👑😊 A	1872	E
1790	P	1817	X	1845	B	1873	🦁👑😊 F
1791	P	1818	I	1846	C	1874	G
1792	U	1819	V	1847	D	1875	H
1793	O	1820	Q	1848	🦁👑 E	1876	J
1794	m	1821		1849	F	1877	K
1795	q	1822	Y	1850	G	1878	L
1796	Z	1823	Z	1851	H	1879	M
1797	🦁👑 X	1824	👑 U	1852	a	1880	N
1798	🦁👑😊 V	1825	a	1853	b	1881	O
1799	E	1826	c	1854	K	1882	P
		1827	d	1855	L	1883	Q
					M		

On smaller objects a crown appears above the date letter. eg 1802

SHEFFIELD MARKS 1884 - 1968

Year	Mark	Year	Mark	Year	Mark
1884	R	1911	(crown)(lion) t	1936	(crown)(lion) t
1885	S	1912	u	1937	u
1886	T	1913	v	1938	v
1887	U	1914	w	1939	w
1888	V	1915	x	1940	x
1889	W	1916	y	1941	y
1890	X	1917	z	1942	z
1891	Y				
1892	(lion)(crown) Z	1918	(crown)(lion) a	1943	A
1893	(crown)(lion) a	1919	b	1944	B
1894	b	1920	c	1945	C
1895	c	1921	d	1946	D
1896	d	1922	e	1947	E
1897	e	1923	f	1948	F
1898	f	1924	g	1949	G
1899	g	1925	h	1950	H
1900	h	1926	i	1951	I
1901	i	1927	k	1952	(crown)(lion)(head) K
1902	k	1928	l	1967	*continuing thus* Z
1903	l	1929	m	1968	A
1904	m	1930	n		
1905	n	1931	o		
1906	o	1932	p		
1907	p	1933	(crown)(lion)(head) q		
1908	q	1934	r		
1909	r	1935	s		
1910	s				

YORK MARKS 1700-1856

Assay office existed from mid-16th century, but closed in 1717. Re-opened 1774 and closed again in 1856. Silver pieces from this area are rare.

Year	Mark	Year	Mark
1700	A	1807	V
1701	B	1808	W *continuing thus*
1702	C	1811	Z
1703	D	1812	a
1704, 1707, 1709, 171, 1712 not on record.		1813	b *continuing thus*
1705	F	1830	t *continuing thus*
1706	G	1836	3
1708	(mark)	1837	A
1711	(mark)	1838	B
1713	(mark)	1839	C
Assay office closed 1717-1733.		1840	D
1774-1777 not on record.		1841	E
1778	C	1842	F
1779	D *continuing thus*	1843	G
1784	J	1844	H
1785	K	1845	I *continuing thus*
1786	L	1848	M
1787	A	1849	N
1788	B	1850	O
1789	C	1851	P *continuing thus*
1790	d	1856	V
1791	e		
1792	f		
1805	T *continuing thus*		
1806	U		

DUBLIN DATE LETTERS

l	1856-7	A	1871-2	Q	1886-7	f	1901-2	A	1916-7	Q	1932
m	1857-8	B	1872-3	R	1887-8	G	1902-3	b	1917-8	R	1933
n	1858-9	C	1873-4	S	1888-9	H	1903-4	c	1918-9	S	1934
o	1859-0	D	1874-5	T	1889-0	I	1904-5	d	1919-0	T	1935
p	1860-1	E	1875-6	U	1890-1	K	1905-6	e	1920-1	U	1936
Q	1861-2	F	1876-7	V	1891-2	L	1906-7	f	1921-2	V	1937
r	1862-3	G	1877-8	W	1892-3	M	1907-8	g	1922-3	W	1938
s	1863-4	H	1878-9	X	1893-4	N	1908-9	h	1923-4	X	1939
t	1864-5	I	1879-0	Y	1894-5	O	1909-0	i	1924-5	Y	1940
u	1865-6	K	1880-1	Z	1895-6	P	1910-1	B	1925-6	Z	1941
v	1866-7	L	1881-2	A	1896-7	Q	1911-2	K	1926-7	A	1942
w	1867-8	M	1882-3	B	1897-8	R	1912-3	m	1927-8	B	1943
x	1868-9	N	1883-4	C	1898-9	S	1913-4	n	1928-9	From Jan 1st 1932 Assay Year and Calendar coincide.
y	1869-0	O	1884-5	D	1899-0	T	1914-5	O	1929-0	
z	1870-1	P	1885-6	E	1900-1	U	1915-6	P	1930-1	Used throughout 1931.

"IRISH REPUBLICAN SILVER"

It may be of interest to note that when a new set of laws was enacted for the Irish Free State, in 1922, the law relating to hall-marking was thought to have been overlooked and the occasion was used by silversmiths to mark articles with a special punch, using a design of a ship for the town mark. The ship forms part of the city arms of Cork. Ultimately the situation was adjusted, but in the meantime a certain amount of silver had been made and marked, and a quantity was sold. The mark illustrated is from a small tray now in possession of the Dublin Assay Office. Pieces bearing this mark will have a certain value as curiosities for collectors.

GLASGOW DATE LETTERS

A 1819 – 0	V 1840 – 1	ℚ 1861 – 2	L 1882 – 3	𝒢 1903 – 4	b 1924 – 5
B 1820 – 1	W 1841 – 2	ℝ 1862 – 3	M 1883 – 4	ℋ 1904 – 5	c 1925 – 6
C 1821 – 2	X 1842 – 3	𝒮 1863 – 4	N 1884 – 5	𝒥 1905 – 6	d 1926 – 7
D 1822 – 3	Y 1843 – 4	𝒯 1864 – 5	O 1885 – 6	𝒥 1906 – 7	e 1927 – 8
E 1823 – 4	Z 1844 – 5	𝒰 1865 – 6	P 1886 – 7	𝒦 1907 – 8	f 1928 – 9
F 1824 – 5	𝔄 1845 – 6	𝒱 1866 – 7	Q 1887 – 8	ℒ 1908 – 9	g 1929 – 0
G 1825 – 6	𝔅 1846 – 7	𝒲 1867 – 8	R 1888 – 9	ℳ 1909 – 0	h 1930 – 1
H 1826 – 7	ℭ 1847 – 8	𝒳 1868 – 9	S 1889 – 0	𝒩 1910 – 1	i 1931 – 2
I 1827 – 8	𝔇 1848 – 9	𝒴 1869 – 0	T 1890 – 1	𝒪 1911 – 2	j 1932 – 3
J 1828 – 9	𝔈 1849 – 0	𝒵 1870 – 1	U 1891 – 2	𝒫 1912 – 3	k 1933 – 4
K 1829 – 0	𝔉 1850 – 1	𝒜 1871 – 2	V 1892 – 3	𝒬 1913 – 4	l 1934 – 5
L 1830 – 1	𝔊 1851 – 2	ℬ 1872 – 3	W 1893 – 4	ℛ 1914 – 5	m 1935 – 6
M 1831 – 2	ℌ 1852 – 3	𝒞 1873 – 4	X 1894 – 5	𝒮 1915 – 6	n 1936 – 7
N 1832 – 3	𝔍 1853 – 4	𝒟 1874 – 5	Y 1895 – 6	𝒯 1916 – 7	o 1937 – 8
O 1833 – 4	𝔍 1854 – 5	ℰ 1875 – 6	Z 1896 – 7	𝒰 1917 – 8	p 1938 – 9
P 1834 – 5	𝔎 1855 – 6	ℱ 1876 – 7	𝒜 1897 – 8	𝒱 1918 – 9	q 1939 – 0
Q 1835 – 6	𝔏 1856 – 7	𝒢 1877 – 8	ℬ 1898 – 9	𝒲 1919 – 0	r 1940 – 1
R 1836 – 7	𝔐 1857 – 8	ℋ 1878 – 9	𝒞 1899 – 0	𝒳 1920 – 1	s 1941 – 2
S 1837 – 8	𝔑 1858 – 9	𝒥 1879 – 0	𝒟 1900 – 1	𝒴 1921 – 2	t 1942 – 3
T 1838 – 9	𝔒 1859 – 0	𝒥 1880 – 1	ℰ 1901 – 2	𝒵 1922 – 3	u 1943 – 4
U 1839 – 0	𝔓 1860 – 1	𝒦 1881 – 2	ℱ 1902 – 3	a 1923 – 4	SINCE 1914-5

GEORG JENSEN

GEORG JENSEN
HANDMADE SILVER

By Appointment to the King of Denmark *By Appointment to the King of Sweden*

159 West 57th Street, New York

MEMBRE DE LA SOCIÉTÉ NATIONALE
DES BEAUX ARTS

Grand Prix · · · San Francisco, 1915
Grand Prix · · · · Barcelona, 1923
Grand Prix · · Rio de Janeiro, 1923

LONDON   PARIS   NEW YORK
ATELIERS   COPENHAGEN

Advertisement for Jenson Silver in New York, 1924. International Studio, November 1924.

Danish silversmith Georg Jensen (1866-1935) was one of the most talented, original, and influential silversmiths of the 20th century.

Following his schooling in Roadvad he moved with his family to Copenhagen where he secured a four year apprenticeship with a goldsmith which he completed in 1884.

In 1887 he became a student at the Royal Academy of Fine Arts graduating five years later.

For the next few years Georg Jensen worked in the fields of sculpture and ceramics until 1900 when he was awarded a travelling scholarship by the Academy.

After a year travelling to Rome, Paris, and Florence, he returned to Denmark to work as a silversmith, establishing his own workshop in 1904, designing his first holloware in 1905 and designing his first flatware the following year.

The first Jensen store outside of Copenhagen was opened in Berlin in 1909, but although closed six years later due to the First World War, the name was soon to expand into an International Company, with stores in Paris (1918) and London (1921).

New markets were sought in the U.S. by 1922 and two years later a store was opened in New York. Barcelona followed in 1925 and by the 1930s the London store relocated to Bond Street and the New York store to Fifth Avenue.

George Jensen had really arrived on the world scene!

Jensen Marks

826 GI
1904 - 1908

GEORG JENSEN COPENHAGEN 826 S GI
1909 - 1914
Used together

ca. 1915 - 1932

GI 925 S
1915 - 1930

GI 925 S
1915 - 1932
The 925 refers to the silver standard; this mark sometimes appears with the number 830, a lower standard.

GEORG JENSEN
ca. 1915 - 1927
(raised lettering)

GEORG JENSEN
1926 - 1932

GJ
1933 - 1944

GEORG JENSEN & WENDEL A/S
1945 - 1951
Used on items sold by the Copenhagen sales shop, Georg Jensen & Wendel.

GEORG JENSEN
1945 - present
(incised lettering)

Country Marks

Danish Hall Marks.

925.S Standard Mark.

222 Standard Mark.

LONDON ASSAY HOUSE MARKS:

GS Signature.

London Hall Mark for Foreign Silver

925 Standard Mark.

Date Mark.

GLOSSARY SILVER

Assay: A test for standard of purity and quality of silver and gold.

Assayer: An officer appointed by an Assay Office. Responsible for testing silver and gold to check standards.

Britannia Standard: Compulsory standard for silverware, set 1697 - 1720 in Britain. Only 10 dwts. of copper were allowed to each pound weight of silver. The figure of Britannia ws the mark used to denote this standard. Replacing the leopard head previously used. 1720, Sterling standard was again used. Higher Britannia standard continued to be used by some silversmiths.

Date Mark: Consists of a cycle of 20 letters of the alphabet omitting j, v, w, x, y, z in various type and shields. Used to denote year.

Hallmark: The distinguishing mark of a British Assay Office. Plural - denotes group of marks, giving maker, date, standard and hall at which assayed.

Maker's Mark: Stamp or punch used by maker, to imprint with device or initials all pieces leaving his workshop. The distinguishing mark of the workshop not always the mark of the actual maker. (In Canada, trade silversmiths marked pieces with the name of the vendor, as in the case of Robert Hendery and Hendery and Leslie.)

Plate: Term used in Europe for items of wrought silver or gold. Now used to desribe Sheffield or Electroplate.

Pseudo Hallmarks: Punch marks sometimes used by early smiths to denote silver and indicate standards. Used in countries where silversmiths had no established guilds or Assay Offices.

Shefield Plate: Copper coated with silver by a special process invented by Thomas Coulsover of Sheffield, 1743. It was hard to distinguish it from silver, so alike was it in appearance, it could be identified best by its weight being heavier than silver. It was made by sandwiching the copper between two layers of silver and fusing the three layers together before manufacturing into vatious articles.

Silverplate: A base metal, usually either nickel silver or copper, coated with a layer of pure silver by electroplating.

Town Mark: The mark applied to denote the location of the Assay Office.

BIBLIOGRAPHY SILVER

John E. Langdon, *Canadian Silversmiths 1700 - 1900,* Toronto 1966.

John E. Langdon, *Clock & Watchmakers in Canada 1700 - 1900,* 1976.

Dorothy T. Rainwater & Judy Redfield, *Encyclopedia of American Silver Manufacturers* - Revised Fourth Edition.

amsay Traquair, *The Old Silver of Quebec,* R1973.

Doris and Peter Unitt, *Canadian Silver, Silverplate & Related Glass,* Peterborough, 1970.

Seymour B. Wyler, *The Book of Old Silver,* New York, 1037.

Dolls

Simon & Halbig early stick body composition doll, ca.1890 with bisque head and pierced ears.

Dolls were among the earliest toys, they have existed in all civilizations and have been traditional gifts for little girls for generations. If you have an old doll from your childhood, or a doll that belonged to your mother or grandmother, you may have a treasure. Old dolls are very collectible and often bring high prices. Marks add to the value because they help identify and date the doll. Some marks are confusing because they don't include the name of the maker. Instead they are marked with initials or symbols.

You might find the maker's mark on the back of your doll's head near the neck, or the shoulder plate, or on the back of the torso. Most bisque and composition dolls were marked or had a paper label identifying the maker.

Doll collectors have their own specialized vocabulary. They call glazed doll heads (china,) and unglazed heads "bisque." Bisque has a matte finish. Early fine-textured white bisque is known as "parian" or "parian type."

Germany was a major producer of dolls and doll parts from about 1870 until the 1930s. Most glass dolls' eyes were made in Germany. Many French dolls had porcelain heads made in Germany. Most German dolls were made for export to the United States, England, and other countries.

Some dolls and doll parts were manufactured in factories, but others were made by families working in their homes. The job of painting, assembling, and dressing the dolls was often done by home workers, which kept the cost of production low.

Dolls were assembled from parts made by more than one manufactuer, and the mark on the doll's head or neck indicates only the manufacturer of the head. To identify the maker of the doll, look for a mark on the torso. Both marks are important for attribution.

ALT, BECK & GOTTSCHALCK

Nauendorf, Thüringia, Germany. 1854 - 1953. Established in 1854 by Gottlieb Beck and Theodore Gottschalk. Friedrich Alt and Christian Ernst Reinhold became co-owners in 1881. They made bisque dolls, character dolls, and bisque heads and were one of the manufacturers of heads for Bye-Lo dolls. They owned several patents for eye and voice mechanisms.

1854 - 1953

ALBEGO
10
Made in Germany

1930 - 1940

AMUSEMENT NOVELTY SUPPLY CO.

Toronto, Ontario. 1932 - 1938. Name changed to Dee and Cee Toy Company Ltd. in 1938.

C and D

MAX OSCAR ARNOLD

Neustadt, Germany. Founded in 1878, the firm of Max Oscar Arnold was noted for its mechanical dolls. Around 1910 he was granted patents for a line of talking dolls.

The firm manufactured bisque heads dating from the early 1920s marked with an eight-pointed star and their firm's initials, the majority being made for Welsch & Co. in Sonneberg.

MOA
150
Made in Germany

Welsch
9/0

BÄHR & PRÖSCHILD

Ohrdruf, Thüringia, Germany. 1871 - 1930s. Founded by George Bäehr and August Pröeschild, who also spelled their names Bähr & Pröschild. They made porcelain heads for other doll manuacturers, bisque dolls, and celluloid dolls. In 1919 the company was bought by Bruno Schmidt. One of several marks used after 1919. The heart shape was originally part of Bruno Schmidt's mark.

1871 - 1930+

1919+

BEAVER DOLL & TOY Co.

Toronto, Ontario. 1917. Marks unknown.

RICHARD BECK & Co.
Waltershausen, Germany. Around 1903 the company advertised leather dolls, ball-jointed dolls and various doll parts.

BISCO DOLL COMPANY
Toronto, Ontario. 1918 - 1920. Marks: Bisco Doll Canada.

GEORGE BORGFELDT & COMPANY
New York City. George Borgfeldt was a skilled businessman with considerable insight whose company commissioned two of the most successful dolls ever made. The Rose O'Neill's **Kewpie** and Grace Storey Putman's **Bye-Lo**.

Realizing that salerooms to display samples would generate sales, in 1881 he established his distribution company in New York and during the next six years opened eight branch offices – three of them in Germany.

When he commissioned bisque heads from other manufacturers, they were always incised with the initials G.B.

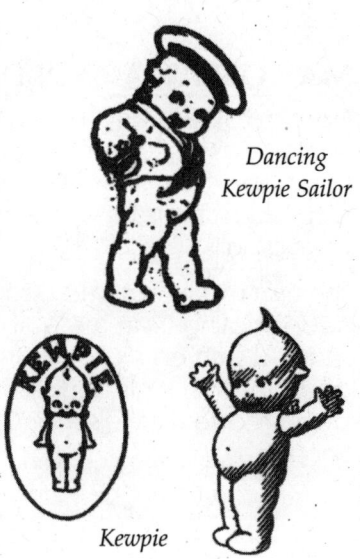

Dancing Kewpie Sailor

Kewpie

BROPHY DOLL COMPANY LTD.
Toronto, Ontario. 1920. Dolls not marked.

BRUYERE TOY MFG. Co. LTD.
Montreal, Quebec. 1920. Marks not known.

C. & W. DOLLS & POTTERY LTD.
Toronto, Ontario. 1919 - 1921. Marks: Toronto C & W Canada.

C.L.S.
Toronto, Ontario. Date unknown. Marks: Toronto CLS Canada.

CANADIAN TOY & NOVELTY Co.
Montreal, Quebec. 1923. Marks unknown.

CHEERIO TOY COMPANY

Toronto, Ontario. 1939 - 1966. Marks: Cheerio Made In Canada.

COMMERCIAL TOY COMPANY

Toronto, Ontario. Ca. 1917. Marks: Commercial Toy Co. Canada.

CUNO & OTTO DRESSEL

Sonnenberg, Germany. This German firm, founded in the 1700s, is the oldest doll manufacturer for which reasonably accurate records exist. The Dressels of the 18th century dealt in small goods, including toys, and in 1789 were included in the group of companies granted exclusive trade rights in Sonnenberg. The firm passed from one generation of Dressels to the next; in 1873 it became known as Cuno & Otto Dressel.

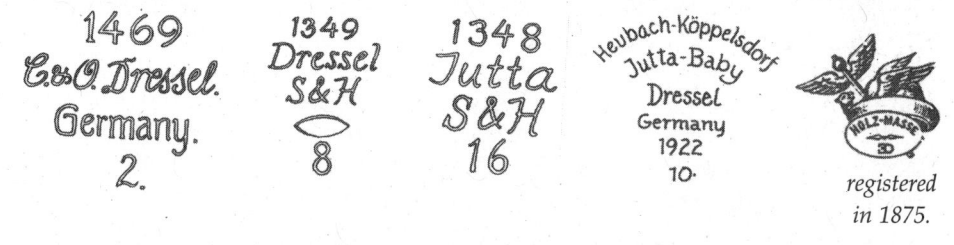

1469
C.&O. Dressel.
Germany.
2.

1349
Dressel
S&H
8

1348
Jutta
S&H
16

Heubach-Köppelsdorf
Jutta-Baby
Dressel
Germany
1922
10.

registered in 1875.

DEE AN CEE TOY COMPANY LTD.

Toronto, Ontario. 1938 - 1962. Owned by Mattel from 1962 - 1964.

Marked their products in many different ways, some marks included "Made in Canada," some did not, but marks included the company name used one way or another e.g. Dee an Cee; Dee & Cee; Dee Cee; DC; D&C; Deeancee.

Dolls manufactured in Canada were not always marked nor was the mark always moulded into a part of the body by the manufacturer. Dolls were often marked with attached cloth labels or stickers or paper tags pinned to clothes. This type of identification was usually removed by children. Moulded marks are usually found on the head, shoulderplate or torso. Many outfits made for dolls were also labelled by manufacturers. A doll made in Canada under licence from a foreign manufacturer usually had the licencer's name included in the mark, e.g. "Mattell," copyright dates and/or patent numbers were sometimes included.

DOMINION TOY MANUFACTURING COMPANY LIMITED

Toronto, Ontario. 1911 - 1932. Owned by Mattel from 1962 - 1964.

Marks included: D.T.M.C.; Dominion Doll Co.; D.T.M.C. Made In Canada; D.T.C.; D.T.M. Co.; Dominion Doll; D.T.Co.; Dominion Brand Dolls & Toys Made In Canada.

Assets were bought by Reliable Toy Company Limited.

THE T. EATON Co. LIMITED
Toronto and Winnpeg.

Eaton's Beauty Dolls

Designated as beauties by The T. Eaton Co. Limited and first marketed in 1900 are treasured by collectors. Made by several manufacturers, European and Canadian, some years dolls were offered in one size only, other years in several sizes.

From 1900 until 1907 – Eaton's Beauty dolls were sold undressed.

From 1904 until 1964 – The dolls were sold wearing a badge, proclaiming that they were an "Eaton's Beauty." Wording later changed to read "Eaton Beauty."

From 1908 until 1943 – Eaton's Beauty dolls were sold dressed in a chemise or slip and wearing shoes and socks. Eaton's 1926/27 catalogue illustrated outfits especially for Eaton's Beauty dolls, also Eaton's Beauty dolls' heads and wigs could be purchased. From 1940 until 1943 doll clothes made especially for Eaton's Beauty dolls were available. Eaton's Beauty dolls sold wearing a slip or chemise were dressed by the purchaser and dolls today wearing the creations first made for them when purchased are considered to be in "original clothes."

1954 onwards – Eaton's Beauty dolls were sold fully dressed.

1965 and 1966 – Eaton Beauty badges not used during these years.

Years Eaton's Beauty dolls not marketed – 1917 - 1923; 1944 - 1953; 1959; 1961; 1967 - 1976.

also see Jointed Dolls.

EFFANBEE DOLL COMPANY

New York, NY; East Brunswick, New Jersey. Ca. 1910 - present. Bernard E. Fleischaker and Hugo Baum founded Fleischaker and Baum in 1910. In 1913 they registered the name EFFanBEE, derived from the initials of their last names. The company sold toys at first, but in 1912 they were making dolls. In 1927, they introduced *Patsy*, the first doll to have extra clothes and accessories. *Patsy* was also the first doll to be part of a "family" of dolls. Effanbee made the first drink-and-wet doll, *Dy-Dee*, in 1934. Effanbee dolls may have a heart-shaped metal bracelet, necklace, or pin, or a gold paper heart label. One of several marks used.

THE FLORENTINE STATUARY COMPANY.

Toronto, Ontario. 1917 - 1932. Marks: Florentine Toronto; Florentine Canada.

FLORADORA DOLLS
By Armand Marseilles.

Made in Germany
Florodora
A 2 M

Florodora

FLORODORA
GERMANY.

Florodora
A 2/0 X M
Made in Germany
D.R.P.

Florodora
A.M. 5½. D R P.
made in Germany.

Florodora
A-4-M
Made in Germa

Label on box of Floradora doll (left).
My Playmate was a name George Borgfeldt used for several models of dolls he imported.

14" Armand Marseille Floradora.
Marks: on head "Made in Germany" and "Armand Marseille Floradora A3-0XM." Bisque head, sleep brown eyes, painted lashes, open mouth, four teeth, blond wig. Compo body, ball-jointed knees and elbows. Pale blue dress trimmed with lace, white lace top with blue ribbon, white bonnet, blue shoes and socks.

FREEMAN TOY COMPANY
Toronto, Ontario. 1943 - 1954. Marked their products in different ways, some marks included "Canada," some did not, but marks included the company name. e.g. Free Toy Toronto; A. Freeman Doll Made In Canada; Freeman Doll Co. Toronto Canada.

THE FRENCH ART DOLL MFG. Co.
Toronto, Ontario. 1927. Marks unknown.

FULPER POTTERY CO.

Flemington, New Jersey. 1805 - 1920. A pottery firm founded in 1805, Fulper began to make bisque dolls' heads in 1918 to compensate for the absence of German ones during the first World War.

Fulper also made all-bisque dolls, including Kewpies and the Peterkin doll designed by Helen Trowbridge. Horsman & Co. assisted in the production and some heads are marked Horsman or Amberg in addition to the Fulper mark.

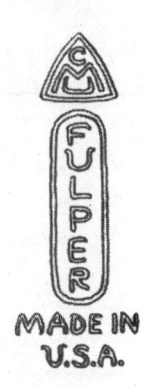

FRANÇOIS GAULTIER (Gauthier before 1875)

St. Maurice and Charenton, France. 1860 - 1899. Became part of S.F.B.J. Dolls' heads and doll parts.

OTTO GANS

Waltershausen and Finsterbergen, Thüringia, Germany. 1922 - 1930. Trade mark registered in 1930. Part of Gans & Seyfarth, 1901 - 1922. Started his own company in 1922 and made bisque dolls' heads, bathing dolls, walking dolls, and voice mechanisms for dolls.

GILTOY COMPANY

Montreal, Quebec. Ca. 1945. Marks: W.O.L.

GOODTIME TOYS

Toronto, Ontario. 1970 - 1977. Marks: Goodtime Toys Inc. Toronto Ontario Canada; 14R; 5. Goodtime Toys bought some of the assets of the Star Mfg. Co. and used some Star moulds. Goodtime dolls may be found with the Star mark.

S. HANCOCK & SONS

Cauldon, England. Founded in 1891, Hancock produced some of the finest English porcelain dolls' heads, most with intaglio eyes. By 1935, the firm had merged with Corona Pottery, Hanley. Marks found on Hancock dolls include S.H. & S.; N.T.I. (on bodies), and Made in England; H & S.P. Hancock.

H.B. CO.

See Standard Toys Ltd.

HERTWIG & CO.
Katzhütte, Thüringia, Germany. 1864 - ca. 1940. Made porcelain dolls' heads, Nanking dolls, bathing dolls, Buster Brown dolls, Snow Babies, and other dolls. The mark is a rebus of the name of the town where the company was located: cat is "katze" and cottage is "hütte" in German.

ERNST HEUBACH
Koppelsdorf, Germany. 1887 - 1932+. Porcelain factory.

HIGH-GRADE DOLL MFG. Co.
Montreal, Quebec. 1923. Marks unknown.

E.I. HORSMAN & Co.
New York, NY. During the 1870s, Edward I. Horsman, a toy distributor, began to import dolls from Europe. By 1900, his firm was manufacturing dolls as well and early on copied the latest American fads and trends. When rag dolls became popular, Horsman produced a line with photographic faces (1907). International events such as Cook's and Peary's North Pole expedition (1909) were recognized, as was the outbreak of the first World War.

After 1925, rights to the Horsman name were purchased by Regal Doll Manufacturing Company, which uses it to this day.

H.C.Q. 1916

© E.I.H. CO. INC.

MADE IN USA HORSMAN DOLL 19©10

© 1924
E.I. HORSMAN INC.
Made in Germany

IDEAL DOLLS
The Ideal Dolls and Toys began as a small home industry 100 years ago in Brooklyn, New York. First making stuffed animals (1903 - 1906) and then progressing to "unbreakable dolls." Morris Michton began a partnership with Aaron Cohn and founded the Ideal Novelty Co. in 1907. The first doll, *The Yellow Kid*, was based on the comic strip character of the same name. Cohn left the partnership in 1912 and the company changed its name to Ideal Novelty & Toy Co.

This company was one of the first American manufacturers to make composition dolls. Composition is a mixture of sawdust, glue, and other ingredients. It is less breakable than bisque, but subject to cracking and crazing.

Hundreds of different Ideal dolls have been made, many of which could walk and had closing eyes. They include *Flossie Flirt* (1924), *Shirley Temple* (1934), *Betsy Wetsy* (1937), *Toni* dolls (1948), *Saucy Walker* (1951), and *Crissy* (1970s).

Date shown is the date the mark was first used.

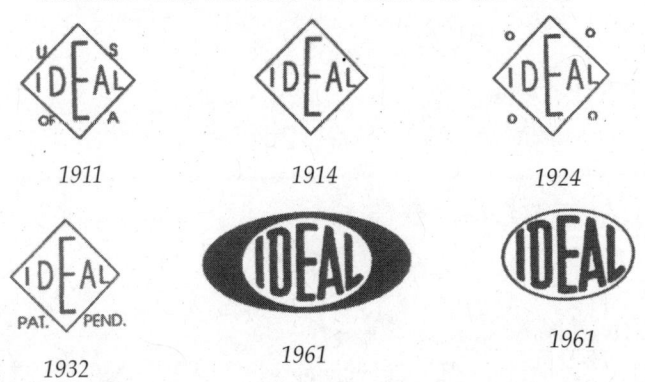

1911   1914   1924

1932   1961   1961

Jointed Dolls

LEFT: 14" Shoulder-Head Girl. Unmarked, in original box labelled "Jointed Doll, T. Eaton Co. Limited, Toronto and Winnipeg. Sleep eyes, open mouth, original mohair wig, imitation kid body and compo arms.

RIGHT: 22" Eaton's Beauty. 1927-1928. By Cuno & Otto Dressel. Marked on head "Cuno Otto Dressel, Germany." Bisque head, blue sleep eyes, painted lashes, open mouth, four teeth, blond replacement wig. Compo body fully jointed, including elbows, knees and wrist.

JUMEAU

Paris, France. Pierre François Jumeau established his doll factory in 1842 for making wood or kid doll bodies and elegant doll clothes. It attained a highly regarded reputation. Son, Emile, joined the business in 1867 and a few years later the company expanded and opened a factory outside Paris in Moutreuil in 1873. Shortly the newly introduced bébé Jumeau dolls were in great demand for export. Their fine bisque heads, jointed composition bodies, innocent facial expressions enhanced with clear blue glass eyes and dressed in the latest fashionable clothing won the company many awards.

Two decades later, due to strong competition from German dollmakers, together with growing economic pressure, Jumeau decided to join with other French companies in 1899 to form the Société Francais de Fabrication de Bébé et Jouets (S.F.B.J.).

Both name and company survived until 1958. Its bee mark introduced in 1891 (as a stamp on the shoe sole), was also used by S.F.B.J. after 1921.

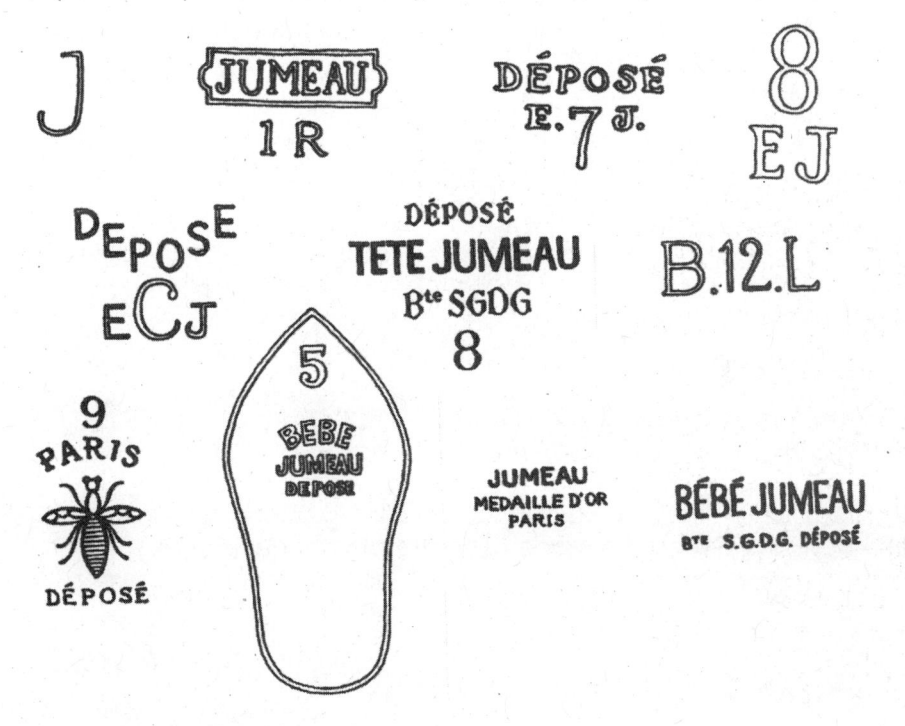

J

JUMEAU
1 R

DÉPOSÉ
E. 7 J.

8
E J

DÉPOSÉ
E C J

DÉPOSÉ
TETE JUMEAU
Bte SGDG
8

B.12.L

9
PARIS
DÉPOSÉ

5
BEBE
JUMEAU
DEPOSE

JUMEAU
MEDAILLE D'OR
PARIS

BÉBÉ JUMEAU
Bte S.G.D.G. DÉPOSÉ

KÄMMER & REINHARDT

Waltershausen, Thüringia, Germany. 1886 - 1930+. Founded by Ernst Kämmer and Franz Reinhardt, the company designed doll heads made by Simon & Halbig and other manufacturers. They also made heads of wood and composition. All K & R dolls made after 1902 have heads designed by K & R and made by Simon & Halbig.

K✡R

LLOYD-HARLAM TOY CO. LTD.
Toronto, Ontario. 1925 - . Changed name in 1926 to Lloyd Toy Co. Marks: on dolls - unknown. On Mama voice box - Trade Lloyd's A1 Mark.

A. LUGE & CO.
Sonneberg, Thüringia, Germany. 1881 - 1930+. made character dolls and kid dolls using dolls' heads made by Armand Marseille, Ernst Heubach, and Gebruuder Heubach.

MATTEL INC.
Hawthorne, California, USA. Some parents were hesitant to buy their little girls the long legged, full figured and somewhat sexy doll that was introduced in 1959. This attitude soon melted with children's insistence that *Barbie* was their heart's desire. *Ken* and the rest of the family, with their selection of clothing and accessories were soon to follow, making ideal gifts to solve the perennial problem of "what would Susie like?"

The *Barbie* success story is history now and the appeal of the infinite variety of the *Barbie* selection to collectors is well established. The values of the scarcer items, especially those in mint conditiion, reflect the desirability of these collectibles.

Even though *Barbie* is over 40 years old, she is still considered a newer doll by seasoned collectors.

ARMAND MARSEILLE
Köppelsdorf, Thüringia, Germany. 1885 - 1950s. From 1900 to 1930, Armand Marseille was one of the largest makers of bisque doll heads in the world, supplying doll heads to many other manufacturers. Composition doll heads were made beginning about 1930. In the 1950s, composition heads were made using the old bisque moulds.

1920 mark.

continued at to of next page

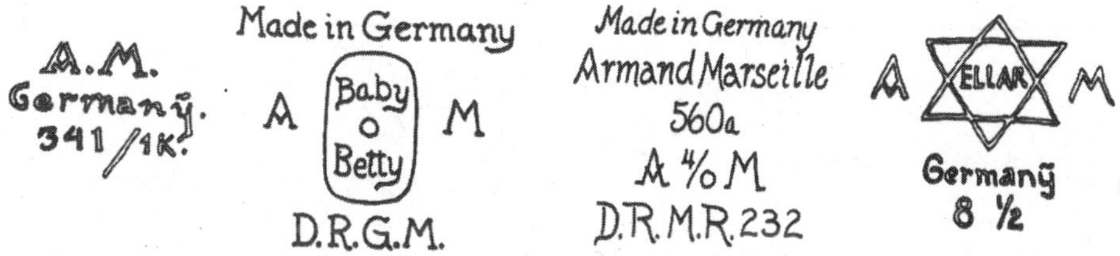

MIGHTY STAR COMPANY LIMITED

Toronto, Ontario. 1977. The Mighty Star Company bought Goodtime Toys and after the change in ownership the company continued to use some Star and Goodtime moulds. Mighty Star dolls may be found with the Star or Goodtime marks.

Marks: 4 Mighty Star Canada; Mighty Star Ltd. Doll Division; Mighty Star.

NOMA TOYS LTD.

Owen Sound, Ontario. 1945 - 1948. Licenced by Cameo Doll Company, New York City to manufacture *Kewpie* and *Scootles* dolls designed by Rose O'Neill.

ROSE O'NEILL

Wilkes-Barre, Pennsylvania, USA. Rose O'Neill's whimsical line drawings of fairy-like *Kewpies* first appeared in the *Ladies Home Journal* in 1909; their instant popularity resulted in a tidal wave of dolls first appearing in 1912, and by the beginning of the first World War, some 21 factories in Germany and the United States were manufacturing *Kewpies* to meet the demand of the George Borgfeldt Co., which distributed them exclusively after 1916.

Most *Kewpies* had O'Neill's signature moulded on one foot; heart-shaped or circular stickers appeared on the chests.

O'Neill designed a follow-up to the *Kewpie, Scootles*, in 1925; its name, or Rose O'Neill, was incised on the sole of the foot.

105

PERFECT DOLL COMPANY
Toronto, Ontario. 1948 - 1949. Marks: Perfect Made In Canada.

DR. DORA PETZOLD
Berlin, Germany. 1919 - 1930+. Mark registered in 1924. Made cloth art dolls with composition heads.

EARLE PULLMAN COMPANY
Toronto, Ontario. 1945 - 1966. Marked their products in different ways, some marks included "Canada," some did not, all marks, but one (*Marjie*, a teen doll) included the company name.

REGAL TOY COMPANY
Toronto, Ontario. 1959 - 1983. Marked their products in different ways, some marks included "Canada," some did not, but marks included the company name. e.g. Regal Made In Canada; Regal Toy; Regal.

RELIABLE TOY COMPANY LIMITED
Toronto, Ontario. 1920 - 1985. Beginning in 1920, Reliable made composition dolls, generally marked as shown on the head or shoulder plate. In the 1920s, the company offered a Mountie, marked Reliable/Made in/Canada on the head, and R.C.M.P. on the uniform's epaulets, followed in the 1930s by a *Shirley Temple* and *Baby Bunting* in 1939. They were taken over by Viceroy Rubber & Plastics Ltd. in 1985.

Marked their products in different ways, some marks included "Made In Canada," some did not, but marks included the company name. eg. A Reliable Doll Made In Canada; Reliable Toy Made In Canada; Reliable Canada; Reliable.

RHEINISCHE GUMMI-UND CELLULOID-FABRIK
Mannheim-Neckarau, Bavaria. Now operating as Schildkröt-Puppen in Rauenstein, Germany. 1873 - present. The turtle mark is a well-known German doll mark and can be found in several variations. The turtle ("schildkröt" in German) is a symbol signifying that the doll's material is as tough as a turtle's shell; "Schutz-Marke" is German for trade mark.

SCHMITT & FILS
Paris, France. 1854 - 1891. Made dolls with pressed bisque heads.

HEINRICH SCHMUCKLER
(Erst Schlesische Puppenfabrik)
Liegnitz, Silesia. 1882 - 1928. Made both dressed and undressed celluloid, cloth, and rubber dolls, including baby dolls and dollhouse dolls. Hesli, which combines the first letters of Heinrich Schmuckler, Liegnitz, was registered as a trade mark for dressed dolls in 1921.

SCHOENAU & HOFFMEISTER
Sonneberg, Thüringia, Germany; Burggrub, Bavaria. 1901 - 1953. Founded by Arthur Schoenau and Carl Hoffmeister. They made their own dolls and also made bisque heads for other doll manufacturers.

Germany
S☆H
914
made in Germany

SCHÜTZMEISTER & QUENDT
Boilstädt, Gotha, Thüringia, Germany. 1889 - ca. 1930. Mark used on bisuqe doll heads. Porcelain factory that made bisque dolls and dolls' heads, jointed dolls, bathing dolls, and cloth dolls.

252
Q&S
Germany
50

S.F.B.J.
(Société Française de Fabrication de Bébés & Jouets)
Paris and Montreuil-sous-bois, France. 1899 - 1963. Syndicate of French doll makers formed to compete with German manufacturers. Most major French doll makers were part of the syndicate, but some of them continued to make dolls under their own names as well.

DÉPOSE
S.F.B.J.
One of several marks used.

SIMON & HALBIG
Gräfenhain, Germany. After Armand Marseille, the firm of Simon & Halbig was the second largest maker of dolls' heads in Germany. The company originated in 1869 as a porcelain factory, but since its co-founder, Wilhelm Simon, was also a toy manufacturer who produced dolls, the new firm took advantage of the growing vogue for bisque-headed dolls by producing dolls' heads, both for its own use and for other companies as well. For this reason, Simon & Halbig's shoulderheads are among the earliest marked bisques available to collectors, because after 1902 they produced all the bisque heads required by Kämmer & Reinhardt, this apparently led to that firm's acquisition of Simon & Halbig in 1920.

Their earliest mark appears to be the seated Chinese registered in 1875. The inclusion of DEP in the mark indicates that the doll was made after 1887. The famous S & H mark first used the ampersand in 1905; SH marks without the ampersand are consequently thought to date before 1905.

Simon & Halbig's successor, Keramisches Werk Gräfenhaim, used the KWG mark after 1930.

Mould numbers and marks used by the Gräfenhain factory are generally incised on one of three places: on the back of the head, the back of the shoulder plate, or the front of the shoulder plate.

S & H
in die Masse gestempelt.   Auf den Etiketten.

S15H 719 DEP

SH 1080 DEP 7

S3H 886   949 S12H

1358
Germany
SIMON & HALBIG
S&H
5

S.H. 1039
Germany
DEP
10½

K.W.G.

S & H 1079
DEP
Germany
15

SMITH DOLL & TOY Co. LTD.
Dunnville, Ontario. 1922. Marks unknown.

STANDARD TOYS LTD.
Bowmanville, Ontario. 1917. Marks: H.B.Co.; Standard Quality Dolls Made in Canada.

STANDARD TOYS LTD.
Hamilton, Ontario. 1923. Marks unknown.

STAR DOLL MANUFACTURING COMPANY
Toronto, Ontario. 1952 - 1970. Marked their dolls in different ways, some marks included "Canada," some did not, but marks included the company name. e.g. Star Doll Canada; Star Doll; Star.

MARGARETTE STEIFF
Giengen, Germany. Steiff established a felt clothing factory in 1877 and began to make felt dolls in 1893. The earliest trade mark, a camel, was registered in 1892; the elephant in 1905; and the circular KNOPF im OHR (button in ear) in 1905, introduced in France as Bouton dans l'oreille (with the cat-like figure) two years later. The Steiff name itself was registered in 1911. Steiff made the first teddy bear, trade marked Petz, in 1903, and later changed its name to Teddy. The firm also produced a number of character dolls after 1911, with most having a metal trade mark button in the left ear. They can also be identified by their very large feet which help them to stand unsupported.

Bouton dans l'oreille.

„Steiff"

TILCO INTERNATIONAL INCORP.
St. Jean, Quebec. 1940s - late 1970s. Marks: Tilly Toy Made In Canada.

TIP TOP TOY Co.
New York City, NY, USA. Founded in 1912, this manufcturer made composition dolls, including novelties such as *Kewpies* intended for use as carnival prizes (under licence from Borgfeldt) and imported bisque heads from German firms.

TIP TOP TOY COMPANY

VALENTINE DOLL COMPANY
Toronto, Ontario. 1949 - 1959. Possibly marked with a small "v".

VICEROY MANUFACTURING COMPANY LIMITED
Toronto, Ontario. Manufactured dolls from the late 1940s - late 1950s. Bought Reliable Toy Company Limited in 1985 and is again making dolls.

Marks: A Viceroy Sunruco Doll Made In Canada; Viceroy Made In Canada; Sun Rubber Co. Made In Canada By Viceroy.

VICTORIA DOLL & TOY MFG. Co. LTD.
Victoriaville, Quebec. 1920. Marks unknown.

VOGUE DOLLS Co.

Medford, Mass, USA. The eight inch *Ginny* doll was created by Jennie Graves in 1937. Many styles of clothing were available for these appealing little dolls, all designed by Mrs. Graves and her daughter Virginia Graves Carlson. Most of the clothing made for *Ginny* dolls has a Vogue cloth label sewn in, however there was a period during the late 1940s when clothes were not labelled. Vogue advertised that *Ginny* was "...the fashion leader in doll society." Outfits for *Ginny* dolls are beautifully designed and made in fine detail. Over the years hundreds of fashionable styles were produced. During the 1950s and 1960s *Buttericks*, *McCalls*, and *Simplicity* offered a number of sewing patterns especially designed for *Ginny* dolls. A full line of accessories was also produced for *Ginny* by Vogue, such as luggage, skates, jewellery, furniture and swing sets.

Vogue Dolls was purchased in 1995 by the Lawton Doll Company.

Marks: **GINNY // VOGUE DOLLS // INC. // PAT PEND. // MADE IN U.S.A.**

Then **PAT PEND** was changed to **// PAT. NO. 2687594 //**

Later some were marked: **MADE IN HONG KONG; MADE IN TAIWAN;** or **MADE IN CHINA.**

The marks can be found on the back of torso, on the head, and on the back.

HERMAN von BERG

Koppelsdorf, Germany. 1904 - 1926+. Doll factory. Made bisque heads.

H.v.B

F. WELSCH

Breslau, Silesia. 1907 - 1930+. Trade mark registered in 1925. Began making dolls in 1922. Made novelty dolls, miniatures, doll clothes, and accessories.

ROSE-PUPPE

WELSCH & Co.

Sonneberg, Germany. Established in 1911, this doll factory at first used dolls' heads from Max Oscar Arnold, but after 1917 purchased heads from Schützmeister & Quendt and Simon & Halbig.

MOA
150
Made in Germany
Welsch
9/0

SIMON & HALBIG
WELSCH

HINTS ABOUT DOLL CARE

If a treasured doll requires repair, unless you have experience in this type of work, it is adviseable that you consult a "doll hospital." If you are unable to locate one in your area, libraries and museums are a good source of information.

It is not always possible to find old dolls in original clothes. Old dolls dressed in their original outfits, in good to excellent condition, are the most desirable to collectors, but if it is necessary to redress a doll it is best to find clothes that were fashionable at the time the doll was made. Clever people who make new garments for dolls can copy the original costume, if available, or redress the doll in a suitable style, often using old textiles and trimmings. Collectors who have acquired new outfits for their dolls usually keep and store the clothing that has been replaced. It is also recommended that old doll's clothes never be dry cleaned.

Dolls or their clothing put in storage should not be wrapped in plastic. Temperature changes cause condensation which will damage stored items.

Many collectors display some, if not all of their dolls, in their home, but it is wiser to display them in a dust free cabinet and away from sunlight.

BIBLIOGRAPHY DOLLS

Jean Bach, *Dictionary of Doll Marks*, Sterling Publishing, 1990

Caroline Goodfellow, *The Ultimate Doll Book*, Reader's Digest, 1993

Polly and Pam Judd, *Hard Plastic Dolls*, Hobby House Press, 1989

Pam Judd, *Cloth Dolls*, Hobby House Press, 1900

Patsy Meyer, *Doll Values - 5th Edition*, Collector Books, 2001

Tom Kelly and Pamela Sherer, *A Century of Dolls*, Courage Books, 1995

Peter and Joan Unitt, *Canadian Price Guide to Dolls and Toys*, Fitzhenry & Whiteside, 1990

GLASS

American enamelled Cranberry perfume bottle, ca. 1880.

Mount Washington
1892

Crown Milano
1892

New England
Glassworkers
1882

Baccarat
Current

Mount Washington Peachblow
1885

Rose Amber
1884

KELVA
NAKARA
WAVECREST
WARE

Quezal

FAVRILE

GLOSSARY GLASS

Agate: Opaque glass resembling the stone agate. Colours: yellow, brown and tan.

Altaglass: Whimsical and decorative art glass pieces manufactured in Medicine Hat, Alberta between 1950 - 1988.

Amberina: Transparent, used for tableware and ornamental pieces. Colours: shading from tones of ruby to pale amber.

Art Glass: A generic term given to glass that came in elegant forms and diverse colour effect. Ornamental glass was often made to imitate other materials, such as satin, marble or porcelain, etc.

Aurene: The trade mark "Aurene" was registered by the Steuben Glass Works, 1904. A lustrous iridescent glass. Colours: blue, gold or combination of colours.

Baccarat: Fine glass ware produced by Compagnie des Cristalleries at Baccarat, France.

Bohemian: The name is taken from Bohemia, a country which is now part of the Czech Republic. Generally, the term refers to colourful cased or flashed glass made late Victorian and early 20th century. Copper wheel

113

engraved scenes are also a feature of this glass, which is still being made in the Czech republic. It is hard to distinguish the old from the new in good quality pieces, but cheap copies, which are plentiful, are very obvious.

Bristol: Includes semi-opaque white glass painted in enamels. This glass was made in England at the numerous Bristol glass houses, the best work was in the mid-1700s. Also made in America during the Victorian era. In the late 1800s great quantities of "Bristol Blue" (bright translucent glass) was manufactured in Bristol, much of it for use as inserts in silverware.

Burmese (American): Mount Washington Glass Company, New Bedford, Mass. Pat. Dec. 15, 1885. Developed by Frederick Shirley. Free blown and shaped with tools also blown moulded in quilted or stretched (expanded) diamond pattern. Soft matte finish, some polished pieces made, but not as lovely as those which are acid finished. Thin and very fragile in delicate yellows with blush rose overtones. Poor imitation reproductions made in Italy in the 1960s.

Burmese (English): Made under a patent granted to Thomas Webb & Sons. Many pieces marked "Queen's Burmese" as it was made in honour of Queen Victoria, who admired the American Burmese, having been presented with a gift of some pieces by Frederick Shirley.

Cameo: Made in two or more layers of varying colours. By cutting or carving the outer layer/layers, the contrasting colour of the background design is revealed.

Camphor: Opaque, cloudy white.

Caramel: Opaque glass in a colour typical of its name.

Carnival Glass: Pressed glass made in vibrant and pastel colours, iridized to give it a rainbow effect. Produced by several American factories as well as factories in Australia, Britain, France and Germany. Carnival glass, a popular collectible today, came into fashion during the early 1900s, and was sold in stores, through catalogues, and during the Depression was offered as prizes at fairs and carnivals.

Clambroth: Grayish, semi-opaque.

Coraline: Made by many factories in England and America. So-called because thousands of tiny glass beads were applied to simulate coral or seaweed patterns on acid etched forms, then fired. Usually yellow beads on lovely blues, greens and peachblow wares.

Crackle: Surface covered in network of fine cracks. Colours: multi-coloured.

Cranberry: Wine-red glass. Colour of cranberries.

Crystal: Also known as flint glass or lead glass. Fine quality colourless glass containing a high proportion of lead oxide.

Crown Milano: Matte finish, with a texture similar to porcelain. Found in white and pastels elaborately decorated with enamel, gold or silver.

Custard: Opaque, colour of milk and egg custard.

Cut: Glass patterned by cutting with a moving wheel.

Depression: Clear and coloured glassware made primarily during the Great Depression which began in 1929. This mass produced type of pressed glass was inexpensive to manufacture and available in a wide variety of designs. Some patterns made before and after the Depression era are included in this category and "depression glass" is the term usually used to describe the many patterns and styles made from the 1920s to the late 1930s..

End-Of-Day: (See spatter glass) So-called because pieces of this type were supposedly made after working hours using remnants of colours and odds and ends of glass remaining in the furnace pots. Most often referred to as spatter glass today.

Foval: Manufactured by the H.D. Fry Glass Co., though seldom marked it can be easily identified. Wares have an opalescent body with brilliant coloured trim, e.g. white opal with blue handle; white to blue opal with brilliant amethyst handle. Most of this glass was produced during the 1920s. The letters FOVAL indicate Fry's Ovenware Art Line.

Iridescent: An iridescent or lustered surface achieved by spraying the form while still hot with metallic salts. Found in a variety of colours. (see (opalescent).

Kelva: See Wavecrest.

Kew Blas: Lustrous or lustre decorated glass, identified by engraved (not acid etched) mark "Kew Blas." Made at Union Glass Co., Somerville, Mass. Colours: deep blue, green, rose, gold, bronze. Scarce.

Lutz: This name is used to describe the striped glass thought to have been produced at the Boston & Sandwich Glass Co. in the mid 19th century. Nicholas Lutz, a Frenchman, worked for several American glass companies. He also produced filigree, threaded and cane glass. Most of the pieces found are similar to those made by Venetian glass makers for hundreds of years and made today by workers in Murano, Venice. Without documentation glass of this nature can only be considered "Lutz type."

Mary Gregory: Clear and coloured glass decorated with white hand painted Kate Greenaway type figures of children.

Matte: A dull surface or finish on glass.

Mercury: Glass with a silver appearance made by filling the space between two layers of clear glass with mercury or nitrate of silver.

Millefiori: "a thousand flowers" A decoration made by fusing short canes of coloured glass to form a floral mosaic.

Milk Glass: Opaque white glass made in imitation of porcelain.

Nakara: See Wavecrest.

Opalescent: Iridescent, like an opal, various colours that can refract light and then reflect it in a play of colours.

Peachblow (Mount Washington): Was made only at the Mount Washington factory from 1886 - 1888. It was an unlined homogeneous glass, the same colour through the thickness of the piece.

Peachblow (New England): Made by Edward D. Libbey, proprietor of the New England Glass Co., which became the Libbey Glass Co. after moving to Toledo, Ohio. New England Peachblow was patented March 2, 1886 and made until 1888. The original name was Wild Rose. Colour is solid through thickness of glass; opaque white to deep red rose at the top. Most pieces have the acid finish, giving it a lovely soft matte effect. A limited number of pieces were left with a polished surface.

Peachblow (Wheeling): The original made in Wheeling, West Virginia by J.H. Hobbs, Brockunier & Co. First produced in 1883. Colour is deep yellow to crimson cased with opal or opaque milk white, acid polished finish.

Pomona: Made at the New England Glass Co. Clear glass with pale amber border at top decorated with tinted flowers and foliage on a background that is covered with fine lines or stippling.

Pressed: Pattern glass made in a mould. Found in clear and colours.

Quezal: Made at the Quezal Art Glass & Decorating Co., New York City, 1901 - 1925 (a company established by two former employees of Tiffany). Iridescent with design in outer layer. Colours: mainly gold and green, some blue, rose and purple. Beautiful glass, made using techniques learned at the Tiffany works.

Rubena Crystal: Transparent, clear at base shading to red.

Rubena Verde: Transparent, yellowish green to green at base shading to red.

Satin: Cased glass, matte finish with satin or velvety texture. Colours: vari-coloured.

Slag: Also referred to as marble glass. Opaque white glass streaked with another opaque colour such as rose, purple, yellow or blue.

Spangle: Multi-coloured, usually cased, with flakes of metal on a dark or pastel ground.

Spatter: Multi-coloured, decorated with an overall blending of melted pieces of coloured glass.

Vassa Murrhina: See Spangle and Spatter.

Vaseline: Resembles the blue yellow colour of petrolium jelly.

Wavecrest (Kelva & Nakara): Made by the C.F. Monroe Co., Meriden, Conn. Used three trade names on toilet articles (dressing table sets) and many covered pieces such as biscuit barrels, frequently having metal hinges and trims. Fine enamel decoration was applied to creamy opal glass. All three of these wares were made in rich, extravagant styles. Only the trade marks which they carry distinguish one from the other. The trade marks were registered in 1892. Wavecrest items appear in the T. Eaton Co. catalogues of that period.

ART GLASS

Following is a selection of marks found on 19th and 20th century art glass. Marks were engraved, stamped or etched on the form or added in the shape of a label.

ENGLAND

GEORGE DAVIDSON & CO.
Teams Glass Works, Gateshead.

late 19th century.

JOHN DERBYSHIRE & CO.
Regent Road Flint Glass Works, Manchester.

late 19th century.

GREENER & CO.
Wear Glass Works, Sunderland.

late 19th century.

JOHN MONCRIEFF LTD.
North British Glassworks, Perth Scotland. Glass manufacturers.

Ca. 1924

JOHN NORTHWOOD
Stourbridge, England. 1836 - 1902.
Mark: **"JOHN NORTHWOOD"**

RICHARDSON'S OF WORDSLEY
at Dennis Glass Works, Amblecote, Stourbridge. Glass manufacturers until 1930 when sold to Thomas Webb.

JOHN SOWERBY
Ellison Flint Glass Works, Gateshead-on-Tyne.

Peacock's head crest used by Sowerby from 1875 to about 1930.

117

STEVENS & WILLIAMS
Brierley Hill Glass Works. 1847 - 1931. Decorative art-glass manufacturers.

ROYAL BRIERLY CRYSTAL
Stevens & Williams is renamed in 1931 to Royal Brierly Crystal, a name it patented after a visit from King George V.

THOMAS WEBB & SONS
Stourbridge England, 1837 - present. Glass manufactures, all kinds. Marks: Queen's Burmese/Thomas Webb & Sons/Patented; Webb; W & W; Woodhall.

WEBB-CORBETT
Coalbournhill Glass Works, Amblecote, Stourbridge. Glass manufacturers. Established in 1897. trade marks many and varied.

FRANCE

ARGY-ROUSSEAU
Paris, France. 1913 - 1931. Marks: **ARGY-ROUSSEAU**

ALMARIC V. WALTER
Nancy, France. 1859 - 1942. Marks: **A. WALTER**

BACCARAT
Baccarat, France. 1764 - present. Marks: **BACCARAT**

D'ARGENTAL
Munzthal (Germany), France. 1809 - present. Marks: **D'ARGENTAL**

DAUM NANCY
Nancy, France. 1875 - present. Marks: **DAUM NANCY; DAUM NANCY, FRANCE** (after 1919); **DAUM** (after 1960)

ANDRE DELATTE
Nancy, France. 1921 - . Marks: **DE LATTE**

EMILE GALLE
Saint Clement, France. 1846 - 1904. Marks: **E GALLE A NANCY; CRISTALLERIE d'E; GALLE NANCY; GALLE; EMILE GALLE**

LEGRAS & CIE
St. Denis, France. 1864 - 1920. Marks: **LE GRAS**

MUELLER FRERES
Croismare, France. 1895 - 1936. Marks: **MUELLER; MUELLER FRERES**

PANTIN (E.S. MONOT)
Pantin, France. 1851 - present. Marks: **DE VEZ**

SCHNEIDER
Epinay-sur-Seine, France. 1913 - present. Marks: **SCHNEIDER**

VAL ST. LAMBERT
Val St. Lambert, France. 1802 - present. Marks: **VAL ST. LAMBERT**

GERMANY

LOETZ, KLOSTERMUHLE
(Bohemia; Austria), Germany. 1840 - 1943. Marks: most pieces not marked, some are marked **LOETZ, AUSTRIA** or with circled crossed arrows.

LUDWIG MOSER & SOHNE
Karlsbad, Germany. 1857 - present. Marks: **LEO MOSER; MOSER; MOSER ALEXANDRITE**

UNITED STATES

STEUBEN GLASS WORKS
Corning, New York. 1903 - present. Marks: etched fleur-de-lis and **STEUBEN** until 1932, later pieces marked **STEUBEN**

THE MOUNT WASHINGTON GLASS CO.
New Bedford, Massachusetts. Glass manufacturers.

BOHEMIAN GLASS

Bohemian glass on the whole is not hard to identify, especially pieces dating from around the late 1800s and early 1900s. They are characterized by heavy decoration with enameling, cut designs and coloured glass overlays.

It is more difficult however to determine the particular manufacturer. Some used cut or acid-etched logos or engraved signatures, some paper labels, but the greater majority were left unmarked.

The following are some identified for being in use around the turn of the 20th century.

ADOLF BECKERT
Ceská Lípa, Bohemia (now Czech Republic). 1884 - 1929. Artistic director of the Lötz glass factory from 1909 to 1911. Taught at Fachschule Steinschönau, a specialized school of glassmaking, from 1911 to 1926 and became director in 1918.

PAUL EISELT
Steinschönau, Bohemia (now Czech Republic). 1887 - 1961. Engraver. Worked at Fachschule Steinschönau in northern Bohemia.

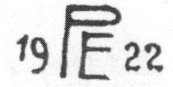

MATHILDE FLÖGL
Vienna, Austria. b.1893 - d.1951. Worked with Wiener Werkstätte doing glasspainting, ceramics, posters, and leatherwork from 1916 to 1931. Had a studio in Vienna from 1931 to 1935.

FRITZ HECKERT
1866 - 1923. In 1923, combined with Josephinenhütte and Neumann & Staebe under the name Jo-He-Ky.

From 1866

After 1900

GRÄFLINCH SCHAFFGOTSCH'SCHE JOSEPHINENHÜTTE
1842 - 1973. In 1923, combined with Heckert and Neumann & Staebe under the name Jo-He-Ky. Worked with Villeroy & Boch after 1973.

Acid etched Ca. 1890

Acid etched Ca. 1925 - 1930

J. & L. LOBMEYR
1823 - present.

Painted or engraved. From 1860

Engraved from 1860. Cut ca. 1928

MEYR'S NEFFE (J. MEYR'S NEFFE)
1841 - 1922, then merged with Ludwig Moser's company. In 1940, became part of Gral-Glashutte. In 1973, became a branch of the state-operated Crystalex.

Acid etched. Ca. 1890

Acid etched, also with "Austria" Ca. 1918 - 1922

LUDWIG MOSER & SONS
1857 - present.

Acid etched. 1870 - 1925. After 1925, "Moser" alone in oval or "Karlsbad" replaced with "Karlovy Vary."

Acid etched. 1895 - 1918 ("M" goblet "M" also used without circle).

JOHANN OERTEL & Co.
Haida, Bohemia (now Nov´y Bor, Czech Republic). Founded in 1869. Johann Oertel died in 1909 and was succeeded by his son.

SCHOTT & GEN.
Jena, Germany. 1884 - present. Otto Schott, Ernst Abbe, and Carl and Roderich Zeiss established the Glastechnisch Laboratorium Schott & Genossen (Schott & Partners Glass Technology Laboratory Jena) in 1884. The name was changed to Jenaer Glaswerk Schott & Gen. in 1920. Now called Schott Jenaer Glas GmbH.

THERESIENTHAL
1836 - present.

Acid etched.

Acid etched. 1920s - 1930s

WIENER WERKSTÄTTE

Vienna, Austria. 1903 - 1932. An association of artists and craftsmen who made a variety of Art Nouveau and Art Deco items, including glass, metal, jewelry, and furniture. Founded by Josef Hoffman and Koloman Moser. Their early work used simple shapes and decorations. When Dagobert Peche became artistic director in 1919, more ornate decorations were used.

CAMEO GLASS

Developed by the Romans over 2,000 years ago, the technique was only utilized in the French and English glass works just over a century ago.

Several layers of different coloured glass form the body. The outer layer(s) are then partly carved away to leave a figure or design against the background colour.

FRENCH MARKS

BURGUN, SCHVERER & Co.

Meisenthal, Alsace-Lorraine. Founded in 1711. Produced some glass for Gallé in the 1880s and 1890s. Etched and painted gilt mark.

DAUM

Nancy, France. 1875 - present. Guillaume Avril and Josué-Victor Bertrand founded The Verrerie Sainte-Catherine in Nancy in 1875 and made plate glass, tableware, and watch glasses. Jean Daum (1825 - 1885) lent them money for the operation of the business. In 1878 he bought the factory and changed the name to Verrerie de Nancy. Daum's son Auguste (1853 - 1909) joined the business in 1879 and his younger son Antonin (1864 - 1931) joined them in 1887. The company, now called Cristalleries de Nancy, is still working. All items made by the Daum glassworks are marked. Marks may be etched, painted, or relief-cut.

DELATTE

Nancy, France. Founded by Andre Delatte in 1921. Etched or relief-cut mark.

GALLÉ

Meisenthal, France. 1874 - 1931. Emile Gallé (1846 - 1904) was a designer who made glass, pottery, furniture, and other items. He worked for Burgun, Schverer & Co. in 1866 and 1867 and established his own glass-making factory in 1874. The firm continued to operate until 1931. Engraved mark. Gilt, enameled, engraved, and relief-cut marks were often hidden in the design of the object.

MICHEL

Eugène Michel worked as a glass engraver for Rousseau in 1867 and later for Léveillé. About 1900 he began working on his own. His work was influenced by 18th and 19th century Chinese glass. Engraved mark **E. Michel.** Not all of his work was signed, and it should not be confused with glass by other makers signed **Michel Nancy** or **Michel Paris.**

CRISTALLERIE SCHNEIDER

Epinay-sur-Seine and Loris, France. 1913 - present. Founded by Ernest and Charles Schneider (1881 - 1962) in 1913. Earlier, he worked as a designer for Gallé and Daum. Schneider made *Le Verre Français* cameo glass from 1920 to 1933. Charles' son, Robert, took over in 1948. The company moved to Loris in 1962. Marks used include **SCHNEIDER; CHARDER;** and **LE VERRE FRANÇAIS** and may be engraved, scratched, or etched.

ENGLISH MARKS (LATE 19TH CENTURY)

THOMAS WEBB
Stourbridge.

1880s etched	1880s etched	1880s etched
THOMAS WEBB & SONS / CAMEO	THOMAS WEBB & SONS / GEM / CAMEO	THOMAS WEBB & SONS
1887 to ca. 1888	1887 to ca. 1888	1887 to ca. 1888
THOMAS WEBB & SONS / CAMEO	THOMAS WEBB & SONS	THOMAS WEBB & SONS / LIMITED

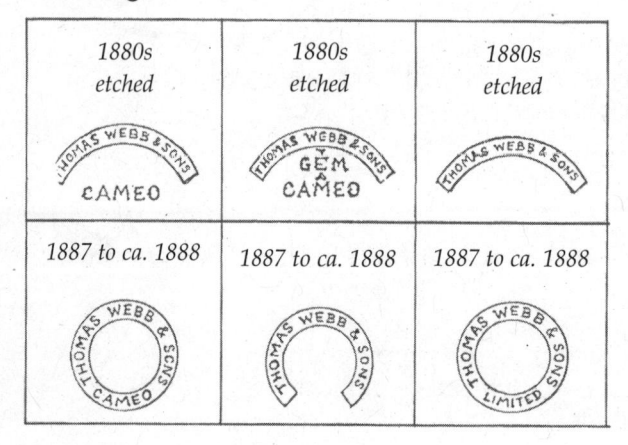

STEVENS & WILLIAMS
Brierley Hill, Stourbridge. *(see marks under "Art Glass")*.

T. & G. WOODHALL
Stourbridge.

T. & G. WOODALL
CAMEO
GLASS
DESIGNERS
STOURBRIDGE

CARNIVAL GLASS

This mass produced glass was made in England, Australia, and in the United States where the major producers were Fenton, Imperial, Millersburg and Northwood. A large amount of the glass is unmarked, many manufacturers having used paper labels.

As a substitute for the average household who could not afford the luxury of cut glass and the iridescent Tiffany, this glass was first called "iridescent glass," "taffeta" and "rhodium glass," but later became generically known as "carnival" due to the fact it was often given away as prizes at carnivals and amusement parks, and also used as a premium at grocery stores, etc.

CAMBRIDGE GLASS COMPANY

Cambridge, Ohio. 1901 - 1954, 1955 - 1958.

FENTON ART GLASS COMPANY

Williamstown, West Virginia. 1905 - present. The company was founded by brothers Frank and John Fenton. In 1908, John left the company and later founded Millersburg Glass Company. Early carnival glass was made from about 1907 to 1921. It was not marked. Carnival glass reproductions have been made sice 1969. Everything made by Fenton since 1971 is marked.

New Fenton mark.

New Fenton mark on glass made from old McKee moulds.

IMPERIAL

Bellaire, Ohio. 1901 - 1984. Made early carnival glass from 1910 to 1924. Reproductions were made beginning in the 1960s. The company went bankrupt in 1984 and the moulds were sold.

Imperial mark.

New Imperial mark used 1951 - 1972.

MOSSER

Cambridge, Ohio. 1964 - present. Mark found on Northwood-style carnival glass and other glass made by Mosser.

NORTHWOOD

Wheeling, West Virginia. 1902 - 1923. Made carnival glass from 1910 - 1918. Harry Northwood opened a glass factory in Indiana, Pennsylvania, in 1896, and another in Wheeling, West Virginia, in 1902. Northwood closed when he died in 1923. This mark was bought by a group of collectors, so no one can use it on reproductions.

L.G. WRIGHT

New Martinsville, West Virginia. 1937 - present. Contracted with Ohio and West Virginia glass factories to reproduce popular carnival and pressed glass patterns. This mark was used on glass made from old Northwood moulds. The colours are slightly different because the production technique is different. Other L.G. Wright marks used include a W or an underlined W in a circle.

125

MARY GREGORY

"MARY GREGORY" TYPE GLASS

Clear and coloured glass decorated with hand painted Kate Greenaway type figures. Many forms were decorated in this manner, such as, cruets, decanters, dressing table sets, pitchers, and vases, etc.

The young lady who was once believed to have originated the paintings of children on this attractive glassware was a decorator in the lamp department of the Boston & Sandwich Glass Company from 1880 to 1884. Rural scenes, rather than children, were most often used as decoration. No one would be more surprised than Miss Gregory herself to find that her name had been associated with this European glassware.

Glass Decorator, Sandwich & Boston Glass Company, Sandwich, Mass., USA

The ware originated in Europe, probably Bohemia, around the mid-19th century, and is known to have been made in countries like Italy, France, Germany, and England for export. Its distringuishing features show tinted faces, lightly coloured clothing, and in some cases gold trim.

Its popularity encouraged a number of USA glass houses to experiment with their own version of the decorating style and the outcome from about 1880 became all white figures and decor. The fashionable colours being cranberry, amethyst, blue, green, amber, and clear. Cranberry examples now command the highest prices. Amethyst is considered rare.

Be alert for reproduction pieces. Many appear in colours not used in the 19th century and are painted in a heavy white enamel not reminiscent of their earlier counterparts.

RENE LALIQUE

Paris, France. Rene Lalique (1860 - 1945) was a successful jeweller, well known for his Art Nouveau designs. During the 1890s and early 1900s he experimented with glass making incorporating some of the glass in his designs for jewelry. He was commissioned by Coty and other perfume manufacturers to design bottles and packaging for their products during this period and by 1915 he was concentrating on glass design and manufacture.

Rene Lalique's main aim was to exploit the luminous properties of the glass metal to its fullest. The proportions of all-coloured glass used for his work is relatively small. A slight concession to the uniformity of the typical Lalique opalescence was made probably during the late 1920s and early 1930s, with the application of dull-blueish colour traces about the edges of the relief decoration, thus breaking the unity of the design. This later period, and through the 1930s date the cigarette boxes, ashtrays, powder boxes, scent bottles, clocks and mirrors with motifs of cupids, lovebirds, nymphs, doves and rabbits.

Characteristic Lalique glass shows a subtly frosted effect. Another distinctive and very beautifu Lalique creation is a moulded crystal glass with an interior, milky-cloud effect, reminiscent of vaseline glass, revealing a pale ochre tinge when held against the light; it is so subtly blended into the metal that it seems difficult to define how this was contrived.

Rene Lalique did not rely on multi-coloured effects of symbolic plant forms to lend expression to his work. There are no over-balanced shapes with narrow rising stems and sudden bulbous protuberances. He relied on the aesthetics of the form itself to satisfy, and on the subtle use of the glass-metal to entrap and reflect natural and artificial light, to give his material its distinctive luminescent quality. Sometimes he decorated his glass with stark enamel colours, applied after completion of the article, and this particular type of embellishment is seen on some of the early heavily sculptured pieces.

R. LALIQUE
FRANCE
Pre-1945

R. Lalique France
Pre-1945

LALIQUE FRANCE
1945 - 1960

Lalique France
1945 - 1960

LALIQUE
1960+

Lalique France
1960+

PAIRPOINT GLASS

A thumbnail sketch of the locations.

- 1837   Mt. Washington Glass Works, founded in South Boston, Mass.
- 1870   Moved to New Bedford, Mass.
- 1876   Reorganized as Mt. Washington Glass Company.
- 1880   Pairpoint Manufacturing Co. established next door.
- 1894   The two companies merged and became the Pairpoint Corporation.
- 1939   Robert Gundersen bought the company, renamed Gundersen-Pairpoint Glass Works.
- 1957   Robert Bryden bought the company, renamed it Pairpoint Glass Co. Inc. and moved it to East Wareham, Mass.
- 1958 - 1970   Glass made in Spain under the Pairpoint name.
- 1970   Company moved back to Sagamore, Mass, now operating as the Pairpoint Glass Company.

Mt. Washington,
1870 - 1894.

Pairpoint Corporation,
1894 - 1939.

Gundersen Glass Works, Inc.,
1939 - 1952.

Gundersen-Pairpoint Glass Works,
1952 - 1957.

Pairpoint Glass Co. Inc.,
1957 - 1958.

Pairpoint Glass Co.
1958 - 1970.

Pairpoint Glass Co.
1972 - present.

LOUIS COMFORT TIFFANY

Tiffany or Favrile* glass is noted for its unique quality, exquisite blending of vibrant colours and its true iridescence. This type of blown glass comprising both ornamental and useful objects was produced by the Tiffany factories during the 1890s until 1918.

The years 1918 to 1928 are known as the Nash period at the Tiffany works. Mr. A. Douglas Nash supervised the factories during this time and changes were made in the type of glass produced, most notably the colours used. Pale colours with thin iridescence instead of the rich colours of previous years. The Tiffany name, signatures and marks continued to be used during this period.

* Favrile: Registered as part of the Tiffany trade mark November 13, 1894. Derived from the old English "fabrile" meaning hand made.

Other Tiffany Products

As well as blown glass the Tiffany enterprises also made other fine decorative items in a wide variety of materials; pressed glass for tiles and jewels; glass for pictorial windows and mosaics; lamps; lamp shades and fixtures; pottery; enamels; jewelry; desk sets; candlesticks; picture frames; boxes; door knockers and paperweights, etc. These pieces can also be identified by the "Tiffany" mark.

The A. Douglas Nash Corporation

The Tiffany furnaces closed in 1928. The Corona, Long Island, New York works were sold to A. Douglas Nash. From December, 1928 until 1931 the A. Douglas Nash Corporation continued to make glass at the Corona works, but a condition of the sale stated that the Tiffany name could not be associated with the firm or its products. Sometimes called "Tiffany-type," this glass is marked **NASH** or **ADNA**.

Marks on Tiffany Glass/Products

Marks are engraved, stamped or etched on the form or added as a label.

On glass, the name or initials were cut or etched by workmen - varying in size and style. Know the glass, signatures have been forged.

It has been said - "Collect glass, not signatures."

L C T & Co or L C T

In block script or monogram

Tiffany Studios
New York

Louis C. Tiffany Furnaces Inc.
Favrile

Louis C. Tiffany and Co., Associated Artists

Tiffany Glass Co.

Tiffany Studios

Tiffany Glass and Decorating Co.

TIFFANY

TIFFANY & Co.

Favrile fabrique

ADNA or NASH

*are the marks used
by the A. Douglas Nash Corporation,
1928 to 1931.*

CUT GLASS MANUFACTURERS

AMERICAN

Marks are engraved, stamped or etched on the form or added as a label.

C.G. ALFORD & COMPANY
New York, NY. 1872 - 1918.

ALMY & THOMAS
Corning, NY. 1903 - 1918.

AVERBECK CUT GLASS COMPANY
New York, NY. 1892 - 1923.

BALTIMORE BARGAIN HOUSE
Baltimore, MD. 1890.

J.D. BERGEN COMPANY
Meriden, Conn. 1880 - 1916.

GEORGE BORGFELDT & CO.
New York, NY. 1912.

T.B. CLARK & COMPANY
Honesdale, PA. 1884 - 1930.

CORONA CUT GLASS CO.
Toledo, OH. 1906.

C. DORFLINGER & SONS
White Mills, PA. 1852 - 1921.

O.E. EGGINGTON COMPANY
Corning, NY. 1899 - 1920.

131

H.C. FRY GLASS COMPANY
Toledo, OH. 1895; Rochester, PA. 1901 - 1934.

T.G. HAWKES & COMPANY
Corning, NY. 1880 - 1964.

A.H. HEISEY & CO., INC.
Newark, OH. 1896 - 1957.
Manufacturers of the Celebrated
Diamond H and Plunger Cut.

J. HOARE & COMPANY
Corning, NY. 1868 - 1920.

HOBBS GLASS COMPANY
Wheeling, WV. 1845 - 1891.

HOPE GLASS WORKS
Providence, RI. 1872 - 1951.

HUNT GLASS COMPANY
Corning, NY. 1895 - .

IRVING CUT GLASS COMPANY INC.
Honesdale, PA. 1900 - 1930.

LACKAWANA CUT GLASS COMPANY
Scranton, PA. 1903 - 1905.

LAUREL CUT GLASS COMPANY
Jermyn, PA. 1903 - 1920.

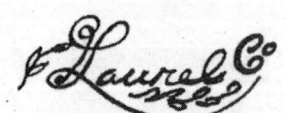

LIBBEY GLASS COMPANY
Toledo, OH. 1888 - 1936.

LOTUS CUT GLASS CO.
Barnesville, OH. 1898.

LYONS CUT GLASS COMPANY
Lyons, NY. 1903 - 1905.

MAJESTIC CUT GLASS COMPANY
Emira, NY. 1900 - 1916.

MAPLE CITY GLASS COMPANY
Hawley, PA. 1901 - 1904.

MERIDEN CUT GLASS COMPANY
(part of International Silver Company)
Meriden, CT. ca. 1896 - 1923.

MT. WASHINGTON GLASS COMPANY
New Bedford, Mass. 1837 - 1894.

NEWARK CUT GLASS COMPANY
Newark, NJ. Dates unknown.

PAIRPOINT CORPORATION
New Bedford, Mass. 1880 - 1938.

P.X. PARCHE & SON COMPANY
Chicago, IL. 1874 - .

PITKIN & BROOKS
Chicago, IL. 1872 - 1920.

QUAKER CITY CUT GLASS CO.
Philadelphia, PA. 1902 - 1927.

SIGNET GLASS COMPANY
Corning, NY. 1913 - 1916.

H.P. SINCLAIRE & COMPANY
Corning, NY. 1904 - 1929

STERLING CUT GLASS COMPANY
Cincinnati, OH. 1904 - 1950.

L. STRAUS & SONS
New York, NY. 1872 - 1919.

STEUBEN GLASS WORKS
Corning, NY. 1903 - .

TAYLOR BROS.
Philadelphia, PA. 1902 - 1915.

TUTHILL CUT GLASS COMPANY
Middleton, NY. 1900 - 1923.

UNGER BROS.
Newark, NJ. 1901 - 1918.

CHARLES VANHEUSEN COMPANY
Albany, NY. 1843 - .

WRIGHT RICH CUT GLASS COMPANY
Anderson, Ind. 1904 - 1915.

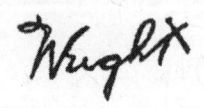

CANADIAN

Marks are engraved, stamped or etched on the form or added as a label.

BELLEVILLE CUT GLASS CO.
Belleville, Ontario. 1912. Not marked.

HENRY BIRKS & SONS
Montreal, Quebec. 1894 - 1907. Glasscutting factory bought by George Phillips & Company, 1907.

CLAPPERTON & SONS LIMITED
GUNDY-CLAPPERTON COMPANY
Toronto & Deseronto. 1905 - 1931.

Gundy-Clapperton mark with retailer's name.

GOWANS & KENT COMPANY LIMITED
Toronto, Ontario. Ca. 1905.

RODEN BROS. LIMITED
Toronto, Ontario. Ca. 1891 - Ca. 1922.

PORTE & MARKLE

Roden Bros. Limited marks with retailer's name.

THE EXCELSIOR GLASS COMPANY
Montreal, Quebec. 1880 - 1883. Mark unknown.

135

LAKEFIELD CUT GLASS COMPANY
Lakefield, Ontario. 1915. Some pieces marked with a small Union Jack.

OTTAWA CUT GLASS COMPANY
Ottawa, Ontario. 1913. Mark unknown.

GEORGE PHILLIPS & Co., LTD.
Montreal, Quebec. 1907. Mark unknown.

THE ST. LAWRENCE GLASS COMPANY
Montreal, Quebec. 1867 - 1875. Mark unknown.

THE WALLACEBURG CUT GLASS COMPANY
Wallaceburg, Ontario. 1913 - 1930. Not marked.

A known but unidentified mark, possibly of a Canadian company.

CANADIAN FACTORIES

Canadian Container Manufacturers and their Marks

From about 1840 onwards glass containers for household and commercial use were manufactured in Canada. Prior to that time items of this type were imported into Canada from Europe and the United States.

Methods of manufacture gradually improved during the late 19th century and with the new technology the factories of Canada were able to satisfy the growing demand for large and small glass containers. During this period the industry was in a state of flux and by the end of the century seven factories had been absorbed by the blossoming Diamond Glass Company Limited which later became the Diamond Flint Glass Company Limited and in 1913 the Dominion Glass Company Limted. The output of the several plants of this large company, now known as Domglas Inc., still includes large quantities of bottles and jars for commercial and domestic use.

Canadian Glass works, their dates of operation and the types of containers produced follows:

NOVA SCOTIA

THE HUMPHREYS GLASS COMPANY
Trenton-New Glasgow. 1890 - 1917. Bottles and fruit jars.

THE LAMONT GLASS COMPANY
Trenton-New Glasgow. 1890 - 1902. Bottles and fruit jars.

NEW BRUNSWICK

THE HUMPHREYS GLASS COMPANY
Moncton. 1917 - 1920. According to *Glass in Canada* research advises bottles were the principal product, but also industrial ware including lamps and chimneys.

THE NEW BRUNSWICK CRYSTAL GLASS COMPANY
Saint John. 1874 - 1878. Thomas B. King in his book *Glass in Canada* states that in the first GLASFAX seminar verbal reports were quoted that window glass, bottles, jars and lamp shades were made.

QUEBEC

THE CANADA GLASS WORKS
Hudson. 1867 - 1871. Advertised that they made several types of food and medicine bottles as well as fruit jars.

CONSUMER GLASS COMPANY LIMITED
Montreal. 1913 - present. Bottles and fruit jars. Consumer Glass Company Limited manufactured containers in Canada with plants at Candiac and Ville Ste. Pierre, Quebec; Milton and Toronto, Ontario; and Lavington, British Columbia.

THE (EARLY) DOMINION GLASS COMPANY
Montreal. 1886 - 1898. Fruit jars, pickle bottles, flasks, medicine bottles.

FOSTER BROTHERS
St. Johns. 1854 - 1860. Advertised that they made a variety of containers including bottles and jars. To date the only type of bottle identified as a product of this factory is a bottle embossed "Foster Brothers St. Johns C.E."

OTTAWA GLASS WORKS
1847 - ca. 1860. Became British American Glass Works in 1857. Exploration of this site has revealed that case gins and druggists' bottles were made there. It is also reported that soda water bottles were a product of these factories, as was window glass.

THE ST. JOHNS GLASS COMPANY

St. Johns. 1875 - 1878. was purchased by William Yuille and became the Excelsior Glass Company from 1879 - 1880. Products include fruit jars, prescription wares, and pressed blown containers.

In 1880 The Excelsior Glass Company moved to Montreal and operated under that name until 1883. The following series of factory names reflect the changes of ownership and reorganization that took place over three decades.

North American Glass Company, 1883 - 1890.
Diamond Glass Company Limited, 1890 - 1902.
Diamond Flint Glass Company Limited, 1903 - 1913.
Diamond Glass Company Limited, 1913 - 1925.

Containers in a variety of types and forms were made over the years at the Delormier Avenue site of these factories; bottles, candy jars, fruit jars and packers.

THE ST. LAWRENCE GLASS COMPANY

Montreal. 1867 - 1873. Bottles, coal oil lamps, glass shades, tableware.

ONTARIO

THE BEAVER FLINT GLASS COMPANY

Toronto. 1897 - 1948. This factory advertised that they sold containers and it is now believed that they were distributors only and not container manufacturers. Medicinals with the mark " B F G Co." on the base usually have a small "D" in a diamond mark as well indicating that the Dominion Glass Comany manufactured some bottles for this firm.

THE BURLINGTON GLASS WORKS

Hamilton. 1874 - 1897. Many types of containers were made at this factory including fruit jars, various bottles, lamp shades and chimneys, and household items.

THE CALEDONIA GLASS WORKS

Caledonia. 1844 - ca. 1848. Produced bottles and bottled the natural mineral waters on the site of the springs near Prescott. To date no examples have been identified.

THE ERIE GLASS WORKS

Port Colborne. 1892 - 1893. Bottles and fruit jars.

THE FOSTER GLASS WORKS

Port Colborne. 1894 - 1900. Local newspapers list fruit jars, gallon jugs, conical inkwells.

THE HAMILTON GLASS WORKS
Hamilton. 1865 - 1898. Re-opened in 1906. Bottles, fruit jars, and tableware.

MALLORYTOWN GLASS WORKS
Mallorytown. 1839 - 1840. A whiskey flask and bottle are illustrated by Gerald Stevens in *Early Canadian Glass* as products of this factory.

THE NAPANEE GLASS WORKS
Napanee. 1881 - 1883. No examples have been identified. A few unidentified shards found on site during a 1968 dig.

THE ONTARIO GLASS WORKS
Kingsville. 1899 - 1902. The "Ferrol" cod liver oil bottle and "Beaver" fruit jars are attributed to this factory.

THE SYDENHAM GLASS COMPANY
Wallaceburg. 1894 - 1913. Bottles and fruit jars, lamps and whimsies.

THE TORONTO GLASS COMPANY
Toronto. 1893 - 1899. Bottles and fruit jars.

MANITOBA

THE MANITOBA GLASS MANUFACTURING COMPANY
Beausejour. 1904 - 1913. Bottles and fruit jars.

MID-WEST GLASS COMPANY
Winnipeg. 1928 - 1930. Bottles, fruit jars, tablewares. lamp chimneys.

ALBERTA

THE DOMINION GLASS COMPANY
Redcliff. 1913 - present. Bottles and fruit jars.

BRITISH COLUMBIA

THE CRYSTAL GLASS COMPANY
Sapperton (now New Westminster). 1907 - 1908. Bottles and fruit jars.

THE VICTORIA GLASS & BOTTLE COMPANY
Saanich, Victoria. 1914 - ca. 1915. Experimetnal glass factory set up by Walter LeDain. John Barclay in The Canadian Fruit Jar Report mentions a report in which it states the factory would make all the various sizes of bottles and jars for firms in Victoria and Vancouver. Hudson Bay company purchased flat whiskey flasks in various sizes. First World War contributed to failure.

The Developement and Structure of the Dominion Glass Company Limited

The **Diamond Glass Company Limited** was formed in 1890 and acquired control of the following glass factories in Canada throughout the period of its incorporation which ended in 1903.

1890: The Burlington Glass Works, Hamilton, Ontario.
North American Glass Works, Montreal, Quebec.
Nova Scotia Glass Company, Trenton-New Glasgow, Nova Scotia.

1893: The Hamilton Glass Works, Hamilton, Ontario.

1897: The Toronto Glass Company, Toronto, Ontario.

1898: The (Early) Dominion Glass Company, Montreal, Quebec.
The Lamont Glass Company, Trenton-New Glasgow, Nova Scotia.

The **Diamond Glass Company Limited** was reorganized in 1903 and the name was changed to the **Diamond Flint Glass Company Limited**. During the period 1903 to 1913 it gained control of two other independant glass companies:

1907: The Manitoba Glass Manufacturing Company, Beausejour, Manitoba.

1908: The Sydenham Glass Company, Wallaceburg, Ontario.

In 1906 the Hamilton Glass Works factory re-opened and a new factory the Canadian Glass Manufacturing Company Limited was built in 1907 at Pte. St. Charles, Quebec.

Reorganization took place again in 1913 and the company became the **Dominion Glass Company Limited**. Expansion continued with the acquisition of the Jefferson Glass Company, Toronto, Ontario. Also in 1913 the company opened a factory at Redcliff, Alberta.

The company became known as Domglas Inc., and manufactured glass containers in Canada with plants in Moncton and Scoudouc, New Brunswick; Montreal, Quebec; Mississauga, Ontario; Redcliff, Alberta; and Burnaby, British Columbia.

Containers were also produced at the Libbey-St. Clair Inc. factory, Wallaceburg, Ontario. Glass items were manufactured at this site since 1894. Libbey-St.Clair Inc. became jointly owned by Donglas Inc. of Canada and the Libbey Division of Owens-Illinois, USA.

TRADE MARKS ON GLASS

CANADIAN

Marks used by Canadian glass factories are illustrated below. Occasionally wholesalers had their trade mark embossed on containers. Although they sometimes designed their own containers, they did not actually make them. Due to the many changes of ownership and amalgamations that took place in the late 1800s and early in the 20th century it is not always possible to date a container by the manufacturer's mark.

ALTAGLASS

Medicine Hat, Alberta is an unassuming western city gaining an international reputation. Not only can "the Hat" lay claim to having once been the home of the numerous pottery factories, including Medalta, it can also lay claim to having been the home of Altaglass, a successful Canadian art glass studio.

From 1950 to 1988 Altaglass manufactured whimsical and decorative art glass pieces, such as animal figures, vases, bowls, candy dishes, ash trays and paperweights.

Altaglass was operated by John Furch, A Czechoslovakian immigrant. Furch and his family moved first to Ontario, but was lured to Medicine Hat in May, 1950 by the local Chamber of Commerce, and their promise of low cost, clean burning natural gas. Furch established his Altaglass studio there.

An experienced glass blower, Furch built his own furnaces, tools and kilns for the Altaglass factory. Altaglass used any one of three glass working processes to create their wares, including pressed glass, mouth blown glass, and freeform glass. Most Altaglass craftsmen were immigrants trained in the art of glass blowing in Europe.

Altaglass markets included the Eaton's department store chain and many small souvenir shops.

John Furch died in 1976, at the age of 80. He had overseen the daily operations of the factory until his death, and many changes took place soon after. As a direct result of the increase in price of natural gas in 1981, the furnaces were

The diamond-shaped sticker used in the mid-1950s. The printing and trim would originally have been gold, but time has turned many of these to silver.

Altaglass began using its maple leaf decal in 1967, the Centennial year.
Both images courtesy of Medicine Hat Museum, and Mary Coward.

141

shut down. Using blow torches and Pyrex glass rods imported from the U.S.A., Altaglass produced drawn animals, birds and decorative objects. But the doors to the factory were closed for good in 1988.

Identifying pieces that are missing the distinctive Altaglass decals is difficult. The earliest items produced by Altaglass have a round black and gold sticker, inscribed with "Hand Made Altaglass Medicine Hat." A diamond shaped black and gold decal followed, but today the gold on many of these stickers is now silver.

And it was in the Centennial year, 1967, that Altaglass began affixing a decal in the shape of a maple leaf. These stickers were used for several years after 1967. Also note that on the bottom of some pieces mounted on a glass pad, there will be a pattern of raised dots. The pattern has the initials "AG" inside a diamond shape. - *G.W.*

BEAVER FLINT GLASS COMPANY

NOTE: Containers marked "B F G Co." were probably made by the Dominion Glass Company and its predecessors.

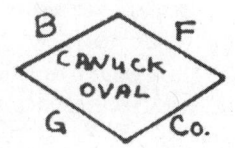

BURLINGTON GLASS WORKS

BGW
1875 - 1877

BURLINGTON
1875 - 1897

BGCo
1877 - 1897

CONSUMER GLASS COMPANY LIMITED

1917 - 1961

1961

Possibly the DIAMOND GLASS COMPANY LIMITED or the (EARLY) DOMINION GLASS COMPANY

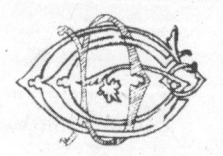

NOTE: A shard from a fruit jar embossed "D G CO" in a maple leaf was found at the Burlington Glass Works site. It seems likely that jars marked in this way were made at Burlington during the period of the Diamond Glass Company's ownership.

(EARLY) DOMINION GLASS COMPANY

DOMINION
1886 - 1898

DOMINION GLASS COMPANY LIMITED

◇ D ◇
1913 -

ERIE GLASS WORKS

⬡ E ⬡
1893 - 1898

ERIE

EXCELSIOR GLASS COMPANY LIMITED

E G Co
1879 - 1883

(monogram)
1879 - 1883

EXCELSIOR
1879 - 1883

EXCELSIOR IMPROVED
1879 - 1883

I L X

NOTE: This type of mark is found on fruit jar lids which are also embossed with the company name.

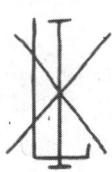

(crossed mark)

NOTE: This type of mark is found on fruit jar lids which are also embossed with the company name. A baby feeder ("Excelsior Feeder") is also embossed with this mark.

HAMILTON GLASS WORKS

HAMILTON
1865 - 1872

(monogram)
1865 - 1895

HAMILTON GLASS WORKS
1865 - 1872

RUTHERFORD & Co.
1872 - 1893.
NOTE: used on fruit jars during George Rutherford's ownership of the Hamilton Glass Works.

SAFETY VALVE PATᴅ MAY 21 1895 (with G in triangle)

◇ HG ◇

HGW

Ca. 1893 - 1898 & 1906 -

NOTE: this note is found on the base of some "Greek Key Safety Valve" fruit jars.

IROQUOIS GLASS LTD.
Candiac, QC.

Current

LAMONT GLASS COMPANY

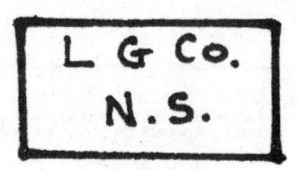

1890 - 1899

L G Co.
N.S.

MANITOBA GLASS MANUFACTURING CO.

B

MIDWEST GLASS COMPANY

M

RICHARDS GLASS COMPANY

NOTE: *This company designed several types of prescription bottles and baby feeders. Although their trade mark often appears on bottles, the Richards Glass Company was a wholesaler and not a manufacturer.*

RIGO

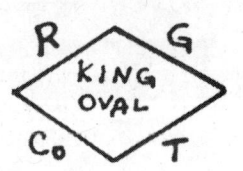

R G
KING
OVAL
Co T

ST. LAWRENCE GLASS COMPANY

STL

TORONTO GLASS COMPANY

T.G.Co

144

AMERICAN

ADAMS & CO.
Pittsburg, PA. 1861 - 1891

A

ARKANSAS GLASS CONTAINER CORP.
Jonesboro, AK. A.B.M. 1958 onwards

A

AKRO-AGATE
Akron, OH. 1991

AKRO AGATES

JOHN AGNEW & SON
Pittsburg, PA. 1854 - 1866

A

AMERICAN ART PRODUCTS CORP.
New York, NY. Before 1950.

HAND CUT MADE IN USA

ANCHOR GLASS CO.
Mount Pleasant, PA. 1907.

(anchor)

ANCHOR HOCKING GLASS CORP.
Lancaster, OH. Current.

(anchor with H)

DURYEA & POTTER
New York, NY. 1901.

ATHOSGLASS

HAZEL-ATLAS GLASS CO.
Wheeling, WV. 1902 - 1964

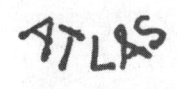

ATLAS

ATLAS

ARMSTRONG CORK CO.
Lancaster, PA. Current

(A in circle) *Armstrong*

STEUBEN GLASS WORKS
Steuben, OH. 1904. Assigned to Corning Glass Works, Corning, NY in 1924.

AURENE

145

MACBETH-EVANS GLASS CO.
Pittsburg, PA. Before 1900.

FREDERICK W. BUNING
New York, NY. 1893.

BARTLETT-COLLINS Co.
Sapulpa, OK. Current

BLENCO GLASS CO.
Milton, WV. After 1913.

GEORGE BORGFELDT & CO.
New York, NY. 1913

BALTIMORE BARGAIN HOUSE
Baltimore, MD. 1890.

Baltimore
Bargain House

BALL BROTHERS CO.
Muncie, IN. 1894

BIBI & CO.
Brooklyn, NY. After 1913.

BEST LIGHT CO.
Canton, OH. 1895

BUCKLEY-NEWHALL CO.
New York, NY. 1910.

BLUE RIBBON

ILLINOIS PACIFIC GLASS CO.
San Francisco, CA. 1910.

BEAVER

CHARLES T. DeFOREST
New York, NY. 1884

BEAUMIROIR

STANDARD GLASS CO.
Marion, IN

BLUE RIBBON

L.A. BECKER CO.
Jersey City, NJ. 1908.

HEMINGRAY GLASS CO.
Covington, KY. 1886.

GLOBE

BELLE VERNON MAPES DAIRY CO.
Cleveland, OH. 1914.

BOTTLERS PROTECTIVE ASSN.
Baltimore, MD. 1888.

HYDRO CARBON CO.
Witchita, KS. 1991.

AIR·O·LITE

KLEPA ARTS
Hollywood, CA

SMALLEY, KILAN & ONTHANK
Boston, MA.

1914

1910

147

GILL BROTHERS CO.
Steubenville, OH

White Star
1884

SAMSON
UNSURPASSED FOR STRENGTH
WARRANTED FINEST QUALITY
PURE LEAD GLASS
1887

WARRANTED BEST LEAD FLINT
OIL FINISHED FIRE PROOF
1890

HAMMER
1896

MONARCH
OIL FINISHED
TRADE MARK
FIRE PROOF
BEST LEAD FLINT
1897

1900

MOROC
TRADE MARK
LEAD GLASS
1901

FINE
ANCO
FLINT
1901

GOOD LUCK
1907

1908

UNICORN
1911

O K
1898
CORONET
1900
ROCK
1901
LUCKY CROSS
1908
PARIAN
1911

GRANITE
1890
VICTOR TOP
1898

ACMELITE
1911
GLORIA
1912

DITHRIDGE & CO.
Pittsburg, PA. 1896.

GOTHAM CO.
New York, NY. 1891.

THE BEST

MACBETH-EVANS GLASS CO.
Pittsburg, PA. 1895.

ZENITH

STANDARD OIL CO.
New York, NY. 1908.

SOCONY

BRYCE BROS. CO.
Mt. Pleasant, PA. 1948

PITTMAN-DRIETZER & CO.
New, York, NY. Mid-1900s.

COLONY CRYSTAL

CAMBRIDGE GLASS CO.
Ohio. 1927 - later.

IMPERIAL GLASS CO.
Ohio.

GENUINE HAND MADE Cambridge MADE IN USA

GENUINE HAND MADE Cambridge & Imperial

CONCORD GLASS MFG. CO.
New York, NY. After 1935.

CONCORD GLASS "handcrafted"

149

CORNING GLASS WORKS
Corning, NY.

1880

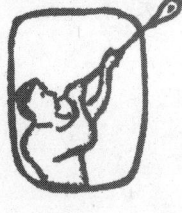

1940

1909

NONEX
1909

NOVIL NULTRA

RESISTAL ULTRA
1914

19104

CANTON GLASS Co.
Hartford City, MD.

CHATANOOGA GLASS Co.
Chatanooga, TN. 1927

T.G. COOK & Co.
Philadelphia, PA. 1873.

CENTENNIAL

First trade mark to be registered in the United States for the marking of tablewares.

COHANSEY GLASS MFG. Co.
Bridgeton, NJ. 1870.

COHANSEY

CORONA CUT GLASS Co.
Toledo, OH. 1906.

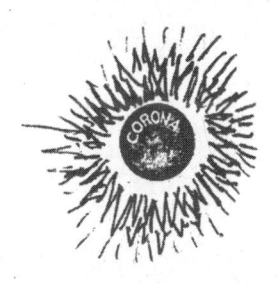

T.B. CLARK & Co.
Seelyville, PA. 1898.

STEAM GAUGE & LANTERN Co.
Syracuse, NY. 1891.

DAULT GLASS & CROCKERY Co.
Toledo, OH. 1909.

DIAMOND GLASS Co.
Royersford, PA.

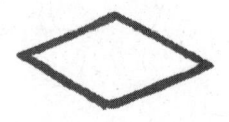

DUNBAR GLASS CORP.
Dunbar, WV. After 1913.

DUNCAN & MILLER GLASS Co.
Washington, PA. After 1913.

CHANDLER SPECIALTY MFG. Co.
Boston, MA. 1905.

WILBUR F. LITCH
Philadelphia, PA. 1890.

CENTURY INKSTAND Co.
New York, NY. 1893.

ONEIDA COMMUNITY LTD.
Oneida, NY. 1914.

COMMUNITY

MCPIKE DRUG Co.
Kansas City, MS. 1904.

CRYSTO

C. DORFLINGER & SONS
White Mills, PA. 1892.

COLONIAL

C.R. DE GOEY
Providence, RI. After 1913.

de Goey CRYSTAL

EMERALD GLASS Co.
Los Angeles CA. After 1913.

C. DORFLINGER & SONS
White Mills, PA. 1894.

LORRAINE

EDMUNDS & JONES MFG. Co.
Detroit, MI. 1904.

E. & J.

O.F. EGGINGTON Co.
Corning, NY. 1899.

EGGINTON

FEDERAL GLASS Co.
Columbus, OH. After 1913.

PROTECTIVE "FREFLO" STOPPLE Co.
Delaware. 1914.

Fredrop

THOMAS DRYSDALE & Co.
New York, NY. 1886.

TERU-TERU

EMPIRE STATE GLASS Co.
New York, NY. After 1913.

ESCO PRODUCTS

152

GLENSHAW GLASS Co.
Glenshaw, PA. Current.

FOSTER-FORBES GLASS Co.
Marion,, IN. Current.

FENTON ART GLASS Co.
Williamstown, WV. After 1913.

GLASS CONTAINERS INC.
Los Angeles, CA. Current.

FOSTORIA GLASS SPECIALTY Co.
Fostoria, OH. 1908.

ACORN

LA BASTIE GLASS Co.
Ottawa, IL. First used 1876.

FOSTORIA GLASS Co.
Moundsville, WV. 1909.

FAIRMOUNT GLASS WORKS
Indianapolis, IN. Current.

FOSTORIA GLASS SPECIALTY Co.
Fostoria, OH. 1905.

NOREC

153

FOSTORIA GLASS Co.
Moundsville, WV. 1891.

FOSTORIA

**FOSTORIA GLASS
SPECIALTY Co.**
Fostoria, OH. 1910.

IRIS

**FOSTORIA GLASS
SPECIALTY Co.**
Fostoria, OH. 1911.

Veluria

FOSTORIA GLASS Co.
Moundsville, WV. Current.

Fostoria

**FOSTORIA GLASS
SPECIALTY Co.**
Fostoria, OH. 1904.

HR
NOBLAC

FOSTORIA GLASS Co.
Moundsville, WV. After 1913.

Fostoria

**EAGLE CE. &
CUT GLASS WORKS**
Brooklyn, NY. After 1913.

GOLD COIN QUALITY EAGLE BROOKLYN

MCKEE GLASS Co.
Jeanette, PA. After 1914.

GLASBAKE OVEN WARE

**SILVER CITY GLASS
Co., INC.**
Meriden, CN. After 1913.

Gold

UNITED STATES GLASS Co.
Tiffin, OH. After 1914.

Glassport

**GENERAL AUTOMOBILE
SUPPLY Co.**
New York, NY. 1905.

GENERAL

RICHARD DOUGLAS & Co.
New York, NY. 1874.

GAME COCK FIRE PROOF TRADE MARK

GULFPORT GLASS CORPRN.
Gulfport, Miss.

HOUZE GLASS CORPN.
Point Marion, PA. Current.

WILLIAM J. TWEED
Milville, NJ. 1904.

GLOBE

GILLINDER & SONS
Philadelphia, PA

GILLINDER
1883

FRANKLIN
1860

1874

EBENEZER CUT GLASS Co., INC.
Buffalo, NY. After 1913

GILLINDER BROS., INC.
Port Jervis, NY. After 1913.

GROZART GLASS Co.
Corona, Long Island, NY. After 1913.

OWENS-ILLINOIS GLASS Co.
Toledo, OH. 1914.

HALEY PRESSWARE DIV. KNOX GLASS ASSOCS., INC.
Knox, PA. After 1913.

HAZEL-ATLAS GLASS DIVISION CONTINENTAL CAN Co.
Wheeling, WV.

GLENSHAW GLASS Co.
Glenshaw, PA. 1904.

T.G. HAWKES & Co.
Corning, NY.

SUSQUEHANNA GLASS Co.
Culumbia, PA. After 1913.

W.H. HAMILTON Co.
Pittsburg, PA

1900

OUR DARLING

1899

UNITED JEWELERS INC.
New York, NY. 1914

HALLMARK

GILLINDER & SONS INC.
Philadelphia, PA.

1907

MICRA
1911

NEBULITE
1911

IMPERIAL GLASS Co.
Bellaire, OH.

1958

1913

1914

1913

1939

1911

A.H. HEISEY & Co.
Newark, OH

1900

1900

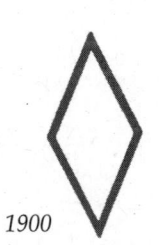

1905

1932

1908

1908

1936

MACBETH-EVANS GLASS Co.
Pittsburg, PA. 1892.

WILLIAM M. DECKER
Kingston, NY. 1893.

157

HUNT GLASS WORKS INC.
Corning, NY. After 1913.

HOD. C. DUNFEE
Charleston, WA. 1910.

IDEAL

M.V. GARNSEY
Spring Lake and Grand Haven, MI. 1906

Japana

JOHN E. KEMPLE GLASS WORKS
E. Palestine, OH

JUSTRITE MFG., Co.
Chicago, IL. 1911.

JUSTRITE

J. HOARE & Co.
Corning, NY. 1895.

ILLINOIS GLASS Co.
Alton, IL. 1915.

JEANETTE GLASS Co.
Jeanette, PA. Current.

HOPE GLASS WORKS
E. Providence, RI.

INDIANA GLASS Co.
Dunkirk, IN. Current.

IMPERIAL GLASS CORP.
Bellaire, OH. Current.

RICHARD MURR
San Francisco, CA. 1905

KIMBLE GLASS PRODUCTS
Toledo, OH. Current.

ANDREW KOCH
New York, NY. 1875

MACBETH-EVANS GLASS Co.
Pittsburg, PA., 1880.

LIBERTY GLASS Co.
Sapulpa, OK. Current.

LORNITA GLASS CORP.
Point Marion, PA. After 1913.

KERR GLASS MFG., CORP.
Sand Spring, OK.

1903

1904

KOEHLER & HINRICHS
St. Paul, MN. 1991.

E. DE LA CHAPELLE & A.M. PATURLE
Brooklyn, NY. 1876.

LAURENS GLASS WORKS
Laurens, SC. Current.

159

LOTUS GLASS Co.
Barnesville, OH. 1911.

Lotus

R.E. TONGUE & BROS.
Philadelphia, PA. 1894.

LUSTRE

KNOX GLASS INC.
Knox, PA. Current.

K

LAMB GLASS Co.
Mt. Vernon, OH. Current.

L52

KRUTH CHINA Co.
St. Louis, MO. After 1913.

KRUTH CUT FINE GLASSWARE

LIBBEY GLASS DIVISION OWENS-ILLINIOS
Toledo, OH. Current.

L

Libbey
1895

Libbey
1896

Libbey
1901

★
1901

Libbey HEAT-TREATED
1933

Libbey Safedge
1933

160

OWENS-ILLINIOS GLASS Co.
Toledo, OH. Current.

JEFFERSON GLASS Co.
Follansbee, WV. 1913.

LUCEo

1910

OSCAR O. FRIEDLAENDER
New York, NY. 1898.

Sometimes with "FIREPROOF" or "INDIFFERENT"

ALBERT LEGRAND
Manchester, NH. 1898.

TRADE MARK.

THE MCBRIDE GLASS Co.
Salem, WV. 1913.

T.C. WHEATON Co.
Milville, NJ. 1903.

M.B.W.

JOHN WILLIAM GAYNER
Salem, NJ. 1903.

LEOTRIC

METRO GLASS
Jersey City, NJ. Current.

(M)

HENRY W. PUTNAM
New York, NY. 1882.

LIGHTNING

MONOGRAM GLASS Co., INC.
Evanston, IL. After 1913.

WHITALL, TATUM & Co.
New York, NY.

MANHATTAN OVAL

161

MOUNTAINEER GLASS Co.
Weston, WV.

MOUNTAINEER GLASS HAND CUT

MARIANI & Co.
New York, NY. 1905.

MARIANI-LIQUEUR
1882

COCA MARIANI

EDWARD MILLER & Co.
Meriden, CN. 1893.

MILLER

MARION FLINT GLASS Co.
Marion, IN. 1894.

Red Cross

MARION GLASS MFG. Co.
Marion, OH. After 1913.

MARION

MARION HAND CUT

MARION

COOK & BERNHEIMER Co.
New York, NY. 1890.

MOUNT VERNON

HENRY MARTIN
Pittsburg, PA. 1883.

G UNION SEAL W

MERRITT GLASS Co.
Morganstown, WV. After 1913.

Merritt Glass Co. Merit Art Morgantown W.Va.

METRO GLASS & CHINA DEC. Co.
Brooklyn, NY. After 1913.

METRO

M.S. BURR & Co.
Boston, MA. 1874.

MEDALLION

WELSBACH Co.
Gloucester City, NJ. 1910.

MULTI-FLEX

OBEAR-NESTER GLASS Co.
St. Louis, MO.

1895   1895

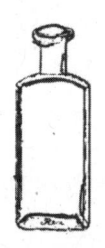

1896   1899    1900

NATIONAL GLASS MFG. Co.
Buffalo, NY. After 1913.

MORITZ KIRCHBERGER
New York, NY.

1898    1903

STANLEY C. CLINE
Philadelphia, PA. 1896.

163

CAMBRIDGE GLASS Co.
Cambridge, OH. 1904.

NEARCUT

NATIONAL STAMPING & ELECTRIC WORKS
Chicago, IL. 1908.

NULITE

ROBERTS & MATHEWS
Ansonia, OH. 1905.

NIGHT DRIVERS FRIEND

MORGANSTOWN GLASSWARE GUILD
Morganstown, WV. Current.

PASSOW & SONS
Chicago, IL. 1914.

NIC=LESS
BULGE
NIC=LESS

QUICKSILVER MINING Co.
New Almaden, CA. 1864.

NORTHWESTERN GLASS Co.
Seattle, WA. Current.

N-W

OIL CITY GLASS Co.
Oil City, PA. Current.

ROBERT A. VANCLEAVE
Philadelphia, PA. 1909.

O-U-KID

PENNSYLVANIA GLASS PRODUCTS Co.
Pittsburg, PA.

AUSTIN D. PALMER
Coshocton, OH. 1892.

164

PILGRIM GLASS CORP.
Huntington, WV.

GEO. BORGFELDT & Co.
New York, NY. 1912.

HAWTHORNE MFG., Co.
Bridgeport, CN. 1910.

OLD SOL

OVINGTON BROS., Co.
New York, NY. 1895.

Ovington's

PIERCE GLASS Co.
Pt. Alleghany, PA. Current.

PHILADELPHIA VACUUM SPECIALTY Co.
Philadelphia, PA. 1911.

CENTRADRINK FILTERS Co.
New York, NY. 1913.

WARREN FRUIT JAR Co.
Fairfield, IW.

PACIFIC COAST GLASS WORKS
San Francisco, CA. 1913.

OTIS A. MYGATT
New York, NY. 1901.

PHOENIX GLASS Co.
Monaca, PA. 1881.

165

MCKEE-JEANETTE GLASS WORKS
Jeanette, PA. 1903.

PRESCUT

CORNING GLASS WORKS
Corning, NY.

GLEASON-TIEBOUT GLASS Co.
New York, NY. 1910.

POLYCASE

ROYAL GLASS Co.
Centralia, IL. 1910.

SCHLOSS CROCKERY Co.
San Francisco, CA. 1910.

C.F. RUMPP & SONS INC.
Philadelphia, PA. 1892.

UNITED STATES GLASS Co.
Pittsburg, PA. 1911.

H. PERILSTEIN
Philadephia, PA. 1908.

JUSTIN THARAUD
New York, NY. After 1913.

REID BROS.
San Francisco, CA. 1909.

F. SCHMIDT. & Co.
Stamford, CN. After 1913.

TAYLOR, SMITH & TAYLOR Co.
East Liverpool, OH. After 1913.

SENECA GLASS Co.
Morganstown, WV. After 1913.

ALART & MCGUIRE
New York, NY. 1908.

CHICAGO HEIGHTS BOTTLE Co.
Chicago Heights, IL. 1913.

SIGNET

SOLAR PRISM Co.
Cleveland, OH. 1899.

SLOAN GLASS Co.
Cumberland, MD. After 1913.

TIFFIN ART GLASS CORP.
Tiffin, OH. After 1913.

L. STRAUSS & SONS
New York, NY. 1894.

THATCHER GLASS MFG. Co.
New York, NY.

167

SILEX Co.
Malden, MA. 1913

SILEX

SILVER CITY GLASS Co., INC.
Meriden, CN. After 1913.

Sterling on Crystal

GENERAL ELECTRIC Co.
Schenectady, NY. 1913.

SudaN

SYL-FAU ART GLASS Co.
S. Hanover, MA. After 1913.

SYL SF FAU

CHARLES BOLDT GLASS Co.
Cincinnati, OH. 1904.

TIP TOP

THOMAS WIGHTMAN
Pittsburg, PA. 1894.

LIVERMORE & KNIGHT Co.
Providence, RI. 1907.

Spookie Shades

EDWARD A. POWER & Co.
Pittsburg, PA. 1897.

UNION A F MADE

UNITED GROCERS Co.
Toledo, OH. 1913.

Un-GRO-CO

WASHINGTON Co.
Washington, PA. After 1913.

WASHINGTON

WHEATON GLASS Co.
Millville, NJ. Current.

(W)

C.E. WHEELOCK & Co.
Peoria, IL. 1898.

RADIANT CRYSTAL WHEELOCK RICH CUT GLASS

168

SUN VAPOR STREET LIGHT Co.
Canton, OH. 1877.

SUN

LIGHTING STUDIOS Co.
New York, NY. 1913.

"Superlux"

FLORENCE TALBOT WESTBROOK
San Francisco, CA. 1912.

VERKO

WESTMORELAND SPECIALTY Co.
Grapeville, PA. 1910.

ALEXANDER HEMSLEY
Philadelphia, PA. 1892.

SUN-FLASH

UNIVERSAL GLASS PRODUCTS Co.
Parkersburg, WV. Current.

UGP

VIKING GLASS Co.
New Martinsville, WV. Current.

early

ERSKINE B. VAN HOUTEN
White Plains, NY.

J.W. TOBIN
New York, NY. 1909.

WHICHWAY

AUSTRIA

EDWARD KAVALIER
Neu Sazawa. 1910

ENGLAND

AERATORS LTD.
London.

PRANA

CLARK'S PYRAMID & FAIRY LIGHT Co., LTD.
London.

BURGLAR'S HORROR
1884

CRICKLITE
1894

S. MAW, SON & SONS
London. 1871.

MOONLIGHT PATENT LAMP Co.
Liverpool. 1894.

MOONLIGHT

PILKINGTON BROS. LTD.
St. Helens. 1877 and later by Pilkington Glass Mfg. Co., Toronto, Canada.

PRICE'S PATENT CANDLE Co.
London. 1884.

FAIRY.

L. ROSE & Co. LTD.
London. 1874.

STUART GLASS WORKS
Stourbridge. Current.

Stuart
STUART CRYSTAL

WEISS & BIHELLER LTD.
London. 1906.

FRANCE

LA COMPAGNIE DE CRISTALLERIES BACCARAT
Meurthe. 1888.

ST. GOBAIN
Paris. 1895.

E. GERARD, DUFRAISSEIX & MOREL
Limoges. 1882.

C F H
G D M

GERMANY

DEUTSCHE GASGLUHLICHT
Berlin. 1902.

DEGEA

EHRICH & GRAETZ
Berlin. 1900.

Graetzin

GRUDER, BLANK & Co.
Berlin. 1903.

Gral

171

FRANZ A. MEHLEM
Bonn. 1890.

GEBR. PUTZLER GLASS WORKS
Penzig, Germany. 1901.

FR. STEUBEN & Co.
Erfurt. 1892.

SCHOTT & GEN
Jena.

1897

1904

1905

BIBLIOGRAPHY - GLASS

Peter & Barbara Sutton-Smith, *Canadian Handbook of Pressed Glass Tableware*. Fitzhenry & Whiteside, Markham, Ontario.

Cyril Manley, *Decorative Victorian Glass*. Van Nosteand Reinhold Company, London/New York.

Walter T. Lemiski, *Elegant Glass with Corn Flower*. Schiffer Books, USA.

Albert Christian Revi, *Encyclopedia of American Cut & Engraved Glass*. Schiffer Books, USA.

David T. Shotwell, *Glass A to Z*. Krause Publications, USA.

Bill Edwards and Mike Carwile, *Standard Encyclopedia of Carnival Glass*. Schroeder Publishing, USA.

Mariam Klamkin, *The Collector's Guide to Depression Glass*. Hawthorn Books, New York.

Phoebe Phillips, *The Encyclopedia of Glass*. Octopus Publishing, London.

Ceramics, China, Porcelain, and Pottery

German Westerwald stoneware punch set, consisting of this large barrel (with matching mugs) 1900-1928.

Company trade marks shown here are not necessarily the same size as those found on ceramics. Each are in proportion according to the item on which they appear. Cups and saucers for instance have smaller centred marks compared to dinner plates or serving pieces.

Since there are more than 4,000 china marks attributed to Britain alone it is obvious that a handbook can contain only a sampling of those most often seen. (See list of reference books for further sources of information).

STYLE OF MARKS FOUND ON CERAMICS

Applied moulded mark.

Impressed mark and artist's incised monogram.

Painted mark.

Printed mark.

Applied Moulded Marks - *Impressed marks in relief on a raised pad. Made separate from the piece and set in place prior to firing.*

Incised Marks - *Marks scratched into the soft clay before the initial firing.*

Impressed Marks - *A metal die imprinted names or initials into the ware before firing.*

Painted Marks - *Applied either under or over the glaze at the time of decorating the ware.*

Printed Marks - Over or under the Glaze.

Identifying marks or symbols on the back or base of a piece can number from one to several and can reveal all kinds of information as to origin. The most common is the company name or trade mark - usually underglaze.

Other possible marks: impressed letters or numbers signifying potters mark and date year; painted decorator/gilder initials, British Registration Diamond; patent number and occasionally name of pattern. During the 20th century a rubber stamp became a popular means of marking.

DATING CLUES

Information as to the age of an item can be acquired from the mark found on ceramic pieces. The following list provides a general time period that various types of information began to appear in the marks of European and North American manufacturers.

Beginning About	Words/Phrases Etc. Marked on Ceramics
1810 - 1820	Pattern names first appeared on china
1813	"Ironstone" patented by Masons
1842 - 1883	Diamond shaped British Registry Mark
1884	Revised British Registry Mark
1891	Country of origin to appear. Items imported to the U.S.A. after 1891 had to be marked with the country it had originated from. e.g. "England or 'Germany" to conform with the McKinley Tariff Act of 1891.
1891 -1921	"Nippon" country of origin name (Japan) or as part of company name.
1892	"copyright" registered with the U.S. Patent Office.
1900	"Bone China" or "English Bone China". Although developed about 1800, the words were not part of the mark until the 20th century.
1900	"Depose" French: registered.
1901	"Semi-vitreous" or "S.V."
1920s	"Warranted 22 Karat/carat gold"
1923	"Cooking Ware" on ceramic ware suitable for use in an oven.
1933	"Oven-proof" or "Oven tested"
1938 - 1952	"Refrigerator Ware"
1944	"Detergent Proof"
1945 - 1949	"U.S. Zone" or "U.S. Zone, Germany". Made in the American occupied zone of Germany following World War II.
1945 - 1952	Made in "Occupied Japan" period of American occupation after World War II
1949 - 1990	"East Germany"
1949 - 1990	"West Germany"
1949	® Registered with the U.S. Patent and Trade mark Office
1955	"Dishwasher Proof"
1960	"Fast Colour or Permanent Colours"
1960s	"Freezer-Oven-Table"
1970	"Microwave Safe"

GLOSSARY - CERAMICS

AGATEWARE: Earthenware made to look like natural agate stone.

APPLIED DECORATION: Ornamentation modelled separately from the body then attached.

BACKSTAMP: Another term for 'mark" made with rubber stamp.

BASALT: Black stoneware used to make ornamental pieces; vases, plaques, figures, etc. Made famous by Josiah Wedgwood.

BISQUE/BISCUIT: Unglazed pottery or porcelain which has been fired only once. Fashionable in late 1700s for figures and groups. Late 19th century figures in pastel shades were popular but lesser quality.

BODY: Ceramic term, e.g. "pottery body" – "porcelain body" – the mixture of clay and other materials used to make a ceramic article.

BLUE & WHITE: White porcelain or pottery body decorated in cobalt blue under the glaze. this form of decoration originated in China at the beginning of the 13th century.

BONE CHINA: Patented in 1748 by Thomas Fry of Bow. The recognized term "bone china" became the standard English body introduced by Josiah Spode II ca. 1794. Translucent, pure white, made with the addition of ash from calcined (burned) bones, which gives it durability, and is used to this day.

CERAMIC: Pottery, Porcelain. From the Greek word Keramos meaning Pottery or potter's earth.

CHINESE EXPORT: Porcelain made in China for the European market during the 16th -19th centuries.

CRACKLE/CRAZING: A network of fine lines. In porcelain the crazing of the glaze was often intentional for decorative purposes. In pottery crazing, a flaw, may have taken place after manufacture due to unequal contraction of glaze or body.

CREAM WARE: Cream coloured, chiefly for tablewares. First made at Staffordshire, England about 1740. Perfected by Josiah Wedgwood, later made by other English potters. Wedgwood's form of creamware became known as Queen's Ware after supplying a tea service to Queen Charlotte (wife of George III). Decorating generally consisted of beading, feather-edge, shell edge or octagon shaped borders.

CROCKERY: Earthenware or Stoneware, usually utilitarian.

DELFT: Tin-glazed ware made in Holland at Delft, decorated in blue, although other colours were sometimes used. Similar wares were made in England.

EARTHENWARE: Flower-pots, dishes and decorative pieces of low-fired baked clayware which are porous. Glazed and unglazed.

ENAMEL PAINTING: Colouring material made from a mixture of metallic oxides and flux. Hand painted enamel decoration is applied over the glaze and fired to fuse it upon the ware. It can be distinguished by its slight relief.

FAIENCE: Tin-glazed earthenwares.

FIRING: A process of converting a clay body into ceramic by heating it to the required temperature in a kiln.

GAUDY DUTCH: English earhthenware with Imari type designs – mostly floral with bright colours. Made for American export trade ca. 1810-1830s. Many later examples.

GAUDY IRONSTONE: Ca. 1850s. Heavier than Gaudy Dutch, similarly decorated in bright colours.

GAUDY WELSH: Imari style flower patterns coloured in cobalt blue, rust, green and red, often highlighted with copper lustre. Originally produced in tablewares on all types of ceramics for ordinary Welsh folk 1830-60. It also became extensively exported to America. Many later productions exist.

GLAZE: A glasslike substance, applied as a thin coating to most porcelain and pottery, then fired making it impervious to liquids.

HARD PASTE: First developed by the Chinese around the 7th century. It consists of a mixture of kaolin (white china clay) and petunse (feldspar rock) and is fired at 1350-1450 degrees. The result is a transluscent body which is strong and resists chipping. It should ring when struck.

IMARI WARE: Originated in Japan, exported to Europe and North America, and acquired its name from the Port Imari from where it was shipped. Gaudily decorated in red, blue and orange floral patterns with green foliage. Copied by English, Chinese and European factories.

IMPRESSED: Mark or decoration pressed into clay using a metal die.

INCISED: Mark or decoration scratched into clay using a pointed instrument.

IRONSTONE: A hard, heavy ceramic patented in 1813 at Staffordshire, England by Charles J. Mason.

JASPER: A hard stoneware made, and perfected, by Wedgwood since about 1775. Slightly transluscent, coloured throughout - blue; green; black, pink; lilac or yellow. Wedgwood's blue Jasperware decorated in white relief is probably the best known and most often copied. "Jasper dipped" is different from Jasper ware, it is dipped and coloured only on the surface.

KILN: A large oven or furnace used to fire ceramics.

LIMOGES: A porcelain making centre in France. Large deposits of kaolin were found in the area, hard and soft-paste porcelain have been made at Limoges since around 1771. By 1850, because of mass production methods, Limoges became one of the largest porcelain producing centres in Europe.

LITHOPHANE: A decorative transparency of translucent porcelain. An illustration becomes visible when viewed by transmitted light. Made for candle and lamp shades, to hang in windows and sometimes found in the base of steins or mugs.

LUSTRE: A thin coating of metal oxides. Irridescent, used to decorate the surface of pottery and sometimes porcelain. Large quantities of lustre ware were made in England from about 1800 to 1850. The metals used were copper, platinum and gold, copper being the most common.

MAIOLICA: Italian tin-glazed earthenware with painted decoration consisting of blue, green, yellow, purple and orange. Made during the 15th to 18th centuries.

MAJOLICA: Pottery decorated in relief beneath a coloured glaze. Introduced by Minton in the 1850s, originally tin-glazed. Made at various factories in England.

MARK: Maker's mark or trade-mark found on the base of many ceramic pieces. Much information can be acquired from a mark, such as revealing factory name, place of manufacture, date, pattern name, artist's name and other things.

MATT: Not Glossy. A dull finish.

NANKING WARE: Blue & White porcelain made in China specifically for export to the U.S. and Europe. Popular during middle and late 1800s.

PARIAN: So-called because of its resemblance to the white marble quarried on the Greek Island of Paros. White unglazed hard-paste porcelain, smooth like marble. Parian ware includes busts, figures, groups, statues and doll's heads.

PATE-SUR-PATE (Clay-on-Clay): A decorative technique. Layers of white or tinted slip clay are applied to the pottery or porcelain body and tooled to give a cameo effect.

PORTNEUF: Crockery, bowls, jugs, mugs, etc. for domestic use. Pieces are sponge decorated with foliage, animal and bird designs. Made at potteries in the U.K. and shipped in large quantities to Canada during the late 1800s and early 1900s.

POTTERY: See Earthenware

PUZZLE JUG: Pottery drinking jug with multi piercing at neck. Rim and handle constructed of hollow tubes, with several spouts. Drinker must block all apertures other than the one from which he intends to imbibe. Popular during the 17th and 18th centuries, and periodically re-introduced, e.g. Torquay ware.

QUEEN'S WARE: See Creamware

RED WARE: Generic term for all types of Red Stoneware.

RELIEF: Carved or moulded decoration, raised above the surface.

ROCKINGHAM GLAZE: Made in England and North America. Pottery made at Bennington, Vermont U.S.A. is called Rockingham ware because the glaze, a rich mottled brown, is a copy of the glaze that was used at the Rockingham pottery in Swinton, England.

SALT GLAZE: Glaze for stoneware produced by throwing salt into a kiln at a certain temperature. Hard, translucent glaze, often with a pitted surface.

SEMI-PORCELAIN: A semi-vitreous body, refined strong earthenware, impervious to heat and cold. Used for tablewares.

SLIP: Liquid potter's clay or paste used to decorate pottery or cover the whole body of an earthenware vessel.

SLIP WARE: Pottery decorated or coated with liquid clay.

SOFT-PASTE: Known as artificial porcelain, it contained ground glass stiffened with white clay. First firing is only 1,200 degrees and subsequent ones even lower. The body is granular when chipped. Over time the formulae has improved. Various substances have been added to stabilize the body.

SPATTERWARE/SPONGEWARE: Pottery decorated by daubing colour on by using a sponge. Popular during the last half of the 19th century.

STAFFORDSHIRE: A generic term to describe pottery made at factories in the district of Staffordshire, England.

STONEWARE: Heavy pottery, fused into a hard vitrified mass, opaque, nonporous.

TERRA-COTTA: Red, unglazed, porous earthenware.

TIN-GLAZE: Lead glaze used in pottery, made opaque by the addition of oxide of tin.

TOBY JUG: A pottery jug made in the form of a person wearing a three cornered hat. First made in Staffordshire, England during the late 1760s. A Toby often portrays a traditional English character – the parson, the snuff taker, the sailor or later a personality from Dickens and frequently well known individuals.

TRANSFER PRINTING: A method of decorating china, introduced about 1755 at Staffordshire, England. Transfer printing made it possible for the same pattern to be reproduced many times. A copper plate with an engraved impression was inked then a print was made on a thin piece of paper and transferred to the surface of the piece of china being decorated, the design was fixed during the firing process.

VITREOUS: Non-porous, glasslike.

MARKS - CERAMICS

ADAMS

William Adams & Sons (Potters) Ltd. Tunstall and Stoke, Staffordshire Potteries. (1769 -) The Adams family have a long history of potting in the area, eventually owning seven different locations. The best known is William Adams & Sons, a name repeatedly used to the present, and now part of the Wedgwood group.

Printed mark 1804-40. Used on blue & white earthenwares.

Printed mark 1879. England added from 1891.

Printed mark 1890-1914. On ironstone type wares.

Printed marks from 1896 onwards on various wares

Printed mark from 1914-1970

Printed mark from 1966-1975 (Adams under Wedgwood)

ADDERLEY'S

Adderley's Ltd., Daisy Bank Pottery. Longston, Staffordshire Potteries. (1906 -) (previously William Alsager Adderley)

Printed mark. (also used 1876-1906 by W.A. Addersley) 1906 - 1926

1912-1926    *1912-1926*    *1926+*    *1926+*    *1929-1947*

Adderley's printed marks 1912-47

1947-1950    *1950-1962*    *1962-*

Taken over by Ridgway Potteries in 1947 but continued under the Adderley name.

181

ALLERTON

Charles Allerton & Sons, Park Works. Longton, Staffordshire Potteries (1859-1942). Operated under Allerton's Ltd. from 1912 when taken over by Cauldon Potteries. Early wares were unmarked.

CHAS ALLERTON &
SONS
ENGLAND

Printed or impressed marks 1890-1942
Individual pattern name often included.

C. A. & SONS

ca. 1890+

ca. 1890+

ca. 1903-1912

Printed marks 1890-1912.

ca. 1912+    ca. 1915+    ca. 1915-1929   ca. 1929-1942

Allerton's Ltd., printed marks 1912-42.

ARKINSTALL & SONS

Harold Taylor Robinson formed the company Arkinstall and Sons, Stoke-on-Trent, Staffordshire, England, using the trade name Arcadian. Taken over by Robinson & Leadbeater in 1908, A.J. Robinson & Sons later, and in 1925 by Cauldon Ltd.

Arcadian China
1904-1920

1904-1924

Introduced around 1910

continued on next page

Introduced around 1912

Mark found on late domestic wares.

G.L. ASHWORTH & BROS. (LTD)

Established 1862 at Hanley, Staffordshire, Enlgand. Manufacturers of earthenware and ironstone etc. Made Mason's Patent Ironstone, used the Mason's mark.

ASHWORTH	G.L.A. & Bros.	A. & BROS.
1862-80	*1862-90*	*1862-890*

1862- 1890

Ca. 1862 used Mason's mark.

1862+ "Ashworths" added to mark. "England" added after 1891.

Royal Arms Mark. 1862+ variations occur.

1880+ variations occur.

20th Century printed mark with "England" or "Made in England" often below.

1932+ variations occur. Pattern names or styles may be included.

...continued on next page

183

1957+   1957+

AYNSLEY

John Aynsley & Sons (Ltd.). Portland Works, Longton, Staffordshire Potteries (1864 -). Early wares were unmarked.

AYNSLEY

Impressed mark, 1875+.

Printed mark, 1875-90.

Printed marks from 1891. Name "England" was added.

BELLEEK (IRISH)

Belleek china has a creamy yellow glaze that looks like a piece of mother-of-pearl. Occasionally, pieces are decorated with gold or very pale colours. The open basketwork designs are the most famous.

Belleek Pottery Limited in County Fermanagh, Ireland, has made Belleek pottery since 1863. The firm, which is still working, gained the legal right to use the name *Belleek* as part of its trade mark in 1929. Since then, no other firms may use the word *Belleek* with a capital B as part of their mark or advertising.

Belleek made in Ireland is almost always marked, although a few unmarked pieces have been identified. The mark is an Irish wolfhound, a harp, a round tower, and a shamrock with the name *Belleek* imprinted on it. This mark can be green, brown, black, red, or blue. The words *Belleek-Fermanagh* were also used.

1863 - 1880

BELLEEK
CO. FERMANAGH

1863 - 1890

FERMANAGH
POTTERY

1863 - 1890

...continued on next page

First mark: Black harp, hound and castle (1863-1890)

Second mark: Black harp, hound and castle (1891-1926) and the words "Co. Fermanagh, Ireland"

Third mark: Black "Deanta in Eirinn" added (1926-1946)

Fourth mark: green, same as third mark (1946-1955)

Not shown
Fifth mark: green "R" inside a circle added (1955-1965)
Sixth mark: green "Co. Fermanagh" omitted (1965-March 1980)
Seventh mark: gold "Deanta in Eirinn" ommited (April 1980-December 1992)
Eighth mark: blue version of the second mark with "R" inside a circle added (1993-1997)
Ninth mark: blue harp, hound and castle and the words "Belleek" (January 1997-present)

BELLEEK (AMERICAN)

Several factories in the United States produced belleek, but the designs are easily distinguished from the Irish products. Ott and Brewer, Willets Manufacturing Company, and Ceramic Art Pottery made belleek. Knowles, Taylor and Knowles Company made true belleek and a similar porcelain called *lotus ware*. Lenox made a ware similar to belleek, but more translucent and warmer in colour.

Note: in 1929 a lawsuit by the Irish Belleek factory made it illegal for any American pottery to use the name "Belleek."

CERAMIC ART COMPANY, Trenton, New Jersey (1889 - present)

Founded by Walter Scott Lenox and Jonathan Coxon in 1889. Lenox bought out Coxon in 1896. The company name was changed to Lenox, Inc. in 1906.

Mark used on belleek 1894-1906. After 1896 the word Lenox was added.

CAC/Lenox Transitional mark, ca. 1896-1906.

Lenox, Inc., 1906-1924

Lenox, Inc., 1906-1930

OTT & BREWER, Trenton, New Jersey (1863+)
Mark used on belleek ca. 1883-1894.

KNOWLES, TAYLOR AND KNOWLES,
East Liverpool, Ohio (1870 - 1929)

Mark used on belleek ca. 1889+.

1889

ETRURIA POTTERY, (OTT & BREWER) Trenton, New Jersey

1882

1883

COLUMBIAN ART POTTERY CO.
Trenton, New Jersey

Ca. 1895

MORGAN BELLEEK, Canton, Ohio

MORGAN BELLEEK AZURE

1923-1929

ORIENT

COXON POTTERY Wooster, Ohio

1926-1929

WILLETS MFG. CO. Trenton, New Jersey

1879-1912

COOK POTTERY CO. Trenton, New Jersey

BELLEEK

C♯ H.C.
TRADE MARK

Ca. 1900

End of Belleek American

JOHN BESWICK (LTD.)
Gold Street, Longton Staffordshire Potteries (1936 -)

Beswick Ware. MADE IN ENGLAND

Print mark, 1936 - .

An impressed mark is sometimes used in conjunction with the above mark. On occasion the impressed mark can be found on its own.

Post-war marks include the words "Beswick, England." This simple form of mark may also be found on earlier wares.

The original mark used mainly on figures from late 1930s. The mark is now used by Royal Doulton.

BING & GRÖNDAHL

Bing & Gröndahl was founded in 1853 in Copenhagen, Denmark, by Frederick Vilhelm Gröndahl and brothers M.H. and J.H. Bing. Gröndahl was a ceramic artist and figure maker who had worked at the Royal Copenhagen Porcelain Manufactory for several years. Meyer Herman Bing and Jacob Herman Bing were art dealers and businessmen who owned a department store in Copenhagen. Gröndahl died in 1856 and other artists were hired.

Overglaze and bisque porcelains were made at first. A line with underglaze blue decoration was introduced at the World Exposition in Paris in 1889. Christmas plates introduced in 1895 became the first collector plates and have been produced ever since. Stoneware was first made in 1914.

Bing and Gröndahl became part of Royal Copenhagen in 1987 and collector plates, ornaments, and figurines are still being made.

Mark	Date
B&G	1853+
Danish China Works COPENHAGEN B. & G.	1895+
DANISH CHINA WORKS B & G	1898+
DANISH CHINA WORKS B & G	1899+
B&G KJØBENHAVN MADE IN DENMARK B & G	1902+
B&G KJØBENHAVN COPENHAGEN B & G	1914+
B&G KJØBENHAVN DANMARK B & G	1915+
B&G KJØBENHAVN DANMARK B & G	1948+
B&G KJØBENHAVN MADE IN DENMARK	1952-1958
B&G KJØBENHAVN MADE IN DENMARK	1958+
B&G KJØBENHAVN DENMARK	1962+
COPENHAGEN PORCELAIN B&G MADE IN DENMARK	1970+
COPENHAGEN PORCELAIN B&G BING & GRØNDAHL (with crown)	current

BLUE MOUNTAIN POTTERY, Collingwood, Ontario (1953 - 2004)

Early pieces had stickers and hangtags.

Three trees mark.
1967 - 1972

Vase and waves mark.
1976 - 1986

BMP mark.
1972 - 1976

BOHEMIAN PORCELAIN

Large quantities of Bohemian porcelain was exported to North America during the late 19th and early 20th centuries.

Production in Bohemia, part of the Austro-Hungarian Empire, was limited to state-owned factories until early in 1800 when several potteries commenced production in the Karlsbad area.

CARL KNOLL, Fischern, Bohemia (Rybare, Czech Republic) (1848 - 1945)

Green underglaze mark used ca. 1916-1918. Founded by Carl Josef Knoll and operated by various owners until 1945.

COUNT THUN'S PORCELAIN FACTORY, Klosterle, Bohemia (Klasterec, Czech Republic) (1819 - ca. 1945)

Green underglaze mark used 1895 - ca. 1945. In 1794 Johann Weber and Johann Sontag began operating a pottery on property owned by Count Josef Matthias von Thun. In 1819 the name became Count Thun's Porcelain Factory. The pottery became part of Duchcovsky Porcelain in Dux in 1947 and is now operating as Thun Karlovarsky Porcelain.

DUX PORCELAIN MANUFACTORY, Dux, Bohemia (Duchov, Czech Republic) (1860 - present)

Mark used ca. 1918 - 1945. In 1992 it became known as Porcelain Manufactory Royal Dux Bohemia. it is now part of the Czech Porcelain Group.

189

FISCHER & MEIG, Pirkenhammer, Bohemia (Brezova, Czech Republic) (1858 - 1918)

Green underglaze mark used 1875 - 1887. In 1853 J.M. Fischer and his son-in-law, Ludwig von Meig, took over the operation. In 1918 it became one of the original members of Opiag (Austrian Porcelain Industry AG).

HAAS & CZJZEK, Schlaggenwald, Bohemia (Horni Slavkov, Czech Republic) (1792 - present)

Green underglaze mark used 1918 - 1939. The first porcelain factory in Bohemia operated under various names and owners from 1792 until 1867, when Georg Hass and Johann Czjzek took over the operation. The company is still in business.

MORITZ ZDEKAUER, Altrohlau, Bohemia (Stara Role, Czech Republic) (1884 - 1909)

Potteries have operated at this site from about 1811 to the present. Moritz Zdekauer bought the pottery in 1884. It was purchased by C.M. Hutschenreuther in 1909 and the name was changed to Altrohlau Porcelain Factories. Since 1992 the pottery has been operating as Starorolsky Porcelain Moritz Zdekauer.

For more information see Bohemian Decorated Porcelain by James D. Henderson, published in 1999 by Schiffer.

End of Bohemian Porcelain

T. & R. BOOTE LTD. (1842 - 1964)

Waterloo pottery (and other addresses) at Burslem, Staffordshire, England. Manufacturers of earthenware, parian, tiles, etc. In 1906 the Waterloo pottery was closed, the firm continued making tiles.

T & R B
1850+

T & R BOOTE
Late 1800s

T B & S

1890 - 1906

1890 - 1906

1890 - 1906

BOOTHS (LIMITED) (1891 - 1948)

Church Bank Pottery (and Swan and Soho Potteries from 1912), Tunstall, Staffordshire Potteries.

Subsequently Booths & Colcloughs Ltd., now part of the Royal Doulton Group.

Printed mark, 1891 - 1906

Printed mark 1912 - with or without England.

1930+ marks or BOOTHS LIMITED ENGLAND with variations to 1948.

BROWN-WESTHEAD, MOORE & CO. (1862 - 1904)

Cauldon Place, Hanley. Staffordshire Potteries. Later became Cauldon Ltd., (also refer to Majolica).

B. W. M.
B. W. M. & CO.

Printed or impressed marks 1862 - 1904. Pattern name is often added.

T. C. BROWN-WESTHEAD MOORE & CO.

BROWN-WESTHEAD MOORE

Impressed marks, 1862+.

Printed or impressed mark, 1884+.

Printed or impressed mark, 1891+.

Printed mark, 1862+.

CAULDON WARE
BROWN-WESTHEAD, MOORE & CO.

POTTERS TO HER MAJESTY

Printed mark, 1890+. Slight variations of wording occur.

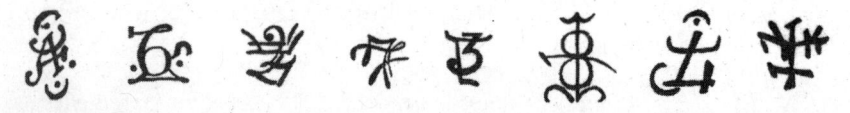

CAUGHLEY-COALPORT MARKS

Caughley-Salopian Works founded by Thomas Turner, 1775. J. Rose & Co. took over and moved the works to Coalport (Colebrook Dale). Later became Coalport Porcelain Works, now part of the Wedgwood group.

TURNER
1770s

1772 - 1785

SALOPIAN
1772 - 1800

1780

1775 - 1790

1775 - 1790

1775 - 1790

Coalbrookdale by Coalport
1805-1815

Coalport   CDale
1810 - 1925

CD
1820

1820 - 1830

JOHN ROSE & CO. ENGLISH PORCELAIN COALPORT
1830 - 1850

JOHN ROSE & CO. COALBROOKDALE SHROPSHIRE
1830 - 1850

1845 - 1855

1850 - 1870
J. R. & CO.

1851 - 1861

1861 - 1875

1870 - 1880

1875 - 1881
COALPORT AD 1750

1881 - 1939
"England" added from 1891

1945 - 1960

1960+

COALBROOKDALE
BY COALPORT
MADE IN ENGLAND

1960+

CAULDON LTD., Cauldon Place, Shelton, Hanley
Staffordshire Potteries (1905 - 1920)

(Previously Brown-Westhead, Moore & Co.) See Cauldon Potteries below and Brown-Westhead, Moore & Co.

Some former Ridgway and Brown-Westhead, Moore & Co. marks used with addition of "Cauldon" or "Cauldon Ltd." and "England", 1905-20.

193

CAULDON POTTERIES LTD., Stoke, Staffordshire (1920 - 1962)

CAULDON ENGLAND Several printed marks of differing design. Name of pattern often added. 1905-20.

Printed mark, 1930-50. Slight variations occur.

Standard printed mark, 1950-62.

CHELSEA PORCELAIN WORKS, London (1745 - 1769)

1745-50
Incised triangle mark, word Chelsea sometimes added.

1748-50
Rare early mark painted in underglaze blue.

1749-52
Raised anchor mark, on small oval raised pad.

1752 - 1758
Red anchor period.

1755   1765   1755   1760

1758 - 1769
Gold anchor period.

1760   1760   1760   1765

NEW CHELSEA PORCELAIN Co. (LTD.), Bagnall St. Longton Staffordshire Potteries (1912 - 1951)

Ca. 1913+   Ca. 1919+   Ca. 1936+   Ca. 1936+   Ca. 1943+

NEW CHELSEA CHINA Co. LTD., Chelsea on St. Longton
Staffordshire Potteries (1951 - 1961)

Printed mark, 1951-61.

CLARICE CLIFF
Worked at Arthur Wilkinson (Ltd.), Royal Staffordshire Pottery, Burslem. Became art director in 1930.

Ca. 1930+   Ca. 1930+

For further marks see ARTHUR J. WILKINSON.

JOSEPH CLEMENTSON
Pheonix Works, Shelton, Hanley, Staffordshire, England, 1839 - 1964.
CLEMENTSON BROS. (LTD.)
Pheonix Works, and Bell Works, Hanley, Staffordshire, England, 1865 - 1916.

J.C.   J. CLEMENTSON
1839 - 1864   1839 - 1864

Variations occur, pattern name and/or Pheonix bird may be included.

CLEMENTSON BROS.
1867 - 1880
Variations occur.

1870+

1910+

1901 - 1913

1913 - 1916

195

JAMES & RALPH CLEWS, Cobridge Works, Cobridge, Staffordshire (1818 - 1834)

Impressed mark usually found on Blue & White printed wares.

The initials G.R. are occassionally found on either side of The Crown, which signifies an early Georgian date.

COALPORT PORCELAIN WORKS

(John Rose Co.) Coalport, Shropshire 1795 - .
(Moved to Stoke-on-Trent in 1926.)

also refer to CAUGHLEY-COALPORT.

COCHRAN/BRITANNIA

R. Cochran & Co., Verreville Pottery, Glasgow, Scotland, 1846 - 1918. Earthenware, china, stoneware.

Cochran & Fleming, Britannia Pottery, St. Rollox, Glasgow, Scotland, 1896 -1920.

Britannia Pottery Co., Ltd., St. Rollox, Glasgow, Scotland, 1920 - 1935.

R C & Co.
1846+

GLASGOW
1846+ - 1918

C & F
1896+

C & F
G
1896+

1896 - 1920

ROYAL IRONSTONE CHINA
COCHRAN & FLEMING GLASGOW. BRITAIN
1900 - 1920

FLEMING PORCELAIN OPAQUE GLASGOW, BRITAIN
1900 - 1920

1920 - 1935
Variations occur.

HIAWATHA
Trade-name
1925+

COLCLOUGH CHINA LTD.

Longton, Staffordshire Potteries (1937 - 1948). Formerly H.J. Colclough. Subsequently Booths & Colcloughs Ltd.

COLCLOUGH
LONGTON,
ENGLAND,
BONE CHINA

Printed mark, 1935 - 1937.

Printed mark, 1939+.

Printed marks, 1945 - 1948.

CROWN DEVON

Established by S. Fielding and Co. Ltd., Stoke-on-Trent, England in 1870 - present. Early marks were an impressed "FIELDING" and "SF & Co" printed with the title of the pattern.

Standard printed marks, ca. 1891 - 1913.

Printed mark, ca. 1913.+

Printed marks, ca. 1917 - 1930.

Printed trade-mark, ca. 1930 - . Slight variations occur.

FIELDING
12 A 52

Impressed mark, showing the date of manufacture, April 12, 1952.

197

CROWN DUCAL

A.G. Richard & Co. Ltd., Gordon Pottery, Tunstall, Staffordshire Potteries, 1915 - , then Britannia Pottery, Cobridge 1934 - .

Printed trade-mark ca. 1916+, with or without A.G.R. & Co. Ltd. under.

1925+.

1930+.

1934+.

Pottery and earthenware. Used up through the 1970s.

CROWN STAFFORDSHIRE PORCELAIN CO. LTD.

Minerva Works, Fenton. Staffordshire Potteries 1889 - . Name changed in 1948 to Crown Staffordshire China Co. Ltd.

Printed mark, 1889 - 1912.

Printed marks, 1906+. "England" or "AD 1801" occassionally added. Used on copies of antique porcelains.

Printed mark, 1930+. The name "CROWN STAFFORDSHIRE" is incorporated.

Standard printed trade-marks from the 1930s onwards. A number of slight changes have been made over the years.

DARTMOUTH POTTERY LTD.
Dartmouth, Devon, 1947 - . Earthenwares.

Impressed,
ca. 1948 - 1953.

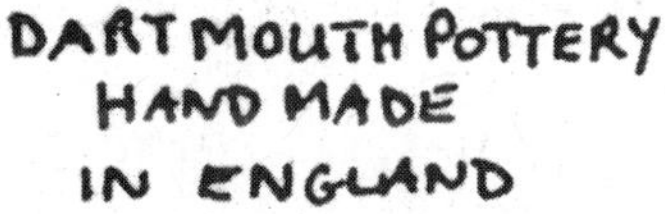

Impressed, ca. 1948 - 1960.

Rubber stamp, 1950s.

Rubber stamp,
ca. 1958 - 1964.

Rubber stamp,
ca. 1965 - 1970s.

Paper label.
1985 - 1987.

DAVENPORT
Factory established at Longport, Staffordshire, England in 1793, closed in 1887. Earthenware main product: porcelain manufactured from about 1820. Much Davenport ware is blue and white printed ware. Tea and dessert services in "Japan" and "India" patterns were popular lines. Landscape plaques were painted by James Rouse.

DAVENPORT
1793 - 1805

Davenport
1793 - 1810

With or without anchor

1795+

1795+

1800 - 1860

1805 - 1820

1805 - 1820

1805 - 1820

continued on next page.

199

DAVENPORT LONGPORT

1815+. With or without anchor, date marks found on earthenware from mid 1800s.

1820s

1820 - 1860. Other variations occur with the factory name and often pattern name.

1830 - 1880

W. DAVENPORT & CO.

1830 - 1882

1840 - 1867

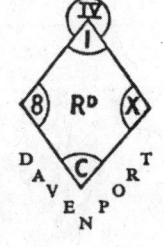

1842 - 1883. With British Registry Mark.

DAVENPORT PATENT

1850 - 1870

1860 - 1870

1860 - 1887

1870 - 1886

DAVENPORTS LTD.

1881 - 1887

DAVENPORTS LIMITED

1881 - 1887

DELFT

Various potteries have operated in and near the town of Delft in Holland since the mid 1700s. This tin glazed Dutch pottery marked with the name "DELFT" dates from the late 1800s to the present.

Since 1879 Delft pottery has been marked with a year code impressed in the base of each piece near the factory back stamp.

Delft Year Code 1879 -

1879 . . . . . . .A	1880 . . . . . . .B	1881 C	1882 . . . . . . .D	1883 . . . . . . .E
1884 . . . . . . .F	1885 . . . . . .G	1886 . . . . . .H	1887 I	1888 . . . . . . .J
1889 . . . . . .K	1890 L	1891 . . . . . .M	1892 . . . . . .N	1893 . . . . . .O
1894 . . . . . .P	1895 . . . . . .Q	1896 . . . . . .R	1897 . . . . . .S	1898 . . . . . .T
1899 . . . . . .U	1900 V	1901 . . . . . .W	1902 X	1903 . . . . . .Y
1904 . . . . . . .Z	1905 . . . . .AA	1906 . . . . .AB	1907 . . . . .AC	1908 . . . . .AD
1909 . . . . .AE	1910 . . . . .AF	1911 . . . . .AG	1912 . . . . .AH	1913 . . . . . .AI
1914 . . . . .AJ	1915 . . . . .AK	1916 . . . . .AL	1917 . . . . .AM	1918 . . . . .AN
1919 . . . . .AO	1920 . . . . .AP	1921 . . . . .AQ	1922 . . . . .AR	1923 . . . . .AS
1924 . . . . .AT	1925 . . . . .AU	1926 . . . . .AV	1927 . . . . .AW	1928 . . . . .AX
1929 . . . . .AY	1930 . . . . .AZ	1931 . . . . .BA	1932 . . . . .BB	1933 . . . . .BC
1934 . . . . .BD	1935 . . . . .BE	1936 . . . . .BF	1937 . . . . .BG	1938 . . . . .BH
1939 . . . . . .BI	1940 . . . . .BJ	1941 . . . . .BK	1942 . . . . .BL	1943 . . . . .BM
1944 . . . . .BN	1945 . . . . .BO	1946 . .BP/BQ	1947 . . . . .BR	1948 . . . . .BS
1949 . . . . .BT	1950 . . . . .BU	1951 . . . . .BV	1952 . . . . .BW	1953 . . . . .BX
1954 . . . . .BY	1955 . . . . .BZ	1956 . . . . .CA	1957 . . . . .CB	1958 CC
1959 . . . . .CD	1960 . . . . .CE	1961 . . . . .CF	1962 . . . . .CG	1963 . . . . .CH
1964 CI	1965 . . . . .CJ	1966 . . . . .CK	1967 CL	1968 . . . . .CM
1969 . . . . .CN	1970 . . . . .CO	1971 . .CP/CQ	1972 . . . . .CR	1973 . . . . .CS
1974 . . . . .CT	1975 . . . . .CU	1976 CV	1977 . . . . .CW	1978 CX
1979 . . . . .CY	1980 . . . . .CZ	1981 . . . . .DA	1982 . . . . .DB	1983 . . . . .DC

and so on -

DENBY

Joseph Bourne & Sons Ltd., Bourne's Pottery. Denby, Derbyshire, 1809 - .
Produced a variety of stonewares for ornamental and domestic requirements.

Impressed or printed mark, in circle from ca. 1895, in square form from ca. 1910.

Impressed or printed marks, ca. 1930+.

Impressed or printed basic mark, ca. 1948 - . Other marks occur with the name of the pattern and the trade-name "DENBY".

Oven-t-table ware "Greenwheat" 1956 - 1977. N.B. First time a designer's name was allowed to appear on Denby wares.

DERBY

Porcelain was made at Cockpit Hill, Derby, England from around 1750 under various owners and managers. The old works were closed in 1848, but some artists and workers joined forces and continued the tradition of Derby porcelain in a small works which they opened on King Street.

1st Crown Derby period.

Chelsea-Derby

1770 - 1780

1782 - 1825

1785 - 1825

1820 - 1840

1825 - 1840

1825 - 1848

1830 - 1840

1830 - 1840

1830+

1830 - 1848

1835

1849 - 1859

1849 - 1863

1859 - 1861

Stevenson & Hancock
King Street Factory mark.
1861 - 1935

DERBY CROWN PORCELAIN COMPANY LTD.   1875

ROYAL CROWN DERBY PORCELAIN CO. LTD.   1890

Continued on next page.

203

1878 - 1900. Dates used in the form of numerals with this impressed mark – e.g. 4.98 indicates April 1898. The word "DERBY" can also occur alone.

1878 - 1890. With year cypher below the printed mark.

1890+. With year cypher below the mark. the word "ENGLAND" used with this mark until 1921. "MADE IN ENGLAND" used with this mark from 1921. The words "BONE CHINA" occured after World War II.

Ca. 1990 mark. This trade name is now owned by Royal Doulton.

Derby Year Cyphers (believed to be correct to within one year)
The 'V' Mark of 1904 is accompanied by the word "ENGLAND"; that of 1942 the words "MADE IN ENGLAND". Similarly in respect of the 'X' Marks of 1901 and 1947.

1880	1881	1882	1883	1884	1885	1886	1887	1888	1889	1890	1891
1892	1893	1894	1895	1896	1897	1898	1899	1900	1901	1902	1903
1904	1905	1906	1907	1908	1909	1910	1911	1912	1913	1914	1915
1916	1917	1918	1919	1920	1921	1922	1923	1924	1925	1926	1927
1928	1929	1930	1931	1932	1933	1934	1935	1936	1937	1938	1939
										I	II
1940	1941	1942	1943	1944	1945	1946	1947	1948	1949	1950	1951
III	IV	V	VI	VII	VIII	IX	X	XI	XII	XIII	XIV
1952	1953	1954	1955	1956	1957	1958	1959	1960	1961	1962	1963
XV	XVI	XVII	XVIII	XIX	XX	XXI	XXII	XXIII	XXIV	XXV	XXVI
1964	1965	1966	1967	1968	1969	1970	1971	1972	1973	1974	1975
XXVII	XXVIII	XXIX	XXX	XXXI	XXXII	XXXIII	XXXIV	XXXV	XXXVI	XXXVII	XXXVIII

DRESDEN

The "Dresden" mark is found on many pieces of porcelain in the Meissen style manufactured since the 1800s. For centuries potteries and porcelain decorators have been established in and near Dresden, Germany. A selection of the many known marks are illustrated.

Decorator marks: Dresden, Germany

Hamman, ca. 1866

Richard Klemm, 1869 - 1916

Donath, 1872+

Used by several decorators, 1883 - 1893

Lamm, 1887+

Wolfsohn, late 1800s. Wolfsohn copied the Augustus Rex mark (left) until an injunction ordered her to cease in 1883.

Meyers & Sons, late 1800s

Hirsch, 20th century

MANUFACTURERS – "DRESDEN"

A selection of marks (see also, Meissen).

1903+
Carl Thieme Saxonian Porcelain Factory, Postchappel, Saxony, Germany.

1905+

1951 – present
Sandizell Porcelain Factory, Sandizell, Bavaria, Germany.

1956+
Dresden Earthenware Work, Dresden, Saxony, Germany.

Ironstone and hotel ware marked "Dresden" was made at East Liverpool, Ohio, USA by The Potter's Co-operative Co. (1882 – 1925).

Ca. 1892

Ca. 1896

Ca. 1905

FORD

T. & C. Ford, Hanley, Staffordshire, England, 1854 – 1871.
Thomas Ford, Hanley, Staffordshire, England, 1871 – 1874.
Charles Ford, Hanley, Staffordshire, England, 1874 – 1904.

1854 – 1871

1871 – 1874

1874 – 1904

1900 – 1904

1900 – 1904

FOREIGN BACKSTAMPS

English translations of words, phrases, and initials frequemtly encountered in backstamps of foreign made china, dolls, buttons, etc.

French
Cie (compagnie) . . . . .company
Fils . . . . .son
Frere, F., Fr., (plural with "s" . . . . .brother
Brevete, Bte. . . . . .patent
Depose, Depe. . . . . .registered
S. D. G. D. (sans garantie
 du gouvernement . . .without government guarantee

German
Komp. (kompanie) . . . . .company
G. M. B. H. (gesellschaft mit
 besh-rankter haftung) . . . . .limited
A. G. (aktiengesellschaft) . . . . .joint stock company
Sohn . . . . .son
Bruder . . . . .brother
Gebr. (gebruder) . . . . .brothers
D. R. P. (Deutsches Reichspatent) . . . . .German patent
Eingetragene . . . . .registered

Spanish
Cia. (companie) . . . . .company
S. A. (sociedad anonima) . . . . .limited
Hijo . . . . .son
Hno., Hnos. (hermano) . . . . .brother(s)
Priv. (patent privilegio) . . . . .patent

Italian
Ca. (compagnia) . . . . .company
Soc. (societa) . . . . .company
S. A. (societa anonima) .limited
Figlio . . . . .son
Frat. (fratelli) . . . . .brother
Patente . . . . .patent

Dutch
Mpy, My. (maatschappij) . . . . .company
N. V. (naamloze vennotschap) . . . . .limited
Zoon . . . . .son
Gebr. (gebroeder) . . . . .brother

FURNIVALS

Jacob & Thomas Furnival, Miles Bank, Shelton, Hanley, Staffordshire, England, 1843. Earthenware.

Thomas Furnival & Co., Miles Bank, Shelton, Hanley, Staffordshire, England, 1844 - 1846. Earthenware.

Jacob Furnival & Co., Cobridge, Staffordshire, England, 1845 - 1870.

Thomas Furnival & Sons, Elder Road, Cobridge, Staffordshire, England, 1871 - 1890. Earthenware.

Furnivals (Ltd.), Elder Road, Cobridge, Staffordshire, England, 1890 - 1964+. Earthenware.

Ca. 1843

T.F. & CO.
1844 - 1846

J. F. & CO.
1845 - 1870

1871 - 1890

1871 - 1890

1871 - 1890

1871 - 1890

1878+

1881 - 1890

FURNIVALS ENGLAND
1890 - 1895

1890 - 1910

FURNIVALS LTD. COBRIDGE ENGLAND
1895 - 1913

1905 - 1913

1913+

GOEBEL

W. Goebel Porcelain Factory, Rodental, Bavaria. Established 1876, made porcelain and earthenware etc. In 1934 introduced figurines based on the drawings of Sister Hummel.

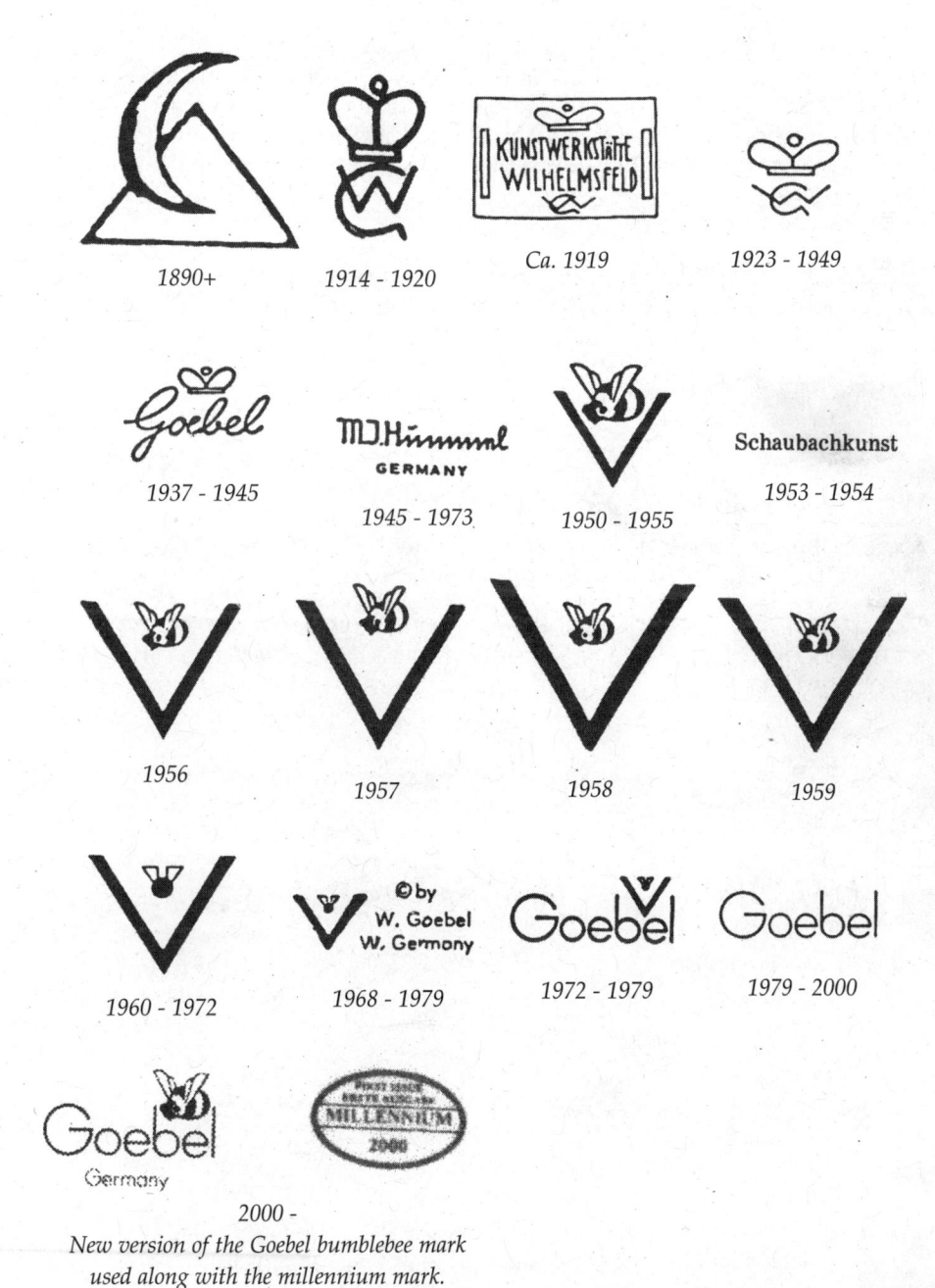

1890+

1914 - 1920

Ca. 1919

1923 - 1949

1937 - 1945

1945 - 1973

1950 - 1955

Schaubachkunst
1953 - 1954

1956

1957

1958

1959

1960 - 1972

1968 - 1979

1972 - 1979

1979 - 2000

2000 -
New version of the Goebel bumblebee mark used along with the millennium mark.

Authenticating Hummel

There are two definitive marks of identification when determining if your Hummel is authentic.

The first is the signature of Sister M.I. Hummel, which is usually incised on the base of the piece. Figurines without bases or an inadequate surface to display the signature are the exception to this rule.

The second source of identification is the Goebel backstamp which is on the underside of every figurine. Since the trade mark has varied since 1935, these can also be used to determine the time frame the piece was made. Most of the known marks used over the years are illustrated on the company's website.

The 70th Anniversary Collection

Each figurine features an anniversary backstamp and porcelain tag, and will have some variations which differentiate it from the first issue.

WILLIAM HENRY GOSS (LTD.)

Falcon Pottery, Stoke-on-Trent, Staffordshire 1858 - 1940. (Retitled Goss China Co. Ltd. from 1934 when taken over by Cauldon Potteries Ltd.)

Manufacturers of parian, earthenwares and porcelain. Known from 1883 for making Heraldic souvenir wares based on antiquities and other tourist attractions.

W H G
W H GOSS

W.H. GOSS
COPYRIGHT

*Ca. 1858 -
Impressed or printed marks.*

GOSS & PEAKE

*Ca. 1868
Recorded by Willis-Fear, M.J.W. The history of the pottery firm of W.H. Goss. 1965. p.36.*

Copyright as Act directs
W. H. GOSS
Stoke-on-Trent.
November 30. 1881.

*Ca. 1866 - ca. 1885
Impressed or printed mark used on portrait busts, figures, etc. The date varies.*

*Ca. 1862 - ca. 1929
Printed mark. The date of the introduction of this mark is based on Patent Office Register for 26/4/1909 which states that this mark had been used "continuously since 13 years before August 13, 1875."*

*Ca. 1929 - 1940
Printed mark.*

GOUDA ART POTTERY

Made at several pottery workshops in the area around Gouda, Holland. Gouda pottery was decorated in the Art Nouveau style from the 1880s to the early 1980s. Pieces are marked with factory names, such as Regina, Zenith, Zuid-Holland, Plazuid Koninklyk, Schoonhoveu, and Arnhemsche etc. Frequently the pattern name and artist's initials are included in the mark. A section of marks are found below.

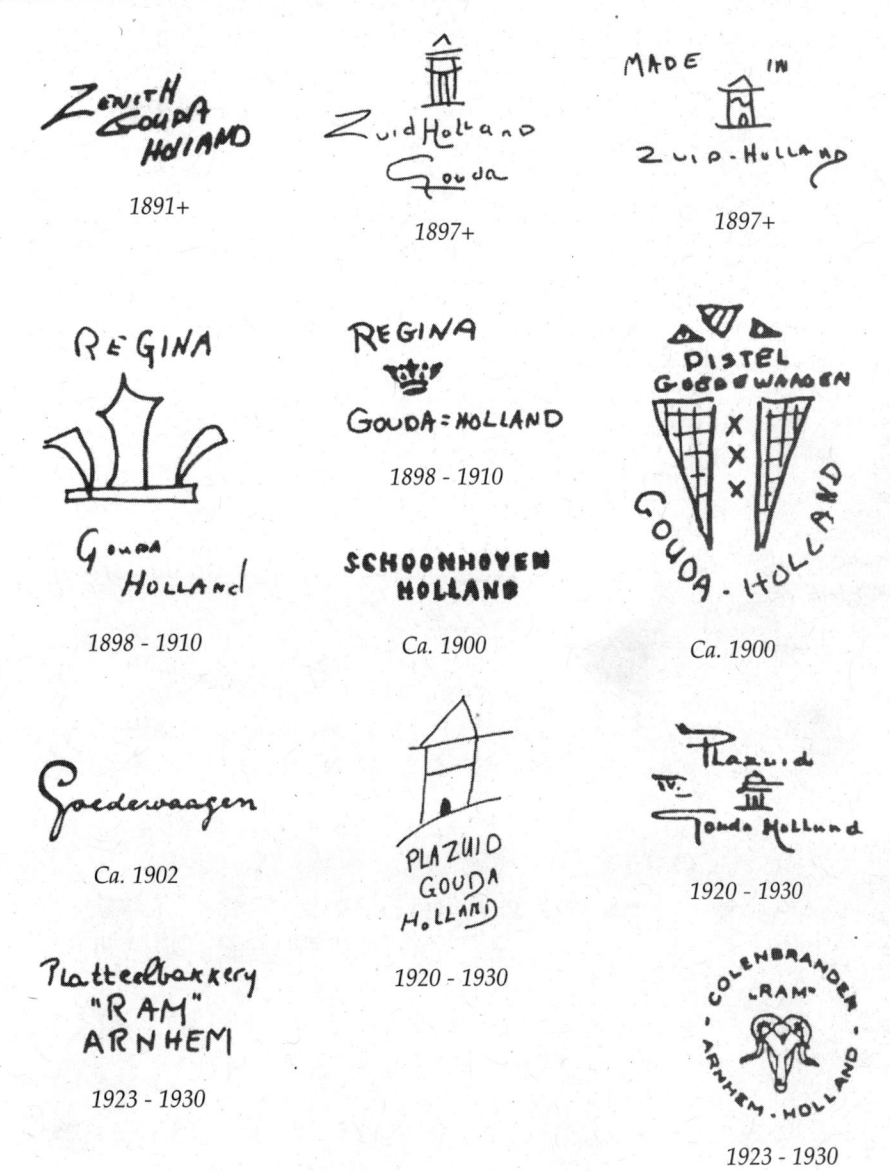

1891+

1897+

1897+

1898 - 1910

1898 - 1910

Ca. 1900

Ca. 1900

Ca. 1902

1920 - 1930

1920 - 1930

1923 - 1930

1923 - 1930

GEORGE GRAINGER & CO. (formerly Grainger Lee & Co.)

George Grainger (& Co.), Worcester, England, 1839 - 1902. Porcelains, parian, semi-porcelain.

GEO GRAINGER CHINA WORKS WORCESTER

1839 - 1860. "& Co." added from ca. 1850.

George Grainger Royal China Works Worcester.

G G & CO
S P

1848+ "Semi-Porcelain" in full on some pieces.

S P
G G W

GRAINGER WORCESTER S P

1848 - 1855 "Semi-Porcelain" in full on some pieces.

G W

1850 - 1860. Pattern name or number may be included.

1850 - 1875

CHEMICAL PORCELAIN GRAINGER & CO MANUFACTURERS WORCESTER

1850 - 1870

G & CO W

1850 - 1889

1860 - 1880

1870 - 1889

In 1889 George Grainger & Co. was taken over by the Worcester Royal Porcelain Co.

1889 - 1902

"England" and year letter added from 1891.

1891 - A	1895 - E	1899 - I
1892 - B	1896 - F	1900 - J
1893 - C	1897 - G	1901 - K
1894 - D	1898 - H	1902 - L

A.E. GRAY & CO. LTD.

Glebe Works, Hanley, ca. 1912-33; Whieldon Road, 1943-61, Stoke. Staffordshire Potteries. 1912-61. Earthenware, (Renamed Portmeirion Potteries Ltd. in 1962).

Printed mark, 1912-30.

Printed marks, 1930-33. Note "Hanley" address.

Printed mark, 1934-61. "England" or "Made in England" were added to this mark.

T.C. GREEN & CO. (LTD.)

Church Gresley, Burton-on-Trent, Derbyshire. 1864 - . Earthenwares & stonewares. Early wares unmarked.

Printed marks, ca. 1892+ with "England".

20th century printed marks.

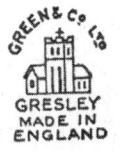

Typical printed marks of the 1930s.

Post-war printed marks; similar marks used for different patterns or styles.

New basic mark introduced in 1962.

213

GRIMWADES *(also see Royal Winton)*
GRIMWADE BROS.
Winton Potteries, Hanley & Stoke, Staffordshire, England, 1886 - 1900. China, earthenware, majolica.

GRIMWADES LTD.
Winton, Upper Hanley & Elgin Potteries, Stoke, Staffordshire, 1900- present. Earthenware, majolica, etc.

1886 - 1890

1900+

1906+

1906+

1906+

1911+

1930+

1930+

1930+

1930+

1930+

1934 - 1939

1934 - 1950

1934 - 1950

1951+

W.H. GRINDLEY & Co. (LTD.)

New Field Pottery (ca. 1880-91), Woodland Pottery (1891-), Tunstall. Staffordshire Potteries. 1880- . Earthenwares, ironstones, etc. Taken over by Alfred Clough Ltd. in 1960.

Printed mark, ca. 1880 - 1914. Early, pre-1891 versions have "Tunstall" in place of "England" as the last word.

Printed marks, ca. 1914 - 25.

Printed marks used from from 1925.

Printed mark, ca. 1936-54. Slight variations occur, with the name of patterns, etc.

Printed mark, ca. 1954- .

HAMMERSLEY & Co.

Alsager Pottery, Longton, Staffordshire Potteries 1887 - 1932. China. Continued as Hammersley & Co. (Longton) Ltd. from 1932 onwards.

H. & C.
H. & CO.

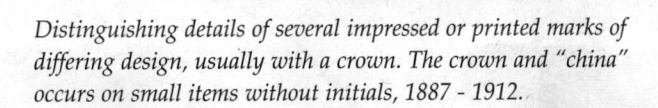

Distinguishing details of several impressed or printed marks of differing design, usually with a crown. The crown and "china" occurs on small items without initials, 1887 - 1912.

Printed marks, 1912-39.

Printed marks, 1939- .

215

HERCULANEUM POTTERY

Liverpool, Lancashire. 1793 - 1841. Earthenwares and porcelains.

Impressed or printed marks, ca. 1796-1833.

HERCULANEUM POTTERY

Impressed mark, 1822- .

Impressed or printed Liver bird marks, 1833-1836.

HEWITT & LEADBEATER

Willow Pottery, Longton. Staffordshire Potteries. 1907-19. China and parian, also made miniature cottages and heraldic ware similar to W.H. Goss but of inferior quality.

Printed mark, 1907-26.*

* This mark was continued by the successors – Hewitt Brothers – to ca. 1926.

HOLLINGSHEAD & KIRKHAM (LTD.)

Unicorn Pottery, (Burslem 1870-1876), Tunstall (1876-1956). Staffordshire, England. Earthenware. Factory purchased by Johnson Bros., 1956.

H. & K.
1870 - 1900

H. & K. TUNSTALL
1870 - 1900

H. & K. LATE WEDGWOOD
1890+

1900 - 1924

1924 - 1956

1933 - 1942

1954 - 1956

HULL POTTERY

Ohio, USA. In 1905 A.E. Hull bought the Acme Pottery Company in Crooksville, Ohio and changed its name to A.E. Hull Pottery Company and commenced making stoneware items.

However, by the time the company closed 80 years later in 1985, it had diversified into a variety of artware, lamp bases and kitchenware. During the 1960s the company accepted a commission from the J.C. Penny Department stores to supply casual use dishes made in a "rainbow" of colours.

Hull's first incised trade mark, most often found on kitchenware, ca. 1915.

Bold "H in circle" mark, used beginning in the 1920s.

Variation of "H in circle," used into the 1930s on kitchenware and artware.

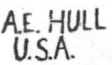

Entire firm name appeared as incised mark by the 1930s. "U.S.A." used on most Hull items by that time, sometimes without "Hull" name.

Foil labels used on artware, kitchenware, and novelties in the late 1930s and '40s. Usually either black or maroon with silver or gold lettering.

"Potter at wheel" label used after about 1950.

Script mark used through the 1950s.

Black foil label with gold lettering used after 1958 on novelty and florist ware.

IMPORTERS' MARKS

Chas. Ahrenfeldt & Co. of New York was one of the importing firms to establish its own foreign factories.

Collectors today often confuse importers' marks with manufacturers' and find difficulty in identifying them.

Bawo & Dotter

Chas. Ahrenfeldt & Co.

The Strobel Wilkins Co.

P.H. Leonard

Lazarus, Rosenfeld & Lehman
(Victoria and Empire Works)

C.L. Dwenger

JACKSON & GOSLING (LTD.)

Grosvenor Works, Longton. Staffordshire Potteries. Various changes in ownership since 1866. *China.*

J. & G.
J. & G.
L.

Distinguishing details of several impressed or printed marks of differing design: name of the individual pattern is often included, ca. 1880 onwards. Early wares were not usually marked.

Ca. 1912+

Ca. 1912+

Ca. 1914+

Ca. 1919+

Ca. 1919+

Ca. 1924+

Ca. 1930+

Ca. 1934+

Note addition of "Ltd."

Ca. 1930s+

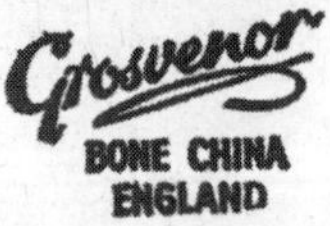

Ca. 1950s+. This mark is also used by Grosvenor China Ltd.

JOHNSON BROS (HANLEY) LTD.
Hanley and Tunstall, Staffordshire 1883 - . Earthenware, ironstone.

1883 - 1913

1900+

1913+

1913+

1955+

A.B. JONES & SONS LTD.
Grafton Works, Longton, Staffordshire, England, 1900 - . China and Earthenwares.

A. B. J. & SONS

A. B J. & S.
1900+

A. B. JONES & SONS

1900 - 1913

1913+

1920+

1930+

1935+

1949+

1950+

1957+

1961+

219

KEELING & Co. (LTD.)

Dale Hall Works (from 1887), Burslem. Staffordshire Potteries. 1886 - 1936. Earthenwares.

K. & CO.
K. & CO. B.
& K. CO.
    Details of several printed marks of differing design; name of the individual pattern is often included, 1886 - 1936.

[mark: figure with 1790 / K & Cº B / LATE MAYERS]
    Trade-mark, printed, 1886 - 1936. "England" may be added after 1891. "Ltd" may be added after 1909.

LOSOL   *Trade-name, ca. 1912 onwards.*

[mark: Losol Ware / KEELING & Cº Lᵀᴰ / crown / BURSLEM ENGLAND]
    Printed mark, ca. 1912 - 1936.

LIMOGES – HAVILAND COMPANIES

Haviland china has been manufactured continuously since the 1840s at Limoges, France. The Haviland family from New York City revolutionized the porcelain industry in France by introducing mass production techniques. Decorated in the English style for the American market this attractive china has wide appeal and is noted for its translucency, hardness and delicate patterns.

Following is a selection from the large number of 19th and 20th century marks.

HAVILAND BROTHERS & COMPANY; HAVILAND & COMPANY

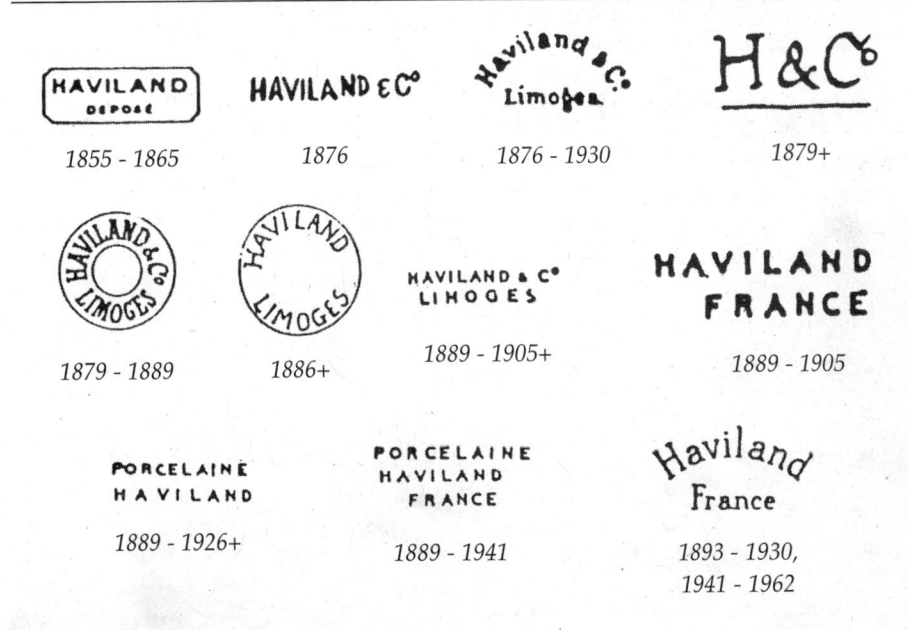

HAVILAND DEPOSE	HAVILAND E Cº	Haviland & C. Limoges	H & Cº
1855 – 1865	1876	1876 – 1930	1879+

Haviland & Co Limoges	Haviland Limoges	HAVILAND & Cº LIMOGES	HAVILAND FRANCE
1879 – 1889	1886+	1889 – 1905+	1889 – 1905

PORCELAINE HAVILAND	PORCELAINE HAVILAND FRANCE	Haviland France
1889 – 1926+	1889 – 1941	1893 – 1930, 1941 – 1962

THEODORE HAVILAND COMPANY

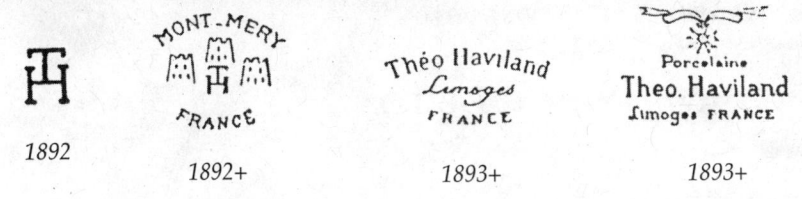

TH	MONT-MERY FRANCE	Théo Haviland Limoges FRANCE	Porcelaine Theo. Haviland Limoges FRANCE
1892	1892+	1893+	1893+

continued on next page...

221

Porcelaine Mousseline
T✳H
Limoges FRANCE
1894+

THEO. HAVILAND
PORCELAINE
FRANCE
1895+

LIMOGES
THEODORE
HAVILAND
FRANCE
1920+

THEODORE HAVILAND
FRANCE
1920 - 1936

La Porcelaine
Theodore Haviland
Limoges
1925+

Theodore Haviland
Limoges
FRANCE
1925+

Theodore Haviland
New York
MADE IN AMERICA
1937 - present

CHARLES FIELD HAVILAND

Æ
Pre 1868

C F H
1868 - 1882

CFM
GDM
1882 - 1891

CFH
GDM
FRANCE
1891 - 1897

GDA
FRANCE
1897 - present

CH. FIELD HAVILAND
LIMOGES
1942

JOHANN HAVILAND

Johann Haviland
Walderstof
1907 - present

HAVILAND
BAVARIA
1910 - 1924

Johann Haviland
BAVARIA
1912 - 1936

JOHANN HAVILAND
BAVARIA
GERMANY
1972

ROBERT HAVILAND & C. PARLON

ROBERT
HAVILAND
LIMOGES
1924

LIMOGES
★ R·H ★
FRANCE
1937 - 1948

222

ROBERT HAVILAND & LeTANNEUR

1929+

FRANK HAVILAND

1910 - 1924

JEAN HAVILAND

1957+   *1957+*

HAVILAND SA

HAVILAND & Cº
LIMOGES
1941+

HAVILAND
FRANCE
1941+

Haviland's
Chantilly
1948 - 1953

HAVILAND
CHINA
1958 - present

HAVILAND
ALUMINITE
TRÉGIER
1964+

Haviland
France
ESTABLISHED 1842
current

Haviland
France
Limoges
current

AMERICAN LIMOGES CHINA CO. INC., Sebring, Ohio

1900 - 1955

MALING
MALING'S OUSEBURN POTTERY
Newcastle, England (1817 - 1859). Earthenware.
C.T. MALING, A & B FORD POTTERIES
Newcastle-Upon-Tyne, England (1859 - 1890). Earthenware.
C.T. MALING & SONS (LTD.), A & B FORD POTTERIES
Newcastle-Upon-Tyne, England (1890 - 1963). Earthenware.

M	MALING	C.T. MALING	C.T.M.
1817 - 1830	1817 - 1890	1859+	1859 - 1890

1875 - 1908

1890+

1908+

1924+

1949 - 1963

MASON'S IRONSTONE

George Miles Mason and Charles James Mason made Patent Ironstone at Lane Delph, Staffordshire England, 1813 - 1829. The firm became Charles James Mason & Co., Patent Ironstone Manufactory 1829 - 1845. From 1845 - 1848 it was designated Charles James Mason – Fenton Works Delph Lane Staffordshire and Longton, 1851 - 1854. Continued by Francis Morley (& Co.) Hanley Staffordshire, ca. 1848 and subsequently by G.L. Ashworth & Bros. Ltd. Hanley, Staffordshire, ca. 1862.

G.M. & C.J. MASON   G. & C. J. M.

Before 1829

MASON'S PATENT IRONSTONE CHINA

1813 - 1825

PATENT IRONSTONE CHINA

1813 - 1825

1813 - 1825

1820+

1825+

FENTON STONE WORKS

1829 - 1845

C. J. M. & Co. GRANITE CHINA

1829 - 1845

1829 - 1845

1829 - 1845

1840+

1845+

MEAKIN POTTERIES

There are a great variety of Meakin marks since there were several firms with that name. A selection of marks follows:

Alfred Meakin (Ltd.) Royal Albert, Victoria and Highgate Potteries, Tunstall, Staffordshire, England. Commenced 1875. "Ltd." added 1897 - 1930. Firm name changed to Alfred Meakin (Tunstall) Ltd. 1913.

Charles Meakin Burslem 1870 - 1882 and Eastwood Potteries, Hanley, Staffordshire, 1883 - 1889.

Henry Meakin, Abbey Pottery, Cobridge, Staffordshire, 1873 - 1876.

J. & G. Meakin (Ltd.), Eagle Pottery and Eastwood Works, Hanley, Staffordshire, 1851 - . Sold the Eastwood Pottery 1958, modernized and enlarged the Eagle Works.

ALFRED MEAKIN (LTD.)

1875 - 1897

1891+

1891+

1897+

1907+

1914+

1914+

Ca. 1920

1930+

1937+

1937+

1937+

1947+. Slight variations occur

1947+. Slight variations occur

226

CHARLES MEAKIN

1870 - 1882

CHARLES MEAKIN HANLEY
1883 - 1889

HENRY MEAKIN

IRONSTONE CHINA H. MEAKIN
1873 - 1876

J. & G. MEAKIN (LTD.)

Ca. 1890

Ca. 1890

1890+

1907+

1912+
Many variations of Sol & Surface mark.

1912+

1939+

1946+

1946+

"ROMANTIC ENGLAND"

1947+
Included in the mark. Found on series of scenic patterns.

1953+

1955+

1958+

1962+

227

MEIGH MARKS

Job Meigh, Old Hall Pottery, Hanley, Staffordshire, England, 1805 - 1834. Became Job Meigh & Son 1812.

Charles Meigh took over 1835 - 1849, became Charles Meigh, Son & Pankhurst, 1850 - 1851 and Charles Meigh & Son 1851 - 1861.

The company name was changed to Old Hall Earthenware Co. in 1861 - 1886. The firm became the Old Hall Porcelain Works Ltd. in 1886 until 1902.

1805 - 1861
Used by J. Meigh and C. Meigh firms.

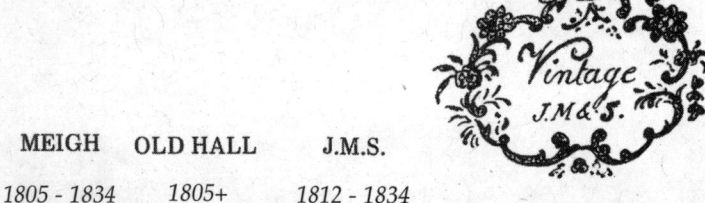

MEIGH
1805 - 1834

OLD HALL
1805+

J.M.S.
1812 - 1834

Vintage J.M.&S.
1815 - 1825

J.M. & S.
1815 - 1825

PLOVER CM
1835 - 1847.
Pattern name often included.

CHARLES MEIGH
1835 - 1849

C.M.
1835 - 1849

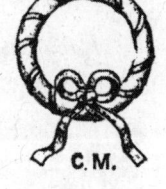

C.M.
1835 - 1849.
Pattern name often icluded.

C.M.S.P.&S.
1850 - 1851

Harebell CM&S
1851 - 1861

JAVA CM&S
1851 - 1861

Continued on next page

CHINA   M & S   C. MEIGH & SON   MEIGH'S   OPAQUE PORCELAIN

1851 - 1861

O.H.E.C.   O.H.E.C. (L)   [1861 - 1886]   IMPERIAL PARISIAN GRANITE (EAGLE CREST) OLD HALL E'WARE CO. (LIMD)

INDIAN STONE CHINA   OPAQUE PORCELAIN   1884+   ENGLAND
1861 - 1886   1891 - 1902

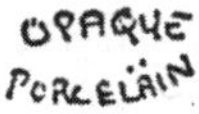

MEISSEN

The Royal Porcelain Manufactory was founded in 1710 at Meissen, near Dresden, Saxony, Germany. It was the first hard paste factory in Europe, and was known for its superior figures, brilliant painted decoration and moulded ornamentation.

Large quantities of porcelain was exported to North America during the 19th century.

The crossed swords mark introduced ca. 1723 has been copied by many manufacturers and many variations occur. For example - Derby, Minton, Bristol, Coalport, Worcester and Sampson, England; Somson Petit and Bloch, France, Dornheim, Koch & Fischer, Germany, to name just a few.

A selection of Meissen (Dresden) marks follows:

1710 - 1725. Augustus Rex mark. Copied often in the 19th century.

1723 - 1725

1720 - 1730

1725 - 1763

Continued on next page

1763 - 1774

1774 - 1815

1850 - 1860

1860 - 1924

1924 - 1934

Ca. 1934

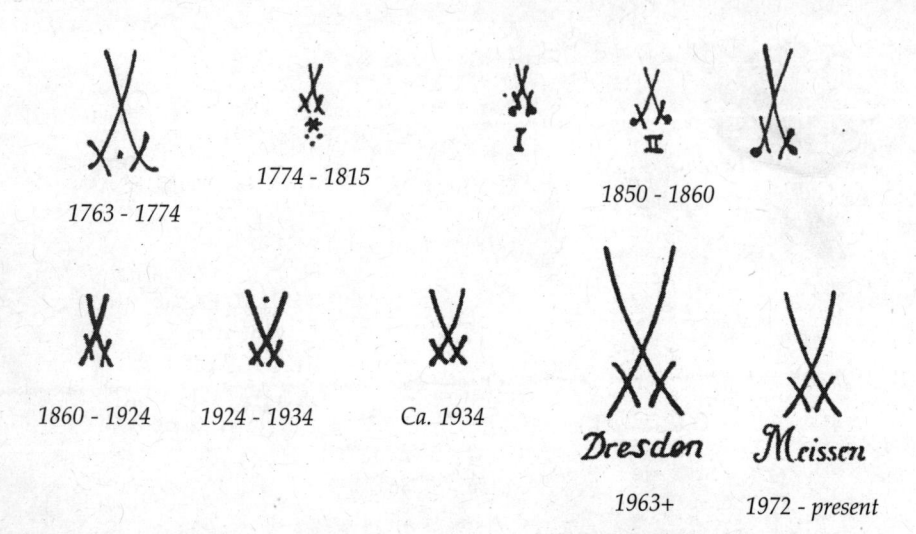

Dresden
1963+

Meissen
1972 - present

Trade marks which can be confused with those of the Royal Manufactory in Meissen.

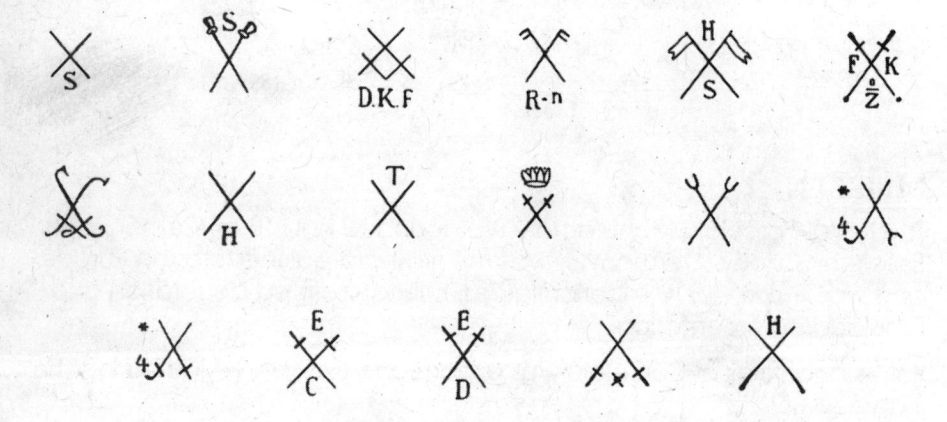

MINTON

Established in 1793, Stoke-on-Trent, Staffordshire, England, by Thomas Minton.

Has operated under various partnerships and names since then. Minton has been part of Royal Doulton Tableware since 1968. Tableware, earthenware, bone china, commemorative and advertising wares, hotel ware, Majolica, art pottery, figurines, Parian, pâte-sur-pâte, tiles, and other items have been made.

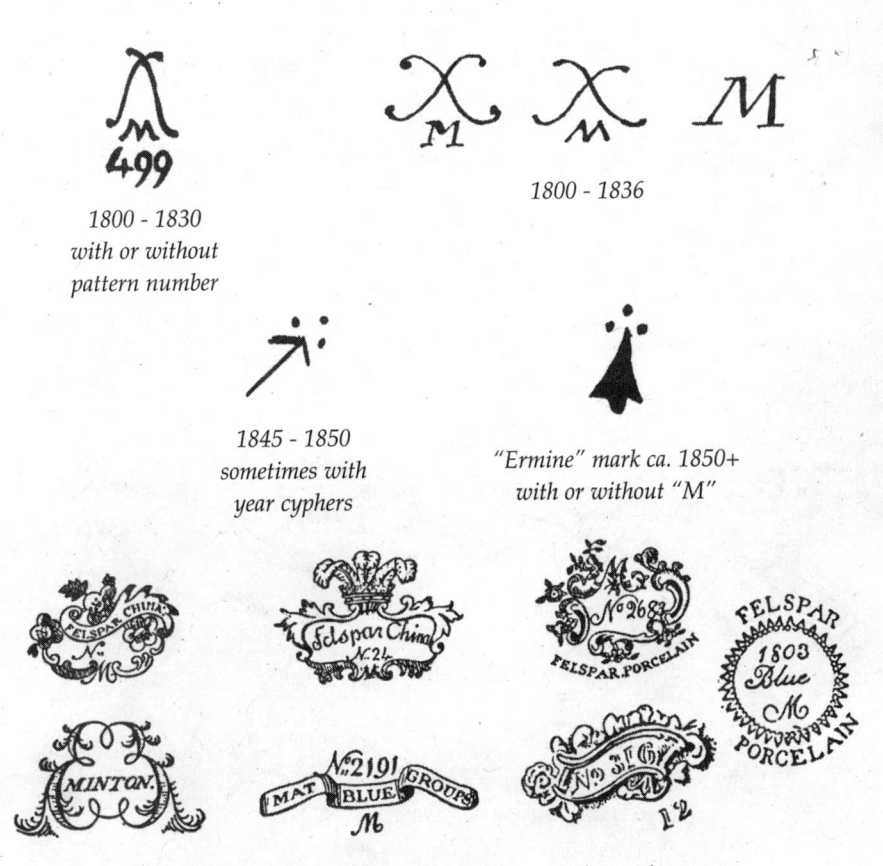

1800 - 1830
with or without pattern number

1800 - 1836

1845 - 1850
sometimes with year cyphers

"Ermine" mark ca. 1850+
with or without "M"

M (Minton) 1822 - 1836. Many other examples are known.

M & B (Minton & Boyle) 1836 - 1841.

Continued on next page

M & H (Minton & Hollins)
1845 - 1868.

M & Co. (Minton & Co.) ca. 1841 - 1873.

Ca. 1851, RARE

1860s

MINTON
1862 - 1841
with year cyphers

1863 - 1872

1868 - 1880
with year of
manufacture.

1871 - 1875

1872

After 1873. Printed. From 1863 to 1873 there was no crown above the globe and the name MINTON was used.
1891 – England below mark.
1901 – On some pieces crown deleted.
1902 - 1911 – Made in England added to mark

Continued on next page

Specialty marks such as this usually include date.

MINTONS ENGLAND

1890 - 1910

MINTONS

1900 - 1908

1900 - 1908

1918+
Uranium Glaze

1951+

MINTON CHINA 3.66.

Impressed on bone china. Last 2 digits indicate year of manufacture.

233

Minton Yearly Marks

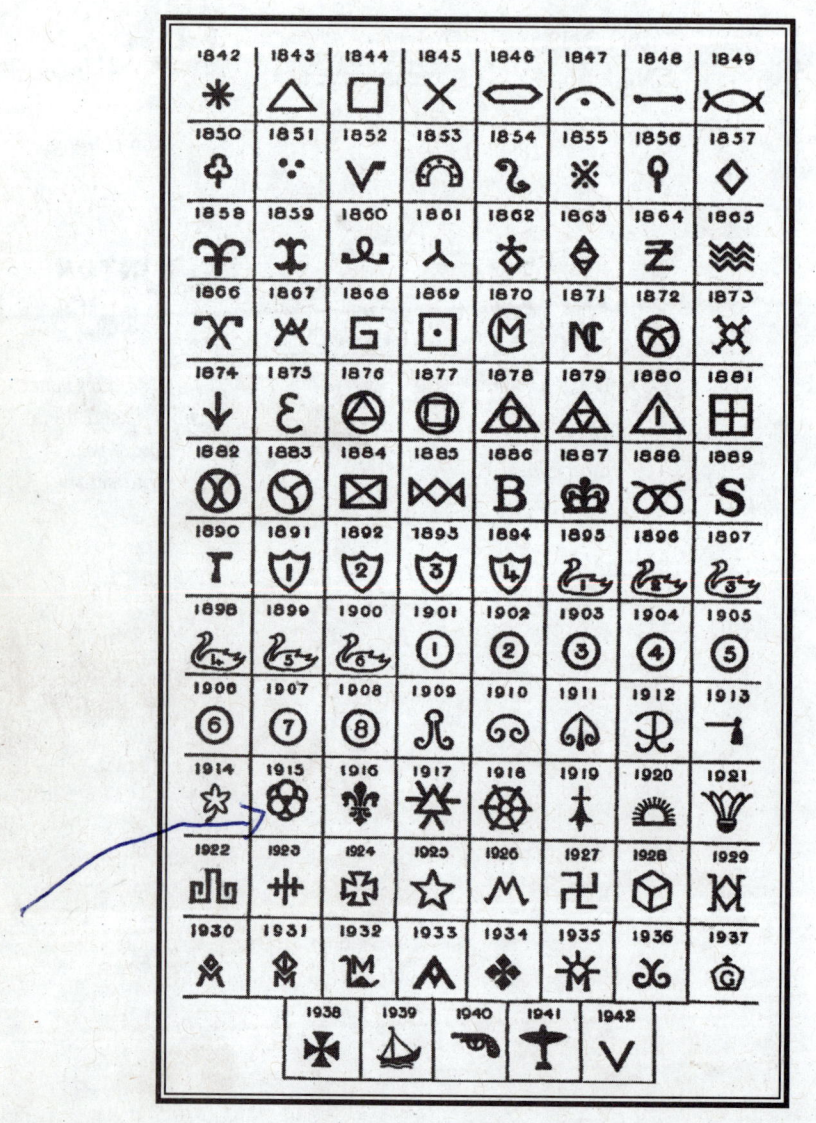

1842	1843	1844	1845	1846	1847	1848	1849
1850	1851	1852	1853	1854	1855	1856	1857
1858	1859	1860	1861	1862	1863	1864	1865
1866	1867	1868	1869	1870	1871	1872	1873
1874	1875	1876	1877	1878	1879	1880	1881
1882	1883	1884	1885	1886	1887	1888	1889
1890	1891	1892	1893	1894	1895	1896	1897
1898	1899	1900	1901	1902	1903	1904	1905
1906	1907	1908	1909	1910	1911	1912	1913
1914	1915	1916	1917	1918	1919	1920	1921
1922	1923	1924	1925	1926	1927	1928	1929
1930	1931	1932	1933	1934	1935	1936	1937
	1938	1939	1940	1941	1942		

Impressed in the clay to show year of manufacture, 1842 - 1942 inclusive. The figures 43, etc., have been used for 1943 onwards. The cyphers occur in sets of three: month, potter's mark, and year cypher.

Minton Month Letters

January (J)	February (F)	March (M)	April (A)
May (E)	June (I)	July (H)	August (Y)
September (S)	October (O)	November (N)	December (D)

MIYAO SHOTEN (1931 - 1962)
MIYAWO COMPANY LTD. (1962 -)

Figured kitchen pieces, dinnerware, lead vases, etc. When founded in 1931 the company was named Miyao Shoten and basically produced dinnerware for export. After the factory was destroyed during World War II they began making novelty items. After rebuilding the production of china recommenced and in 1962 the name became Miyawo Company Ltd.

Most china made from 1949 - 1961 was marked Miyan, although some was unmarked. The attribution of the PY trade mark was not known until the book *PY/Miyao: Fun Kitchen Collectibles*, by Belinda Evans was published in 2003 by Hobby House Press.

Items made from the 1930s until 1961 are very much sought after today, especially pieces marked made in Occupied Japan which are extremely hard to find.

Torii Gate mark. Green ink. 1949 - 1952.
The Torii Gate mark was first used ca. 1933. Pieces made in Occupied Japan are hard to find today.

PY in elipse mark. Green ink.
Shown with the C over N mark, which was also used by other companies.

Miyao mark. 1949 - 1961.
Used both with and without the C over N mark.

E.S.D. mark.
Mark used on Regal Rose by E.S.D. (Enterprise Sales & Distributors).

Geo. Borgfeldt & Company mark.
PY and C over N ink stamp with Borgfeldt coronet sticker.

MOORCROFT

The first pieces of Moorcroft Pottery were designed by William Moorcroft shortly after he was employed as designer by James Macintyre & Co., at the Washington Works, Burslem (England) in 1897.

In 1913 Moorcroft left Macintyre's to set up his own pottery in a custom-built works nearby.

Throughout the 1920s and the 1930s, designs were evolved to suit changing tastes and the pottery continued through World War II with William in charge until his death in 1945, when Walter took over his father's role. He introduced new exotic colours and also improved the working conditions of the employees. He continued to use the Royal Warrant originally granted to his father by Queen Mary.

Today W. Moorcroft PLC is still an independant business, with William's younger son John in charge, Walter having retired in 1987. The method of production developed by William in 1897 is unchanged, but the pattern range has been expanded and the pottery is selling more all over the world today, than it ever did in its previous heyday in the mid 1920s.

1897 - 1945

1945 - 1987

Signatures used with other marks.

1987 -

MOORCROFT

Transfer printed or impressed. With "Burslem" 1918 - 1929. "Made in England" 1916 - added to comply with international tariff regulations.

Printed paper Royal Warrant label 1928 - 1978 changed to POTTER TO H.M. QUEEN MARY in 1936 following death of her husband King George V, and to the late Queen Mary in 1953.

FRANCIS MORLEY (& CO.)

Broad St., Shelton, Hanley. 1845 - 1858. Formerly Ridgway & Morley. Subsequently Morley & Ashworth.

F. M.
F. M. & CO.
F. MORLEY & CO.

Distinguishing details of several impressed or printed marks of differing design: name of the individual pattern is often included, 1845 - 1858.

Masons' printed Ironstone mark continued by Francis Morley from ca. 1845.

MYOTT

Myott, Son & Company took over the Alexander Pottery (1888 - 1898) already at Stoke, Staffordshire, England. Moved to Cobridge 1902 - 1946 then to Hanley in 1947.

Alexander Pottery, 1888 - 1898. George T. Mountford, Proprietor.

1898 - 1902

1900+

1907+

1930+

1930+

1936+

1959+

1961+

1961+

237

NIPPON

The McKinley Tariff Act of 1891 specified that items imported into the United States be marked with the name of country of origin.

Nippon is the Japanese word for Japan, it was used as the country of origin name from ca. 1891 to ca. 1921 when regulations in the US required that the word Japan be used to specify country of origin.

There is a large and varied amount of marks, many are shown.

239

ROYAL
NISHIKI
NIPPON
IMPERIAL • NIPPON
HAND PAINTED
HAND • PAINTED •
NIPPON
HAND PAINTED
NIPPON
MADE IN
NIPPON
HAND PAINTED
T T
MADE IN NIPPON
Hand Painted
G
NIPPON
THE YAMATO
NIPPON
NO 1
HORSMAN
NIPPON
HAND PAINTED
W
PICKARD
CHINA
NIPPON
Hand Painted
T
NIPPON
NORITAKE
NIPPON
HAND PAINTED
SNB
NIPPON
DOLLY
HAND PAINTED
T
NIPPON

241

242

BABY BUD NIPPON   NIPPON
                         D

MADE IN   NIPPON   NIPPON 84
NIPPON

NIPPON 144   221   L.W & Co.
                 NIPPON   NIPPON

NORITAKE   NORITAKE   Studio
NIPPON   NIPPON   Handpainted
                                Nippon

Royal Sometuke   Hand Painted   ROYAL SOMETUKE
NIPPON   NIPPON   Nippon

Hand Painted   HAND PAINTED   Hand Painted
Nippon   NIPPON   NIPPON

                 Handpainted
                 NIPPON

243

PALISSY POTTERY LTD.

Chancery Lane, Longton. Staffordshire Potteries, 1946 - . Earthenware.

Formerly A.E. Jones (Longton) Ltd., whose marks continued.

Ca. 1948+

Ca. 1948+

Ca. 1950+

Ca. 1957+

Ca. 1959+

PARAGON CHINA (CO.) LTD.

Atlas Works, Longton. Staffordshire Potteries, 1920 - . Porcelain. Formerly Star China Company who had used the trade-name "Paragon" from 1900.

Ca. 1932+

Ca. 1939 - 1949

Ca. 1949 - 1952

Ca. 1952+

Ca. 1952+

Ca. 1956+

Ca. 1957+

R.H. & S. L. PLANT (LTD.)

Tuscan Works, Longton. Staffordshire Potteries, ca. 1898 - . China. Several marks incorporate the initials R.H. & S.L. P, or the trade-name "Tuscan" from 1898.

Ca. 1898+

Ca. 1902+

Ca. 1907+

Ca. 1936+

Ca. 1936+

Ca. 1947+

Ca. 1961+

Note: Later marks have year numbers, (eg. 62 refers to year 1962.)

POOLE POTTERY LTD.

Poole, Dorset, 1963 - . Earthenwares. Originally Carter, Stabler & Adams Ltd., whose marks continued to be used.

Impressed monogram mark of initials, C.S.A. ca. 1921+.

Impressed or printed ca. 1921+, with or without border lines.

Impressed or printed mark, ca. 1921+. N.B. A pre-1925 version omits "Ltd." after the style.

Dolphin mark introduced in 1950-1951 (not 1919 as has been recorded in other books, in error).

Special printed marks on individual "Studio" wares, first exhibited in October 1963.

Redrawn version of above previous printed mark, used from 1956 onwards.

Version of standard mark used on oven tableware introduced ca. 1961.

245

QUEBEC IMPORTERS

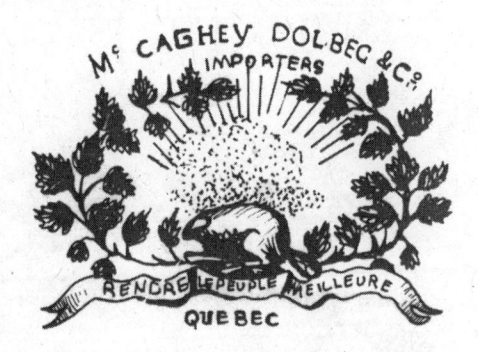

Marks of makers and importers of ceramics.

Mark stamped on blue and white ceramic pieces with historic scenes, made by Enoch Wood & Sons, ca. 1840 in England.

QUIMPER (SAY "KAM-PAIR")

By Susan and Al Bagdade

Quimper pottery derives its name from a town of the same name in Brittany, in the northwest corner of France, where the potteries were located. Jean Baptiste Bousquet settled in Quimper in 1685 and produced functional faience wares. His son Pierre succeeded him in 1708. In 1731, Pierre Bellevaux, Pierre's son-in-law was included in the business.

Pierre Clement Caussy joined the factory in 1739, took over the direction of the faiencerie and expanded the works. Through marriage Antoine de la Hubaudiere took over the Caussy factory in 1782 and it became known as the Grande Maison de HB.

Francois Eloury opened a rival factory in 1776 and in 1778 Guillaume Dumaine opened a third. By 1780 there were three rival faience factories operating in Quimper.

The Eloury factory passed to Charles Porquier and later to Adolphe Porquier. In 1782 the master artist Alfred Beau joined the factory.

continued on next page

In 1884 Jules Henriot took over the Dumaine factory and later purchased the Porquier factory in 1904. Noted artists Meheut, Sevellec, Maillard and Nicot worked at the Henriot concern.

The HB factory introduced the Odetta line of stoneware in the 1920s.

The Henriot factory merged with the Grande Maison HB in 1968 with each retaining its individual characteristics and marks. The factory was closed in the early 1980s, but has been taken over by an American couple and is still producing pottery today.

GRANDE MAISON HB

PC
Pierre Caussy
late 18th century.

de la Hubaudiere
early 19th century.

de la Hubaudiere
late 19th century.

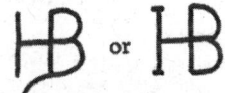

HB or **HB**
de la Hubaudiere
1882 - 1883.

HB Quimper
de la Hubaudiere
late 19th century to 1910.

ELOURY-PORQUIER-BEAU

P
Eloury-Porquier
1843.

A
Adolphe Porquier
1880s - 1890s.

B
Porquier-Beau
1898.

JULES HENRIOT FACTORY

HR
Jules Henriot
1904.

HENRIOT QUIMPER
Faiencerie Henriot after 1922.

HB QUIMPER
Les faienceries de Quimper.
Mark used ca. 1970 - 1984.

VATOFEU
B
QUIMPER

*Faiencerie de la
Grande Maison.
Quimper, ca. 1958.*

**Henriot
Quimper**
France

ca. 1970s mark.

**HB HenRiot
Quimper France
PeinT moig**

*Quimper Faience Inc.
Stonington, CT. This mark is used by
a Quimper, pottery owned by an
American firm since 1984.*

Many early pieces were unmarked. The following guidelines will help identify these unmarked examples as Quimper.
1. Body is often thick. Plates may appear wobbly, and large pieces asymmetrical.
2. Pinkish red clay used on early pieces and often shows through the glaze.
3. Prior to World War I, pieces were fired in wood burning ovens. Pits and streaky glaze are common on these pieces.
4. Unglazed rest spots or scars are often found on the bottoms of pieces fired in the wood burning ovens.
5. Florals and exotic birds were common subjects. After 1860, peasant figures dominated.
6. Due to the nature of the glaze, rim wear is common and often indicated age.

Additional notes on marks:
1. Many pieces were made on consignment for department stores and carry the store mark, i.e. "MACY."
2. Numbers and letters in conjunction with Quimper marks are usually pattern or style numbers.
3. Souvenir pieces were potted for various resorts and were marked as such.
4. Many pieces were re-issued. Museum quality reproductions were often marked in brown.
5. The word "France" added to the mark after 1891.
6. Peasant pieces with the mark PBx are not from Quimper, but from Malicorne, near Paris, and were an attempt to capitalize on the popularity of the Quimper peasant theme.

R.S. PRUSSIA, R.S. GERMANY, R.S. POLAND & R.S. TILLOWITZ

Made by the Schlegelmilch family during the mid-19th to 20th centuries. A wide variety of this popular china was made, both tableware and decorative pieces.

ERDMAN SCHLEGELMILCH

Suhl, Thuringia, Saxony-Prussia, Germany. 1861 - ca. 1938.

1881 - 1925

1891+

1891+

1891+

1891+

1891+

1896 - ca. 1938

1900 - 1938

1902 - 1938

Ca. 1904

1904+

1909 - 1938

Ca. 1938

REINHOLD SCHLEGELMILCH

Tillowitz, Silesia, Prussia, Germany (German-Poland). 1869 - ca. 1938.

1891+

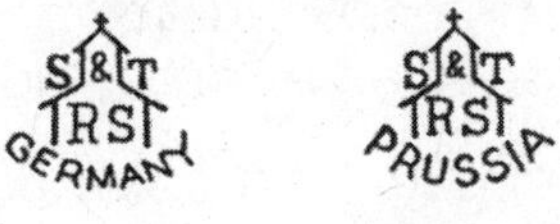

Ca. 1898 - 1908

1904+

1919 - 1921

1932 - 1938

249

OSCAR SCHLEGELMILCH

Langewiessen, Thuringia, Germany. 1892 - ca. 1972.

| 1892+ | 1896+ | 1900+ | 1904+ | 1950+ |

RIDGWAY

A long time family of Staffordshire potters founded by Job Ridgway in 1802 and continuing through many generations. Due to a variety of partners a considerable amount of impressed and printed marks showing distinguishing details and many variations for each type of ware and differing designs exist. The partnership of John William Ridgway 1814 - 1830 is considered one of the best periods.

RIDGWAY, SPARKS & RIDGWAY

Bedford Works, Shelton, Hanley, Staffordshire, England, 1873 - 1879.

RIDGWAYS

Bedford Works, Shelton, Hanley, Staffordshire, England, 1879 - 1920.

RIDGWAYS (BEDFORD WORKS) LTD.

Bedford Works, Shelton, Hanley, Staffordshire, England, 1920 - 1952.

RIDGWAY & ADDERLEY LTD.

1952 - 1955.

RIDGWAY POTTERIES LTD.

1955 - .

Companies that formed the Ridgway Group – Booths, Tunstall; Colcloughs, Longton; North Staffordshire Pottery, Cobridge; Portland Pottery, Cobridge and Adderley Floral China Works, Longton.

A selection of marks

R
R within Chinese style square is considered as mark of Job Ridgway.
1802 - 1808.

**J. R.
JOHN RIDGWAY
JHN RIDGWAY
I. RIDGWAY**
Impressed marks of differing design, name of pattern often included.
1830 - 1841.

Royal Arms mark, came with and without initials. Many variations occur.

John and William Ridgway, Cauldon Place and Bell Works.
Three differing impressed or printed marks. 1814 - 1830.

R.S.R.
1873 - 1879

1873 - 1879

Pattern name may be included.

1880+

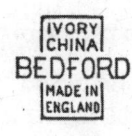

1905+

1905+

1912+

1912+

1927+

1927+

1930+

1930+

1930+

1934+

1934+

251

1950+

1950+

1962+

1962+

ROBINSON & LEADBEATER (LTD.)

Stoke, Staffordshire, England, 1864 - 1924. Parian, etc. Taken over by J.A. Robinson & Sons Ltd., and subsequently Cauldon Potteries Ltd.

1855+

1905 - 1924
Variations occur.

ROSENTHAL

Decorators and manufacturers of fine porcelain, tableware, figurines and Christmas plates, etc.

Philipp Rosenthal began producing dinnerware in Selb, Bavaria, Germany, about 1879, and the marks used clearly date the pieces. In the early years, undecorated china from Hutschenreuther was painted by Philipp and his wife, Maria. In 1914, Rosenthal produced his first dinner set, "Maria" pattern. It was octagonal-shaped, all white, with an embossed band. It is still one of Rosenthal's most popular designs.

Philipp Rosenthal fled the country in 1935 and died in 1937. His son, Philip (different spelling) Rosenthal, returned to Germany after World War II and took over the business.

1879 - 1891

1891 - 1904

1901 - 1956

Ca. 1900

Ca. 1900

Ca. 1901

1917 - 1952

Selb, Bavaria. 1907 - 1933. Selb, Germany. 1934 - 1956.

1922+

1925+

1935 - 1956

1937+

1939

1948

1957+

Current

253

ROYAL BAYREUTH

Established in 1794. Continues today as Tettau Porcelain Factory. Noted for floral, scenic and portrait china, and fruit and vegetable forms, as well as figural and souvenir articles.

Many versions of the mark are known, slight variations occur.

1870 - 1914

Ca. 1919

1946 - 1949

1957+

1968 - present

1972+

ROYAL COPENHAGEN PORCELAIN MANUFACTORY

Copenhagen & Fredericksberg, Denmark. Established in the 1770s. Supported and owned by the Danish Royal family until it went into private ownership in 1868. Produced tableware, figurines and decorative items etc. Christmas plates were introduced in 1908.

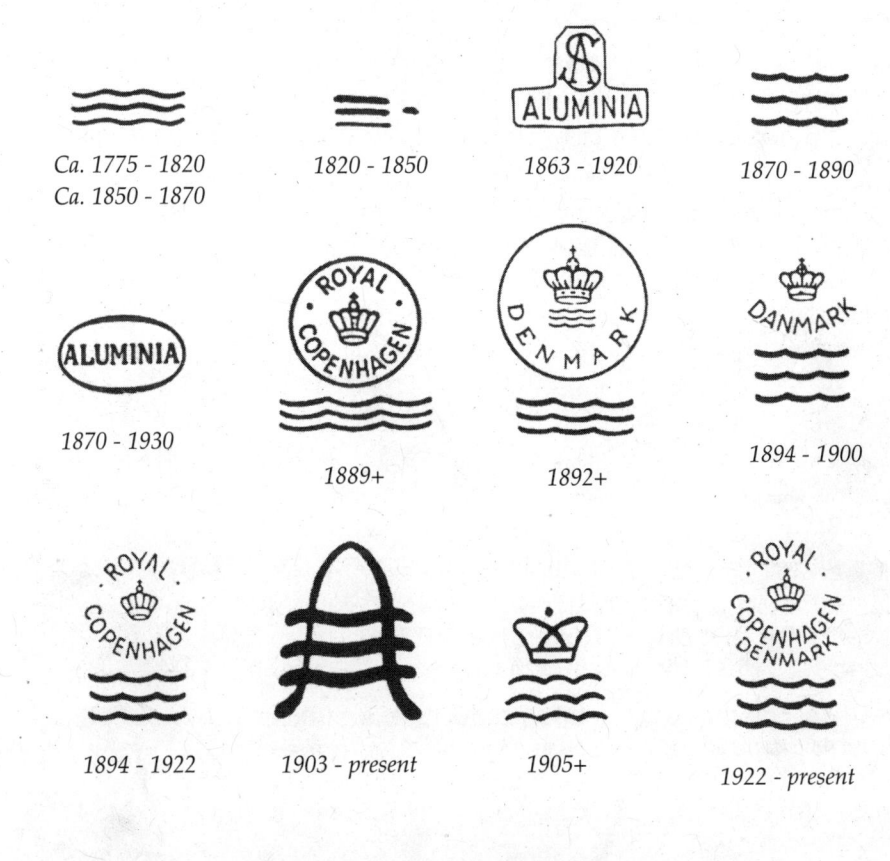

Ca. 1775 - 1820
Ca. 1850 - 1870

1820 - 1850

1863 - 1920

1870 - 1890

1870 - 1930

1889+

1892+

1894 - 1900

1894 - 1922

1903 - present

1905+

1922 - present

Ca. 1923

1929 - 1950

1929 - present

ROYAL DOULTON

Date marks and other marks found on some Doulton pieces.

Often, numbers and/or initials are found along with the manufacturer's mark. Examples of methods used by Doulton:

- **A-Mark:** A factory control mark. used by Doulton, ca. 1939 - ca. 1955. Found along with the back-stamp on some character jugs, series ware and tableware.
- **HN Prefix:** Found on figurines, first used in 1913. Henry Nixon was the artist in charge of painting Royal Doulton figurines, his initials, HN, prefix the number assigned to each figure.
- **M Prefix:** Miniature. 1932 - 1949.

Between 1902 and 1914 a lower case letter in a shield is found marked on some pieces: c for 1902, d for 1903, e for 1904 and so on to the letter o for 1914.

Between 1913 and 1930 Doulton used a date-number method to specify when a mould was made. 21 - 11 - 13 would indicate that a mould was made on the 21st day of November, 1913. Only two numbers, for instance, 11 - 13 indicates month and year – November 1913.

After 1927 another way Doulton dated some of their products was by adding a two digit number to the right of the mark. To ascertain the year of manufacture, add the number, for example, 16 to the year 1927 to arrive at the year of production, 1943.

DOULTON & WATTS, DOULTON & CO., ROYAL DOULTON

Lambeth, London, England, 1827 - 1956.
Burslem, Staffordshire, England, 1882 - present.

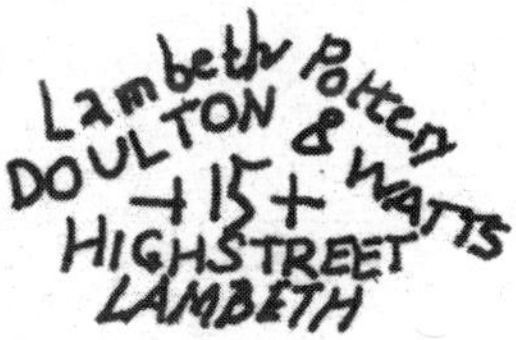

Ca. 1827 - 1858

DOULTON LAMBETH

1858 - ca. 1910. England added from 1891.

1869 - 1877. Often year of production in centre.

Ca. 1873 - ca. 1914

Ca. 1873 - ca. 1914. Occasionally with year of production in centre.

1877 - 1880

1877 - 1880

1879 - 1900

1880 - 1902. England added from 1891. Occasionally with year of production.

1881 - 1910. Also without word "Crown".

1881 - 1912. England added from 1891.

DOULTON

1882+

1882 - 1902.
England added from 1891.

1882 - 1914

DSP
1886 - 1914.
(Doulton & Slater's Patent).

1887 - 1902.
With variations in wording.

1888 - 1898

1891 - 1956

Ca. 1900 -

Ca. 1900 -

1902 - ca. 1930

1912 - 1956

1918 - 1932
RARE.

1920 - 1936

1922 - 1956

1930+

1930+

Royal Doulton – Artists

Artists who worked at Doulton & Co. signed their work with initials or a monogram. The following is a list of artists and their years of employment at Doulton.

Margaret Aitken
Ca. 1875 - Ca. 1883

Elizabeth Atkins
Ca. 1876 - Ca. 1899

Eliza S. Banks
Ca. 1876 - Ca. 1884

Arthur B Barlow
Ca. 1871 - Ca. 1878

Florence E. Barlow
Ca. 1873 - Ca. 1909

Hannah B. Barlow
Ca. 1871 - Ca. 1913

Lucy A. Barlow
Ca. 1882 - Ca. 1884

Harry Barnard
Ca. 1880 - Ca. 1890

John Broad
Ca. 1873 - Ca. 1919

Frank A Butler
Ca. 1872 - Ca. 1911

Mary Butterton
Ca. 1875 - Ca. 1890

Mary Capes - C
Ca. 1876 - Ca. 1888

Miss F.M. Collins
Ca. 1875 - Ca. 1880

Minna L. Crawley - C
Ca. 1876 - Ca. 1883

Louisa J. Davis
Ca. 1873 - Ca. 1895

W. Edward Dunn
Ca. 1882 - Ca. 1895

Emily J. Edwards
Ca. 1872 - Ca. 1876

Louisa E. Edwards
Ca. 1873 - Ca. 1890

Herbert Ellis
Ca. 1879 - Ca. 1928

John Eyre
Ca. 1884 - Ca. 1890

Elizabeth Fisher
Ca. 1873 - Ca. 1888

Arthur Leslie Herradine
Ca. 1902 - Ca. 1914

Miss Agnete Hoy
Ca. 1952 - Ca. 1957

Vera Huggins
Ca. 1923 - Ca. 1950

Francis E. Lee
Ca. 1875 - Ca. 1890

Florence Lewis
Ca. 1875 - Ca. 1897

Florence Linnell
Ca. 1880 - Ca. 1885

Edith D. Lupton
Ca. 1875 - Ca. 1889

Mark V. Marshall
Ca. 1876 - Ca. 1912

John H. McLennan
Ca. 1880 - Ca. 1910

Isabella Miller
Ca. 1880 - Ca. 1884

Mary Mitchell
Ca. 1874 - Ca. 1887

William Parker
Ca. 1879 - Ca. 1892

Arthur E. Pearce
Ca. 1873 - Ca. 1920

Francis C. Pope
Ca. 1880 - Ca. 1923

Florence C. Roberts
Ca. 1879 - Ca. 1930

Edith Rogers
Ca. 1881 - Ca. 1884

Kate Rogers
Ca. 1880 - Ca. 1892

Martha M. Rogers
Ca. 1881 - Ca. 1884

William Rowe
Ca. 1883 - Ca. 1939

Eliza A Sayers
Ca. 1877 ca .1881

Harry Simeon
Ca. 1894 - Ca. 1936

Eliza Simmance
Ca. 1873 - Ca. 1928

Elizabeth M. Small
Ca. 1881 - Ca. 1884

Emily E. Stormer
Ca. 1877 - Ca. 1892

Katie Sturgeon
Ca. 1880 - Ca. 1883

George Hugo Tabor
Ca. 1878 - Ca. 1890

Margaret E. Thompson
Ca. 1900

George Tinworth
Ca. 1866 - Ca. 1913

Linnie Watt
Ca. 1880 - Ca. 1886

Bessie J. Youatt
Ca. 1873 - Ca. 1890

ROYAL DUX - *Also refer to Bohemian.*

The Dux Porcelain Manufactory was founded in 1860 by E. Eichler, at Dux in Bohemia, Austria (after 1918 Duchcov, Czechoslovakia). The Dux Porcelain Company specialized in making statues, busts, figurines and decorative vases.

| 1860+ | Ca. 1860 - 1900 | Ca. 1900 - 1918 | pre 1918 |

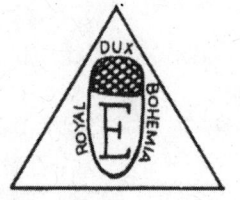

ROYAL WINTON - *also refer to Grimwades*

What is the first thing you think of when you hear this name? A tea table set with a flowery chintz pattern. Inexpensive when they were first introduced, but nothing chintzy about the prices realized on today's market.

Leonard Grimwades began operating a pottery in Stoke-on-Trent, Staffordshire, England, in 1885. His brothers joined the firm in 1886 and the pottery operated at Grimwade Bros. The company name was changed to Grimwades Ltd. in 1900, the same year Grimwades bought Stoke Pottery and Winton Pottery. Both of those names were used in some Grimwades marks. Other potteries were acquired in the next few years, and their names were sometimes also included in marks.

Queen Mary bought a Winton teaset when she visited the pottery with King George V in 1913, and soon afterwards the company began using 'Royal' in their advertising. In 1929 Royal Winton became the company's trade name.

In their early years Grimwades included commemorative items and souvenir china together with their utilitarian products such as toilet wares and a whole range of everyday items, egg cups, mugs, cake stands, toast racks, etc.

Royal Winton introduced its firts chintz dinnerware pattern in 1928. More than 60 different chintz patterns were made until the early 1960s, when they were discontinued because of high production costs.

New pieces of Royal Winton chintz are now being made, but they can usually be identified as the year of production is normally included in the backstamp.

New owners bought the company in 1995. The company is now registered as Grimwades Ltd. trading as Royal Winton.

See marks on next page

Grimwade Bros.
1886 - 1900

Grimwades Ltd.
ca. 1900+

Grimwades Ltd.
ca. 1911+

Grimwades Ltd.
ca. 1930+

Grimwades Ltd.
ca. 1930+

Grimwades Ltd.
ca. 1934 - 1939

Grimwades Ltd.
ca. 1934 - 1950

Grimwades Ltd.
ca. 1951+

SAINT-JEAN POTTERY
Quebec

Mark of the famous Saint-Jean pottery, ca. 1850, and the later mark, used in the late 19th century.

SAMPSON HANCOCK (& SONS)

Sampson Hancock (& Sons), Bridge Works, Stoke, Staffordshire, England. 1858 - 1937. (At Tunstall 1858 - 1870) Earthenware.

S. HANCOCK	S.H.	S.H. & SONS	S. H. & S.
1858+	1858 - 1891		1891 - 1935

Name of pattern may be included with mark.

1900 - 1906    1900 - 1906    1906 - 1912    1906 - 1912

1906 - 1912    1912 - 1937

SAMPSON SMITH (LTD.)

Longton, Staffordshire Potteries. 1846 - 1963. Earthenware, figures, etc., China in the 20th century.

S SMITH LONGTON 1851 — *Most 19th century wares unmarked. Very rare relief mark on earthenware dogs, Toby jugs or figures.*

SS — *Impressed marks very rarely used in the 19th century.*

SEVRES MANUFACTORY

France. Orignally founded in Vincennes in 1738 and became renowned for its soft paste porcelain, and in particular its flowers which were mounted on stems or applied to vases, chandeliers, etc. The factory was moved to a new building in Sevres in 1756 and through the influence of Madam Pompadour the King became the chief shareholder and controlled the manufacture of the luxury pieces. The interlaced "l" mark was used during his reign.

After the French Revolution the company fell into disfavour but was eventually revived as a leading manufacturer of hard paste porcelain in Europe.

Distinctive colours, artistic scenic painting and extensive use of gilding are the characteristics of the earlier wares.

In the 20th century the company was completey re-vamped.

Soft Paste
1753 - 1793

Hard Paste
1753 - 1793

1793 - 1804

1804 - 1814

1810 - 1814

Date letters were used with the "crossed L" mark from 1753 until 1793. The letters in either upper or lower case were either inside or beside the "crossed l" mark.

1753 - A	1759 - G	1755 - C	1756 - D	1757 - E
1758 - F	1764 - L	1760 - H	1761 - I	1762 - J
1763 - K	1769 - Q	1765 - M	1766 - N	1767 - O
1768 - P	1774 - V	1770 - R	1771 - S	1772 - T
1773 - U	1779 - BB	1775 - X	1776 - Y	1777 - Z
1778 - AA	1784 - GG	1780 - CC	1781 - DD	1782 - EE
1783 - FF	1789 - LL	1785 - HH	1786 - II	1787 - JJ
1788 - KK		1790 - MM	1791 - NN	1792 - OO
1793 - PP				
1754 - B				

For six years it appears no date code was used and in 1801 Sevres began using another method to refer to the year.

1801 - T₉	1802 - X	1803 - ll	1804 - ≑
1805 - ⫪	1806 - ∿	1807 - 7	1808 - 8
1809 - 9	1810 - 10	1811 - oz	1812 - dz
1813 - tz	1814 - qz	1815 - qn	1816 - sz
1817 - ds			

After 1817 Sevres indicated the year of manufacture in their mark by using the last two digits of the year.

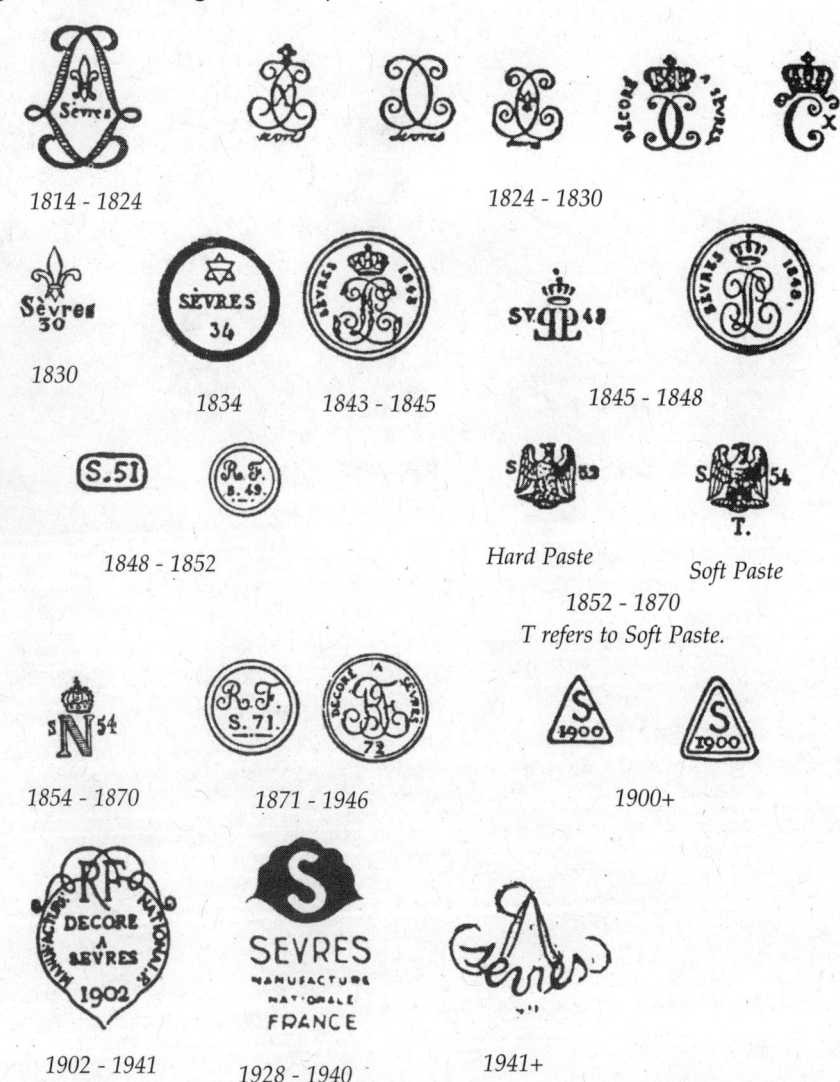

1814 - 1824

1824 - 1830

1830

1834

1843 - 1845

1845 - 1848

1848 - 1852

Hard Paste

Soft Paste

1852 - 1870
T refers to Soft Paste.

1854 - 1870

1871 - 1946

1900+

1902 - 1941

1928 - 1940

1941+

SHELLEY POTTERIES LTD.

(Shelley, ca. 1925 - 1929). The Foley, Longton. Staffordshire Potteries. 1925 - . China. Formerly Wileman & Co., who used the name "Shelley".

ca. 1925 - 1940   ca. 1945

Printed marks.

SHIP CHINA

Research information is readily available on examples that have survived from the early 19th century, such as the Arctic Scenery, the H.M.S. Discovery and the steamships that serviced the St. Lawrence.

Not so much however has been recorded on what one would term commercial dinnerware used on the ships and the railroads.

Until the 1960s these would have had distinctive patterns and logos, but after then more utilitarian products came into use.

More information can be found in *Restaurant China*, by Barbara J. Conroy, published by Collector Books.

Admiral Line. Pacific Steamship Co. United States, 1916 - 1936 Operated between Seattle and San Diego.

Baltimore Steam Packet Co. Old Bay Line. United States, 1840 - 1962 Operated between Norfolk, Virginia, and Baltimore, Maryland in Chesapeake Bay.

California Navigation and Improvement Co. United States, Late 1880s - 1927. Bought by the California Transportation Company in 1928, operated in San Francisco Bay area.

Detroit & Cleveland Navigation Co. United States, 1898 - 1951.

Grand Trunk Pacific Steamship Co. Canada, 1910 - 1920.
Operated between Seattle, Vancouver Island and Alaska.

Morgan Line. United States, 1834 - 1885.
From 1886 owned by Southern Pacific.

Ulysses Cruise Line. Greece, 1979 - 1984.
Later renamed Dolphin Cruise Line.

White Star Line. Great Britain and United States, 1850s - 1934. Operted transatlantic service. 1902 bought by International Mercentile Marine Co. 1926 bought by Royal Steam Packet Co. 1934 merged with Cunard, operated as Cunard White Star Ltd. 1950 White Star dropped from name.

SOHO POTTERY (LTD.)

Soho Pottery, Tunstall. Staffordshire Potteries. 1901 - 1906. Elder Works, Cobridge from 1906 - 1944. Note Cobridge on later marks and trade name "Solian" introduced ca. 1913. Earthenwares.

Printed mark, ca. 1901 - 1906.

ca. 1906 - 1922

ca. 1913 - 1930

ca. 1930+

ca. 1930+

ca. 1930+

ca. 1930+

ca. 1930

J. SPODE, W. COPELAND, T. GARRETT

Josiah Spode, Stoke-on-Trent, Staffordshire, England, 1784 - 1833. Manufacturers of earthenware, porcelain and bone china etc. William Copeland became a partner about 1813 and Thomas Garrett joined the firm in 1833. In 1833 the company name was changed to Copeland & Garrett and in 1847 to W.T. Copeland & Son. Became Royal Worcester Spode Ltd. 1976 - .

A selection of 19th and 20th century marks.

SPODE
1805+

SPODE Stone-China
Black: 1805 - 1815
Blue: 1815 - 1830

SPODE'S NEW STONE
1805 - 1820

SPODE Felspar Porcelain
Ca. 1810

1805 - 1833

Spode Felspar Porcelain
1815 - 1827
Variations occur.

N. S.
1820 - 1840

C. & G.

COPELAND & GARRETT
1833 - 1847

COPELAND & GARRETT NEW BLANCHE

COPELAND AND GARRETT
1833 - 1847

COPELAND & GARRETT LATE SPODE THE TIBER

1833 - 1847

COPELAND & GARRETT LATE SPODES FELSPAR PORCELAIN

COPELAND & GARRETT NEW JAPAN STONE

COPELAND
1847 - 1851

COPELAND
1847 - 1867

COPELAND, LATE SPODE
1847 - 1867

267

COPELAND
1850 - 1867

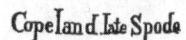

Copeland Late Spode
1850 - 1890

Copeland Stone China
1850 - 1890

COPELAND
1851 - 1885

W. COPELAND & SONS
1867 - 1890

1875 - 1890

SPODE COPELANDS CHINA ENGLAND
1891+

COPELAND SPODE'S TOWER ENGLAND
1891+

COPELAND SPODE ENGLAND
After 1891 and early 20th century.

COPELAND SPODE ENGLAND New Stone
After 1891 and early 20th century.

1894 - 1910

COPELAND
Ca. 1900

Spode's Velamour ENGLAND
1930s & 1950s

SPODE BONE CHINA ENGLAND
1950+

Spode Impl ENGLAND

Spode FORTUNA England.
1950s

Spode Flemish Green England

Spode BONE CHINA ENGLAND
1960+

X COPELAND SPODE ENGLAND Fine Stone
1962+
"x" omitted after 1962.

SUMIDA POTTERY

Asakusa, near Tokyo, Japan. 1828 - (about) 1941.

The Sumida River that flows near the Asakusa pottery district, gave this ware its name.

The pottery is heavy, usually brightly glazed and has human and animal-like figures applied in relief.

The vessels are soft as the clay is fired at a low temperature, causing the glaze to flow off the surface.

Most of the products were household objects made for export to the West, and came from the studio of Inoue Ryosai. This name was used by three generations, father, son, and the grandson who moved the manufacturing site to Yokohama in 1924.

Other Sumida marks are on pottery attributed to Ishiguro Koko, Hara Gozan, Fuji and Sezan.

Marks are from Sumida... *According to Us*, by Herbert Karp and Gardner Pond.

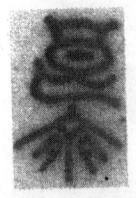

Inoue Ryosai

Inoue Ryosai

Ishiguro Koko

Ishiguro Koko

Hara Gozan

Sezan

Fuji

SUSIE COOPER POTTERY (LTD.)

Burslem. Staffordshire Potteries, ca. 1930 - 1950. Earthenwares and china.

Printed marks, also signature alone, ca. 1930 - . The name "Crown Works" does not occur before 1932.

SUSIE COOPER CHINA LTD.
Longton, ca. 1950 - 1959. Burslem, ca. 1959+. Staffordshire Potteries, 1950 - 1961. Bone China.

Printed mark, 1950 - .

SUSIE COOPER LTD.
Staffordshire Potteries, 1961.

Same mark used

SWINNERTONS LTD.
Various addresses, Hanley. Staffordshire Potteries, 1906 - . Earthenwares.

Ca. 1906 - 1917

Ca. 1917 - 1930

Ca. 1930+

Ca. 1930+

Ca. 1930+

Ca. 1946+

Ca. 1946+

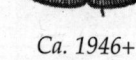

Ca. 1946+

Ca. 1962+

Printed marks, 1906 - .

270

SYRACUSE

The company began as Onondaga Pottery in 1871 in Syracuse, New York. As a trade name in 1892, 'Syracuse' became the company name in 1966.

The pottery made tableware, toilet sets etc., until 1971 when they concentrated entirely on commercial ware, and are now one of the few American companies continuing to make commercial ware for hotels and airlines etc.

Lion and Unicorn Arms of England.
Mark used on earthenware 1871 - 1873.

Great Seal of the State of New York.
Mark used on earthenware 1873 - 1897.

O.P. Co./China.
Mark used on earthenware 1890 - 1895.

China Dragon.
Mark used on fine (vitrified) china 1892 - 1895.

Western Hemisphere.
Mark used on Syracuse china (vitrified china) 1895 - 1897.

O.P. Co./Syracuse/China
Mark used on commercial ware (vitrified china) 1897 - 1920 with impressed date code; 1897 - 1926 on dinnerware.

Syracuse China Shield
Mark used on Empire and Wellington pattern vitrified china 1966 - 1970. Similar marks were used on other patterns. Some marks include the pattern name.

271

THE TORQUAY POTTERIES

South Devon, England. 1870 - 1960s. Torquay is the term used today when referring to the clay pots created in the South Devon potteries in England from 1869 - 1962. Earlier, "Devonware" was the term used and is still being used today by many collectors. There are three categories of Torquay: Classical, Art Pottery and Mottoware.

Torquay Pottery Marks

Black stamp Transfer printed 1884 - 1890	Incised 1901 - 1920	Black stamp 1902 - 1915
Impressed 1915 -1920	Black stamp 1918 - 1927	Black stamp 1935 - 1962
Impressed Exeter Art Pottery 1892 - 1896	Impressed Hart & Moist 1896 - 1935	Devon Tors Impressed 1920 - 1939
Black stamp Subsidiary, TPCO 1922 - 1930	Black stamp Lemon & Crute 1925 - 1928	Plymouth Pottery Impressed 1925 - 1926

Torquay Pottery Marks

ALLERVALE Serifs Imprssed 1885 - 1893	**ALLER VALE** Impressed 1891 - 1910	**ALLER VALE H H & CO.** Impressed 1897 - 1902
Aller Vale Devon Black ink, brush 1902 - 1924	**LONGPARK TORQUAY** Impressed 1903 - 1909	*Tormohun Ware* Incised 1903 - 1914
LONGPARK TORQUAY. Black stamp 1904 - 1918	**LONG PARK TORQUAY DEVON** Black stamp 1925 - 1957	**TORQUAY TERRA COTTA CO LIMITED** Black transfer 1875 - 1890
TC STAPLETON Impressed 1890 - 1905	*Torquay Pottery* Brush, black ink 1905 - 1920	**ROYAL TORQUAY POTTERY ENGLAND** Black stamp 1924 - 1940

WADE

WADE & CO.
Union Pottery, Burslem, Staffordshire, England. 1887 - 1927.

GEORGE WADE & SON LTD.
Manchester Pottery, Burslem, Staffordshire, England. 1922 - .

WADE HEATH & CO., (LTD.)
Royal Victoria Pottery, Burslem, Staffordshire, England. 1927 - .

WADE (ULSTER) LTD.
Portadown, Co. Armagh, Northern Ireland. 1953 - .

Wade & Co.

W. & CO.
B.
1887 - 1927

WADE'S
1887 - 1927

G. Wade & Son

1936+ *1936+* *1947+*

Wade Heath & Co.

1927+ *1934+* *1934+*

1936+ *1936+* *1939+*
With or without
"Flaxman"

1953+ (ROYAL VICTORIA WADE ENGLAND POTTERY)

1953+ (WADE MADE IN ENGLAND HAND PAINTED)

1957+ (WADE ENGLAND)

1953+ (WADE (ULSTER) LTD. PORCELAIN)

1953+
Variations occur
(Irish Porcelain E MADE IN IRELAND)

1954+ (Irish Porcelain WADE. CO. ARMAGH.)

1955+ (Irish Porcelain MADE IN IRELAND R)

JOSIAH WEDGWOOD (& SONS LTD.)

Burslem, Etruria and Barlaston, Staffordshire, England. Josiah Wedgwood's name in Staffordshire pottery is famous for its wide variety of products, such as bone china, jasper, basalt, majolica, etc. The firm Wedgwood continues today and through acquisitions and mergers many well known potters have joined the Wedgwood group.

A selection of marks.

wedgwood
1759 - 1769

WEDCWOOD
1759+ From 1860 with date code (see table)
From 1891 "ENGLAND" "MADE IN ENGLAND" occurs in the 20th century.

WEDGWOOD

WEDGWOOD & BENTLEY
1768 - 1780

W. & B.
Ca. 1775

(WEDGWOOD & BENTLEY ETRURIA)
1769 - 1780
Variations occur

Wedgwood
1780 - 1798

WEDGWOOD
1812 - 1822

275

WEDGWOOD ETRURIA 1840 - 1845	**PEARL** 1840 - 1868	**P** 1868+

WEDGWOOD

Standard mark. Occurs with date mark. "ENGLAND" added from 1891. "MADE IN ENGLAND" added ca, 1910.

E Lessore

Artist signature.
Emile Lessore
Ca. 1858 - 1876

WEDGWOOD
1878+ "ENGLAND" added 1891.

WEDGWOOD ETRURIA. ENGLAND
1891 - 1900

WEDGWOOD
1900+ With "ENGLAND" or "MADE IN ENGLAND"

WEDGWOOD BONE CHINA MADE IN ENGLAND
1920+

N W or NORMAN WILSON
1927 - 1962
with standard mark.

WEDGWOOD
1929 - present

Of ETRURIA WEDGWOOD MADE IN ENGLAND BARLASTON
1940+

WEDGWOOD BONE CHINA MADE IN ENGLAND
Post WWII

ENGRAVED BY WEDGWOOD STUDIO
1952+

WEDGWOOD Bone China MADE IN ENGLAND

1962+
Pattern name or number may be included.

WEDGWOOD DATE CODE 1860 - 1906

A set of three capital letters was used by Wedgwood as a date mark – the first for the month of manufacture, the second for the potter and the last letter indicates the year. This system is somewhat confusing because in 1886 Wedgwood began to repeat the letters used from 1860 until 1885. From 1891 onwards the word "ENGLAND" should be included in the mark.

Year Marks 1860 - 1906

1860 - O	1866 - U	1872 - A	1863 - R	1864 - S
1865 - T	1871 - Z	1877 - F	1868 - W	1869 - X
1870 - Y	1876 - E	1882 - K	1873 - B	1874 - C
1875 - D	1881 - J	1887 - P	1878 - G	1879 - H
1880 - I	1886 - O	1892 - U	1883 - L	1884 - M
1885 - N	1891 - T	1897 - Z	1888 - Q	1889 - R
1890 - S	1896 - Y	1902 - E	1893 - V	1894 - W
1895 - X	1901 - D		1898 - A	1899 - B
1900 - C	1906 - I		1903 - F	1904 - G
1905 - H	1862 - Q			
1861 - P	1867 - V			

Month Marks 1860 - 1864

January - J	February - F	March - M	April - A
May - Y	June - T	July - V	August - W
September - S	October - O	November - N	December - D

Month Marks 1864 - 1906

January - J	February - F	March - R	April - A
May - M	June - T	July - L	August - W
September - S	October - O	November - N	December D

Wedgwood Date Code 1907 -

In 1907 Wedgwood changed the month code from a letter to the number 3 or 4, but continued using letters of the alphabet to indicate the year.

Year Marks 1907 - 1929

1907 - J	1908 - K	1909 - L	1910 - M	1911 - N
1912 - O	1913 - P	1914 - Q	1915 - R	1916 - S
1917 - T	1918 - U	1919 - V	1920 - W	1921 - X
1922 - Y	1923 - Z	1924 - A	1925 - B	1926 - C
1927 - D	1928 - E	1929 - F		

Wedgwood date mark code changed again beginning in 1930. For the month of manufacture, a number from 1 to 12 is used, the potter is identified by a letter and the year by two digits, for example, 43 idicated the year, 1943.

WEDGWOOD & CO. (LTD.)

Unicorn and Pinnox Works, Tunstall, Staffordshire, England. 1860 - . Earthenware, stoneware, etc. **NOTE: Not to be confused with Josiah Wedgwood & Sons Ltd.**

WEDGWOOD & CO.

1860+ Date and body type often incuded.

1862+

1890 - 1906

WEDGWOOD & CO. LTD.

1900+

1906+ Variations occur.

1908+ Pattern name & body type included.

1908+

1925+

1925+

1936+

1951+

1956+

1956+

1957+

1962+

Some other companies that used a "Wedgwood" or "Wedgewood" mark: Ferrybridge Pottery (1792 -), Hollingshead & Kirkham (1870 - 1956), Podmore, Walker & Co. (1834 -), William Smith & Co. (1825 - 1855), Ralph Wedgwood & Co. (1766 - 1837) and John Wedge Wood (1841 - 1860).

WILEMAN & CO. *Foley*
Foley Potteries, Foley China Works, Fenton, Longton, England. 1892 - 1925. Earthenware and china.

Became Shelley Potteries Ltd., Foley, Longton, Staffordshire, England. 1925 - . China.

1892+

1911+

1923+

1925 - 1940

1925 - 1940

1945+

ARTHUR J. WILKINSON (LTD.)
Royal Staffordshire Pottery, Burslem, Staffordshire, England. 1885 - . Earthenware.

1891+

Ca. 1896
Variations occur.

Ca. 1907

Ca. 1910

1930+

1930+

279

1930+

1947+

This mark is ca. 1970s. Old version of mark has words below banner in place of Wilkinson.

WILTSHAW & ROBINSON (LTD.)

Carlton Works, Stoke, Staffordshire, England. 1890 - 1957. China, earthenware, re-titled Carlton Ware in 1958.

CARLTON WARE LTD.

Carlton Works, Stoke, Staffordshire, England. 1958 - . China, earthenware.

1890+

1894+

1906+ Mark continued by Carlton Ware Ltd.

Ca. 1914

1925 - 1957

1925+ Mark continued by Carlton Ware Ltd.

1958+

ENOCH WOOD & SONS

Fountain Place, Burslem, Staffordshire. 1818 - 1846. Enoch Wood was in business with various partners from 1784. When his three sons joined him in 1818 the business became Enoch Wood & Sons.

Impressed mark 1818 - 1846. Many similar marks occur on blue and white ware made for the American market.

WOOD & SON(S) LTD.

Trent and New Wharf Potteries, Burslem, Staffordshire. 1865 - . Earthenwares, Ironstones, etc.

Changes: SONS from 1907; LTD. from 1910; WOOD & SONS (Holdings LTD., from 1954.

Printed mark, 1891 - 1907.

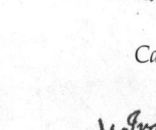

Ca. 1910+

Ca. 1910+

Ca. 1917+

Ca. 1930+

Ca. 1930+

Ca. 1931+

Ca. 1936

Ca. 1940+ and similar marks with different

Ca. 1952+

Ca. 1957+

Ca. 1958+

Ca. 1960 -

WORCESTER PORCELAINS

Produced at the main factory at Worcester, England, ca. 1751 - .
Selecton of Worcester marks:

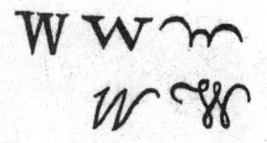

W W W
W W

1755 - 1770

C
Flight

1783 - 1788

Flight

1788 - 1792

B or **B** incised

1792 - 1807

Flight & Barr

1792 - 1807

Barr Flight & Barr

1807 - 1813

BFB

1807 - 1813

CHAMBERLAINS

1847 - 1850

Flight Barr & Barr

1813 - 1840

CHAMBERLAIN & Co
WORCESTER

1850 - 1852

K&B

1854 - 1862

Chamberlain & Co, Worcester.

After 1840

*George Grainger.
Royal China Works
Worcester*

1846

1852 - 1862

G & Co
W

1870 - 1890

The Royal Worcester Factory Tree

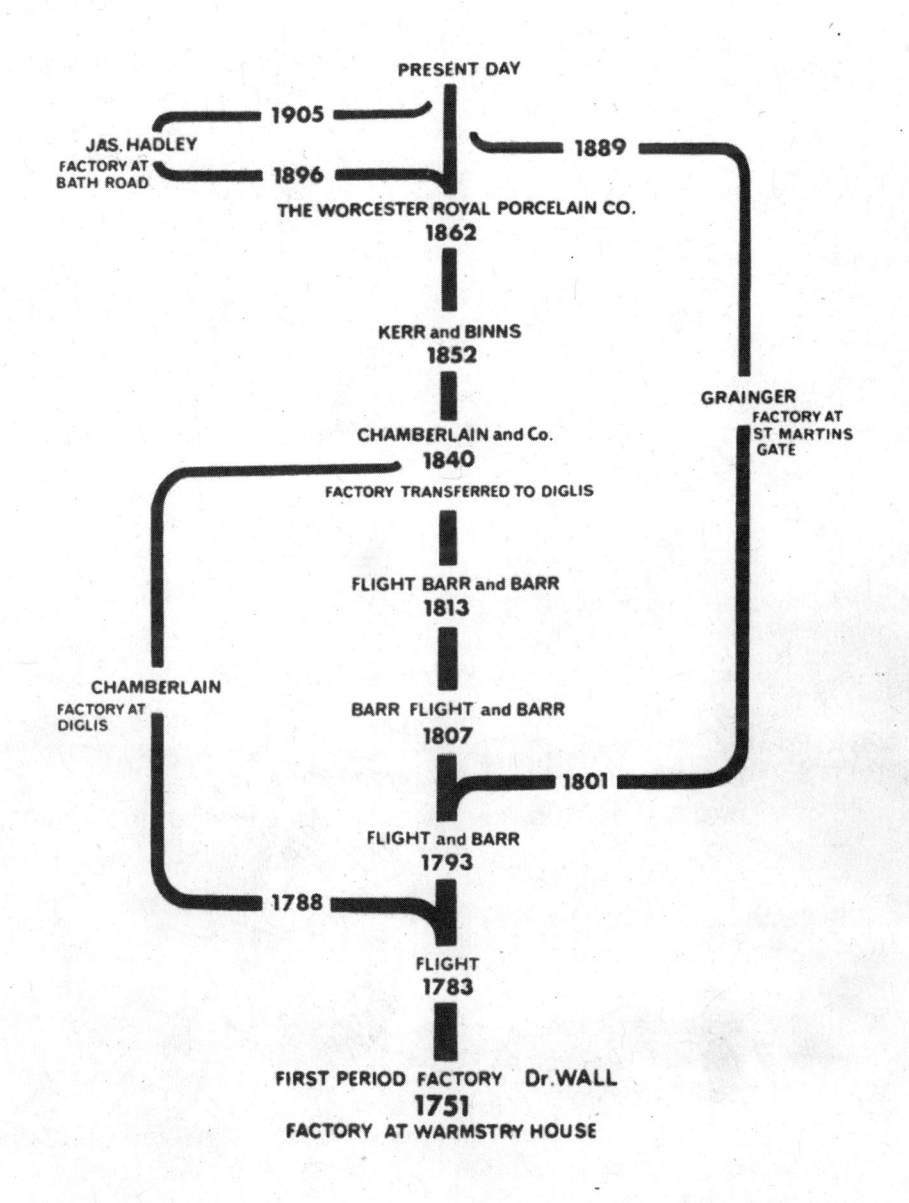

PRESENT DAY

JAS. HADLEY
FACTORY AT BATH ROAD — 1905 / 1896

1889

THE WORCESTER ROYAL PORCELAIN CO.
1862

KERR and BINNS
1852

CHAMBERLAIN and Co.
1840
FACTORY TRANSFERRED TO DIGLIS

GRAINGER
FACTORY AT ST MARTINS GATE

FLIGHT BARR and BARR
1813

CHAMBERLAIN
FACTORY AT DIGLIS

BARR FLIGHT and BARR
1807

1801

FLIGHT and BARR
1793

1788

FLIGHT
1783

FIRST PERIOD FACTORY Dr. WALL
1751
FACTORY AT WARMSTRY HOUSE

ROYAL PORCELAIN WORKS WORCESTER
1865 – 1880

1897 – 1900

1900 – 1902

1902 – 1905

283

1862 -1875. Numbers or a letter below the mark indicate year. (i.e. 73 for 1873, A for 1867. See key below)

1876 - 1891, Letter below the mark indicates year. (i.e. a for 1890).

Key to System of Dating by Letters

1867 - A	1871 - E	1875 - K	1879 - P	1883 - U	1887 - Y
1868 - B	1872 - G	1876 - L	1880 - R	1884 - V	1888 - Z
1869 - C	1873 - H	1877 - M	1881 - S	1885 - W	1889 - O
1870 - D	1874 - I	1878 - N	1882 - T	1886 - X	1890 - a

1891 - . Note: addition of words "ROYAL WORCESTER ENGLAND" round the mark. From 1892 onwards the following system was used to indicate year.

1892   one dot between "ROYAL" and crown.
1893   two dots - one either side of crown.
1894   three dots, this method, adding a dot each year, continued until 1915 when 24 dots were used to indicate year. These dots are found on either side of the crown and also below the mark.
1916   star - below the mark.
1917   star and one dot - below the mark.
1918   star and two dots - below the mark. Marking with the star and adding a dot to indicate year continued until 1927 when eleven dots had been added.
1928   small square.
1929   small diamond.
1930   –
1931   two interlinked circles.
1932   three interlinked circles.
1933   three interlinked circles - one dot.
1934   three interlinked circles - two dots. Marking with three interlinking circles and adding a dot each year continued until 1948 when 16 dots had been added.
1949   "V" under mark.
1950   "W" under mark.
1951   "W" with one dot, again a dot was added for each year until 1956.
1957   "W" or "R" under mark, with a dot added for each following year until 1963.
1964   "W and 14 dots.

ZSOLNAY

Pécs, Hungary, 1853 - . Established over 150 years as the Zsolnay Hard Tile Manufactory mainly producing wash basin sets, flower pots and architectural ornaments.

As styles changed, around 1897 Zsolnay was making Art Nouveau style pottery, which today is very collectible.

Some pieces from this earlier period have been re-issued but of an inferior quality from the 1897 - 1920 period, but they are clearly marked with one of the later marks.

1868 - 1876

1871 and after.
Five churches mark.
During medieval times, the name of the town was Five Churches, or Fünfkirchen in German.

1878 - 1900.
Mark with five churches and the initials of the children of Vilmos Zsolnay; Térez, Júlia, and Miklós.

1893 - 1903

1899 - 1920

1900 and after.

Mark using the five steeples was first used during the Victorian era. This ca. 1900 mark is registered to M & M Associates of the United States.

285

BIBLIOGRAPHY - CERAMICS

E. Paul and A. Pterson, *Collector's Handbook to Marks on Porcelain and Pottery*. Modern Books and Crafts Inc., USA

Ralph M. and Terry H. Kovel, *Dictionary of Marks: Pottery and Porcelain*. Crown Publishing, New York.

Donald Blake Webster, *Early Canadian Pottery*. McClelland & Stewart, Toronto.

Geoffrey A. Godden, *Encyclopedia of British Pottery and Porcelain Marks*. Barrie & Jenkins, London.

Joan F. Vanpatten, *Encyclopedia of Nippon Glass*. Collectors Books, USA.

J.P. Cushion, *Handbook of Pottery & Porcelain Marks*. Faber & Faber, UK.

Richard and Jean Symonds, *Medalta Stoneware & Pottery for Collectors*.

Geoffrey A. Godden, *Minton Pottery & Porcelain of the First Period 1798 - 1850*. Barrie & Jenkins, London.

Elizabeth Collard, *Nineteenth Century Pottery & Porcelain in Canada*. McGill University Press, Montreal.

Henry Sandon, *Royal Worcester Porcelain from 1862 to Present Day*. Crown Publishing, New York.

Llewellynn Jewitt, *The Ceramic Art of Great Britain*. Sterlng Publications Co., New York.

Wolf Mankowitz, *Wedgwood*. Spring Books, London.

Majolica

French Majolica Vase, 25" high, early 19th century.

Distinctive in style, this imaginatively mould modelled eathenware, decorated in brightly coloured lead glazes, with relief designs, was first introduced in 1850 by the English Staffordshire company, Minton, and exhibited on their stand at the Great Exhibition of 1851 in London. It was well received and praised and thereafter became enormously popular throughout much of the 19th century.

Inspiration for the wares came from the works of centuries old Italian potters, called Maiolica, but the most influential was the 16th century French potter Bernard Palissy whose Faience wares were characterized by naturalistic designs of insects, shells, snakes, lizards and other specimens of nature, seen in high relief and glazed in bright colours on oval dishes, plaques, and a range of objects.

The earliest Minton majolica wares endeavoured to imitate the 14th century Italian Maiolica in which the pottery was covered with an opaque white tin glaze giving a fine white surface upon which the design was freely painted.

Minton used his leading artists for the new production line intended to attract the new emerging middle-class with artistic aspirations, but lacking the financial means of the wealthy for the more refined art objects. Filling this need, and typical of the Victorian taste at the time, large ornamental fountains, jardinieres, garden seats, umbrella stands and architectural pottery intended for facing pillars, walls, staircases and balconies, all in colourful, semi transluscent glazes, became the new fashion.

It wasn't long before domestic and utilitarian pottery followed. Such items are usually moulded into intricate floral shapes, or has vegetation or garden creatures encrusted on it. Decoration such as flowers, vines, frogs, snakes or fish, if not an integral part of the mould design are moulded separately or fashioned by hand and applied to the article. The beautiful glazes which are painted on, vary in tint with the numerous factories that ultimately produced the ware. The domestic line ran from vases, wall brackets, candlesticks, compotes, plates, jugs and a variety of dishes to huge ornamental vases, all elaborate and excessive in ornament. For the next quarter century designs followed the trends of Victorian interests, whether serious, humerous or sophisticated all were ablaze with glorious colour. And most important it followed the current trends and was affordable to the average family. The most renowned English makers of Majolica, in addition to Minton, include Wedgwood, George Jones, Joseph Holdcroft, and Brown-Westhead Moore & Co. In time most English potteries made the ware. In the U.S. the better pieces came from the Bennett Pottery in Baltimore, Eureka Pottery in New Jersey and from about 1878 to the early 1890s Griffin Smith & Hill of Phoenixville, Pennsylvania, marked their product "Etruscan Majolica". It was also made on the Continent by Sarreguemines in France and Villeroy & Boch in Germany, the most noted, and in Canada at St. Johns, Quebec, the Brantford Pottery and Newton Brook Pottery of Toronto.

Look for crisp moulding and glazes that have been carefully applied and show no sign of blurring, Cobalt-blue background is one of the more highly valued. George Jones became best known for his whimsical characters surrounding tureens, game-pies, pitchers and the like, with rabbits and chicks and similar subjects. Backs of plates and bottoms of dishes often have a mottled effect.

The latter part of the 19th century saw almost every pottery making its own style of majolica, unfortunately with many of the lesser companies quality was questionable and left a lot to be desired. British interest was on the wane and much of the production was being exported to America, where interest was still high. In due course, like any mass marketing, quantity became the over riding factor and quality declined. Ultimately this had an enormous affect on the overall market. By the end of the century interest had reached zero, majolica, was virtually over.

It took nearly a hundred years for interest to be revived, and now there is a considerable interest and market for the older better quality Victorian majolica. **B.S.S.**

For those wishing to study the subject further, there are a number of good books available.

SAMUEL ALCOCK & CO., Burslem, Staffordshire (1828 - 1859)
Marked their rare majolica pieces "S. Alcock & Co."

BENNETT POTTERY, Baltimore, Maryland U.S.A. (Ca. 1850)
Majolica, Parian ware.

E. & W. BENNETT
CANTON AVENUE
BALTIMORE MD.   1846 - 1856.

T.C. BROWN-WESTHEAD, MOORE & CO., Hanley, Staffordshire (1862 - 1904)
Produced a limited line of quality majolica.
1870s - 1880s printed or impressed.

B.W.M.
B.W.M. & Co.

S. FIELDING & CO. (LTD.), Stoke-on-Trent, Staffordshire (1879 -)
(Not all Fielding majolica was marked)

FIELDING   Ca. 1879.

SF & Co.   1880 - 1917

GRIFFEN, SMITH & HILL, Phoenixville, Pennsylvania USA (1878 - 1889)

Impressed mark.
1878 - 1889

D.F. HAYNES & CO. Chesapeake Pottery Co., Baltimore, Maryland USA (1881 - 1914)

Mark used 1882 - 1884
(on Avalon Faience)

Mark used 1882 - 1885
(on Clifton Majolica)

JOSEPH HOLDCROFT Sutherland Pottery, (from ca. 1872), Longton. Staffordshire Potteries (1865 - 1939)
Earthenwares, Majolica, Parian, etc.

Printed or impressed monogram (J H) marks, 1865 - 1906.

GEORGE JONES (& SONS LTD.), Staffordshire, England
Trent Pottery, (1864 - 1907), Crescent Pottery (1907 - 1957)

Printed or impressed mark 1874 - 1924.

Printed or impressed mark 1924 - 1951.

MINTON, Stoke, Staffordshire, England (1865 - 1939)

MINTON 1140

Impressed mark 1862 - 1871.
Impressed year cypher 1867.

GEORGE MORLEY & COMPANY,
Wellsville and East Liverpool, Ohio USA (1879 - 1885)

Known for gurgling fish and other figural pitchers.

MAJOLLICA *Early work.*

MORLEY & CO./MAJOLICA/WELLSVILLE, O. 1879 - 1884

GEORGE MORLEY'S/MAJOLICA/EAST LIVERPOOL, O. 1885

C.C. THOMPSON POTTERY CO.
East Liverpool, Ohio USA (Ca. 1915)
Ironstone ware, Majolica.

Eureka
1868 - 1938

WARDLE & COMPANY, Hanley, Staffordshire (1871 - 1910)
Popular patterns, Bird & Fan, and Fern & Bamboo.

WARDLE *Impressed mark plus English registry mark.*

JOSIAH WEDGWOOD (& SONS LTD.),
Burslem, Etruria, & Barlaston, Staffordshire, England (1769 - present)

WEDGWOOD *Standard impressed mark 1759 -*

Canadian Potters

John Kulp Grimsby

G BEECH/MAKER/ BRANTFORD/1863

MEDALTA POTTERIES CANADA MEDICINE HAT. ALTA.

W.E. WELDING BRANTFORD. ONT

Cap Rouge Pottery

STONE CHINAWARE CO. ST JOHNS. P.Q.

BRANTFORD CANADA

MEDALTA STONE WARE LTD. MEDICINE HAT. ALTA.

G. LAZIER PICTON. C.W.

Glass Bros Co London

Among the many types of stoneware pottery made in Canada were utilitarian ware such as crocks, jugs, butter churns and flower pots etc., as well as household and hotel-ware including tableware, tea pots, vases and decorative ornaments.

Canadian-made pottery items that are marked with a potter's or pottery name were usually marked using one of the following methods.

INCISED: mark scratched into the clay using a pointed instrument.

IMPRESSED: a metal die was used to imprint names or initials into the clay.

PRINTED: marked using a stencil or rubber stamp.

MOULDED: when the maker's mark was part of the mould used in casting or pressing of pottery. It is usually found on the base.

NOTE: Place names and/or initials such as Berlin; C.E.; C.W. on pottery/stoneware gives an indication of when a piece was made, but can only be used as a general guide because often the "old name" continued in use after a new place name was assigned.

L.C. LOWER CANADA (1792 - 1840) Part of what is now known as Quebec.

U.C. UPPER CANADA (1792 - 1840) Part of what is now known as Ontario.

C.E. CANADA EAST (1840 - 1867) Part of what is now known as Quebec.

C.W. CANADA WEST (1840 - 1867) Part of what is now known as Ontario.

N.W.T. NORTH WEST TERRITORIES. Prior to joining Confederation in 1905 Alberta and Saskatchewan were part of the North West Territories.

ACADIA POTTERY – See: James Prescott & Sons

JACOB H. AHRENS, Paris, On (1860 - 1883)
marks:
- J.H. AHRENS / PARIS, C.W.
- J.H.AHRENS

ALBION POTTERY, Bolton, On (1898 - 1904)
mark:
- ALBION POTTERY / C. SAUNDERS / BOLTON, ONT.

FRANCIS BAILEY, Cartwright Twp., Durham Co., On (1855 - 1862)
mark:
- F. BAILEY

ORRIN L. BALLARD, St. Johns, QC (1858)

ORRIN L. BALLARD, Cornwall, On (1864 - 1869)
marks:
- ORRIN L. BALLARD / ST. JOHNS, C.E.
- BALLARD / CORNWALL, C.W.

GEORGE BEECH, Brantford, On (1851 - 1869)
marks:
- G. BEECH / MAKER / BRANTFORD / 1863
- MADE BY G. BEECH / APRIL 1862 / BRANTFORD / CANADA WEST
- G. BEECH

BELLEVILLE POTTERY CO., Belleville, On (1901 - ca. 1914)
marks:
- BELLEVILLE POTTERY CO / SUCCESSORS TO / HART BROS. & LAZIER / BELLEVILLE, ONT.
- B P & CO / BELLEVILLE / ONT. – in a heart shape

BELLEVILLE STONEWARE CO., Belleville, On (1870 - 1879)
mark:
- BELLEVILLE / STONEWARE / COMPANY

BERTRAND & LAVOIE, Iberville, QC (ca. 1888 - 1890)
mark:
- MFG / BY / BERTRAND & LAVOIE / IBERVILLE, P.Q.

ADAM BIERENSTIHL, Bridgeport, On (1867 - 1900)
mark:
- BIERENSTIHL

JACOB BOCK, Waterloo Co., On (1820's)
marks:
- WATERLOO UPPER CANADA / SEPTEMBER 17, 1825 / JACOB BOCK POTTER
- WATERLOO / THE 4 JAN / 1825

BOEBLER & WEBER – See: Huron Pottery

JOSEPH BOEHLER, New Hamburg, On (1874 - 1894)
mark:
- JOSEPH BOEHLER / NEW HAMBURG

BRANTFORD POTTERY

Justus Morton was the first to establish a stoneware pottery in Brantford, Ontario in 1849. Although several ownership/partnership changes occurred and two fires destroyed the factory, temporarily interrupting production, pottery was made at the Brantford site under several proprietorships from 1849 until 1907. "Brantford" pottery is the term often used when referring to the various products of the following firms: Morton & Co. (1849 - 1856); Morton & Bennet (1856); James Woodyatt & Co. (1857 - 1859); Morton Goold & Co. (1859 - 1867); Welding & Belding (1867 - 1872); Belding (1872); Welding (1873 - 1894); Brantford Stoneware Manufacturing Company (1894 - 1907).

BRANTFORD STONEWARE MANUFACTURING COMPANY, Brantford, On (1894 - 1907)
marks:
- B S MFG. CO. LTD. / BRANTFORD
- BRANTFORD STONEWARE MFG. CO. / BRANTFORD, ONT.
- BRANTFORD / STONEWARE
- BRANTFORD / CANADA
- *See also: F.P. Goold*

JOHN, JOSEPH & WILLIAM O. BROWN, Toronto and Bowmanville, On (1860's - 1870's)
marks:
- BROWN with initials J & J or J & W O

THOMAS BROWN, Strathroy, On (1881 - 1899)
mark:
- T. BROWN / STRATHROY

BROWNSCOMBE & GOODFELLOW, Peterborough, On (1880 - 1881)
mark:
- BROWNSCOMBE & GOODFELLOW / PETERBORO, ONT.

SAMUEL BROWNSCOMBE, Owen Sound, ON (1882 - 1907)
mark:
- S. BROWNSCOMBE

WILLIAM BROWNSCOMBE, Peterborough, ON (Estab. 1852)
mark:
- W. BROWNSCOMBE / PETERBOROUGH

BURNS & CAMPBELL, Toronto, ON (1879 - 1881)
mark:
- BURNS & CAMPBELL / TORONTO

DAVID BURNS, Holmesville, On (ca. 1860 - ca. 1900)
mark:
- D. BURNS / MAKER

JAMES R. BURNS, Toronto, On (1881 - 1887)
marks:
- J. R. BURNS / TORONTO
- JAMES R. BURNS / TORONTO

SAMUEL BURNS POTTERY, Markham, On (1870's)
mark: • S. BURNS POTTERY / MARKHAM, ONT.

R. CAMPBELL & SONS, HAMILTON POTTERY, Hamilton, On (ca. 1890 - 1928)
mark: • CAMPBELL / CANADA

CANADA POTTERIES LTD., Hamilton, On (1928 - 1929)
mark: • CANADA / HAMILTON / POTTERIES

CAP ROUGE POTTERY CO., Cap Rouge, QC (Estab. 1860)
mark: • CAP ROUGE / POTTERY – *is a mark used by the Cap Rouge Pottery Co. mid 1870's to early 1880's. Other potteries in the area also marked their wares with "Cap Rouge."*

CORNWALL POTTERY, Cornwall, On
mark: • CORNWALL / POTTERY, C.W. – *a mark used by O.L. Ballard or Flack and VanArsdale.*

CROWN BRICK AND POTTERY CO., New Glasgow, N.S. (Estab. 1867)
mark: • CROWN BRICK & POTTERY WORKS, NEW GLASGOW, N.S.

JOHN DAVIS & SON, Davisville, On (1890 - ca. 1928)
mark: • JOHN DAVIS & SON / DAVISVILLE, On

JOSEPH DAVIS, Davisville, On (1845 - 1890)
mark: • JOSEPH / DAVIS / MAKER / SEPT 1878

DERBY POTTERY, Kilsyth, On (1869 - 1909)
mark: • DERBY

NICHOLAS EBERHARDT, Toronto, On (1865 - 1879)
marks:
• EBERHARDT
• N. EBERHARDT / TORONTO, C.W.
• N. EBERHARDT / TORONTO, ONT.
• N. EBERHARDT

EBERHARDT & HALM, Toronto, On (1863 - 1865)
mark: • EBERHARDT & HALM / TORONTO, C.W.

WILLIAM EBY, Conestogo, On (Estab. 1856)
marks:
• EBY
• EBY, CONESTOGO

ELMSDALE POTTERY, Elmsdale, NS (Estab. 1856)
mark: • R. MALCOM / ELMSDALE POTTERY

FARRAR, St. Johns and Iberville, QC
marks:
- MOSES FARRAR / ST. JOHNS, L.C. (1840)
- E.L. & M. FARRAR / ST. JOHNS, C.E. (1841- 1850)
- E.L. FARRAR / ST. JOHNS, C.E. (1850 - 1857)
- E.L. & G.W. FARRAR / ST. JOHNS, C.E. (1857)
- G.W. FARRAR / ST. JOHNS, C.E. (1857 - 1871)
- ST. JOHNS / STONEWARE (1857 - 1871)
- ST. JOHNS / QUEBEC (1870's)
- FARRAR & DENEAU (mid 1870's)
- G.H. & L.E. FARRAR / ST. JOHNS, P.Q. (1871 - 1873)
- E.L. FARRAR / IBERVILLE, P.Q. (1880's)
- ELF(1880's)
- E.L FARRAR / POTTERY WORKS / IBERVILLE (1880's)
- POTTERIES / FARRAR / IBERVILLE (1886)
- ST. JOHNS POTTERY (1850's or 1860's) **
- ST. JOHNS POTTERY WORKS (1873 - 1876) **

** Thought to be Farrar marks

FLACK & VANARSDALE, Cornwall, On (1869 - 1907)
mark:
- FLACK & VANARSDALE / CORNWALL, On

EBAN T. GILBERT, Port Ryerse, On (1886 - 1900)
mark:
- EBAN T. GILBERT / PORT RYERSE

GILLESPIE & MACE, St. Johns, QC (1857 - 1858)
mark:
- GILLESPIE & MACE / ST. JOHNS, C.E.

GLASS BROS. & CO., London, On (1888 - 1899)
marks:
- GLASS BROS / & CO / LONDON
- GLASS BROS / LONDON, ONT.
- G B & CO / LONDON
- GLASS BROS CO / LONDON
- G
- GLASS BROS / FIREPROOF / LONDON, ONT>
- MANUFACTURED / BY/ GLASS BROS & CO / LONDON, ONT

FRANKLIN P. GOOLD, Brantford, On (1859 - 1867)
marks:
- F.P. GOOLD & CO / BRANTFORD, C.W.
- F.P. GOOLD / BRANTFORD
- BRANTFORD STONEWARE WORKS

GRAY & BETTS, Tillsonburg, On (1883 - 1886)
mark:
- GRAY & BETTS / TILLSONBURG, Ont.

GRAY & GLASS, Tillsonburg, On (1886)
mark:
- GRAY & GLASS / TILLSONBURG

JOHN GROH, Waterloo Co., On (ca. 1863 - ca. 1873)
mark:
- JOHN GROH PR

HAMILTON POTTERIES, Hamilton, On (1930 - 1947)
marks:
- HAMILTON / POTTERIES
- HAMILTON / CANADA / POTTERIES / OVEN / PROOF

H. HANDLEY, Picton, On (1894 - 1899)
mark:
- H. HANDLEY / MANUFACTURER / PICTON / ONT.

HANDLEY BROTHERS, Picton, On (1891 - 1894)
mark:
- HANDLEY BROS. / PICTON

W. HART & CO., Picton, On (1849 - 1855)
marks:
- W. HART & CO. / PICTON, C.W.
- *See also: Samuel Skinner, Picton, On*

HART BROS. & LAZIER, Picton, On (1879 - 1887)

HART BROS. & LAZIER, Belleville, On (1879 - 1901)
marks:
- H B & L
- H B & L PICTON / C.W.
- HART BROS & LAZIER / BAY OF QUINTE WORKS / PICTON, C.W.
- HART BROS & LAZIER / PICTON, C.W.
- H B & L / BELLEVILLE, ONT.
- HART BROS & LAZIER / BELLEVILLE, ONT.
- HART'S SELF BASTING ROASTER

SAMUEL T. HUMBERSTONE, Newton Brook, On (1872 - 1920)
marks:
- S.T. HUMBERSTONE
- S.T. HUMBERSTONE / NEWTON BROOK
- S.T. HUMBERSTONE / NEWTON BROOK / ONT.

HURON POTTERY, Egmondville, On Established 1852
by Valentine Boehler, who formed a partnership in 1873 with Jacob Weber.

marks:
- (1873-76) BOEHLER & WEBER / MAKERS / EGMONDVILLE
- (1876) Jacob Weber became sole owner
- (1876-97) J.B. WEBER / HURON POTTERY / EGMONDVILLE, ONTARIO
- (1897) Jacob Weber sold the business to his brother, Joseph, who rented the pottery to John Allan.
- (1900) Ferdinand Burgard took over the pottery and it became F. Burgard & Son. Closed 1910.
- Miniature souvenir jugs with painted signatures often included F BURGARD or EGMONDVILLE.

J. A. KENNEDY, Brantford, On (1889 - 1897)
mark:
- J.A. KENNEDY / BRANTFORD, ONT.

JOHN KULP, Grimsby, On (1829 - 1868)
mark: • JOHN KULP / GRIMSBY

GEORGE I. LAZIER, Picton, On (1864 - 1879)
marks: • G.I. LAZIER / PICTON, C.W.
- G.I. LAZIER
- A.J. LAZIER / PICTON, C.W.

B. LENT, Lincoln, On (ca. 1836 - 1841)
marks: • B. LENT / U.C.
- B. LENT

THE LONDON CROCKERY MANUFACTURING COMPANY, London, On (1886- 1888)
mark: • LONDON CROCKERY MFG. CO. / LONDON, ONT.

LONDON POTTERY MFG. CO. London, On (1905 - ca. 1939)
mark: • LONDON POTTERY / LONDON, ONT.

J.M. MARLATT & CO., Paris, On (1859 - 1868)
marks: • J.M. MARLATT / PARIS, C.W.
J.M. MARLATT & CO. / PARIS, C.W.

MCGLADE & SCHULER, Paris, On (1868 - 1873)
mark: • McGLADE & SCHULER / PARIS, ONT.

MEDALTA STONEWARE COMPANY, Medicine Hat, AB (1916 - 1924)
mark: • MEDALTA STONEWARE LTD / MEDICINE HAT, ALTA.
- Became Medalta Potteries Limited in 1924 and continued in business at Medicine Hat until 1959.

mark: • MEDALTA / POTTERIES LTD. / MEDICINE HAT / ALBERTA

The Medalta pottery produced many types of stoneware articles: art ware, oven ware as well as tableware and used many variations of their mark on their goods, eg. Medalta, Medicine Hat; Medalta, Canada; also pattern names and numbers were included.

Medalta pottery with the place name Redcliff dates from 1966 when the business began again at Redcliff producing the same styles and using some of the moulds from the Medicine Hat factory.

JAMES MOONEY, Prescott, On (ca. 1847 - ca. 1856)
mark: • JAMES MOONEY / PRESCOTT

MORTON & BENNETT, Brantford, On (1856 - 1857)
mark: • MORTON & CO. / BRANTFORD, C.W.
- MORTON & CO. / BRANTFORD.

MORTON & GOOLD, Brantford, On (1859)
mark: • MORTON GOOLD & CO. /BRANTFORD, C.W.

ORANGEVILLE POTTERY, Orangeville, On (ca. 1865 - 1880)
mark: • ORANGEVILLE / POTTERY

DANIEL ORTH, Campden, On (1851 - 1903)
marks:
- D. ORTH
- CAMPDEN / D. ORTH

OWEN SOUND POTTERY CO., Owen Sound, On (1894 - 1907)
mark: • OWEN SOUND

CHARLES E. PEARSON, Iberville, QC (1880)
mark: • CEP

JAMES PRESCOTT & SONS, Enfield, NS (ca. 1880 -?)
marks:
- HENRY PRESCOT (sic)
- HP - monogram mark
- ACADIA POTTERY / ENFIELD, N.S.

PRINCE EDWARD ISLAND POTTERY, Charlottetown, PEI (ca. 1880 - 1895)
marks:
- P.E.I. / POTTERY
- P E ISLAND / POTTERY

JOHN & JAMES RICHARDSON, Kerwood, On (1860 - 1886)
marks:
- RICHARDSONS / EGYPTIAN WARE
- RICHARDSONS WARE

ST. JOHNS STONE CHINAWARE COMPANY, St. Johns, Qc (1873 - late 1890's)
marks: • Two types of "Royal Arms" mark with –
- STONE CHINAWARE CO. / ST. JOHNS, P.Q. or QUE.
- IRONSTONE CHINA / ST. JOHNS, P.Q. or QUE.
- also without P.Q. or QUE.

HENRY SCHULER, Paris, On (1873 - 1884)
mark: • H. SCHULER / PARIS, On

W. SCHWAB, Beamsville, On (1853 - 1875)
mark: • W. SCHWAB / BEAMSVILLE

SIMCOE STREET POTTERY, Beaverton, On (1876 - 1904)
mark: • SIMCOE STREET / POTTERY / BEAVERTON

SAMUEL SKINNER, Picton, On (1855 - 1867)
Samuel Skinner, a one-third owner of the William Hart & Co. pottery managed the firm from 1855 - 1867. The S. Skinner & Co. mark appeared on the wares made at the Hart pottery during his management.

marks:
- S. SKINNER & CO. / PICTON, C.W.
- S. SKINNER
- S. SKINNER & CO. / PICTON P.O.

STAR POTTERY, London, On (1892 - 1905)
mark:
- STAR

TARA POTTERY, Tara, On (1867 - 1884)
mark:
- TARA POTTERY

WILLIAM TAYLOR, Beaverton, On (1873 - 1875)
mark:
- J.W. TAYLOR / BEAVERTON

FRED B. TILLSON, Tillsonburg, On (1870 - ca. 1883)
mark:
- F.B. TILSON / TILLSONBURG

TILLSONBURG POTTERY CO., Tillsonburg, On (1880's)
mark:
- TILLSONBURG / ONT / POTTERY CO.

The Toronto Pottery Company was a subsidiary of the Robertson Clay Products Co., Akron, Ohio. Pottery marked by the Toronto firm was made in the U.S.A.

JOSEPH WAGNER, Berlin (Kitchener), On (1869 - 1880)
mark:
- JOSEPH WAGNER / BERLIN POTTERY

WARNER & CO., Toronto, On (1856 - 1863)
mark:
- WARNER & CO. / TORONTO

J.B. WEBER – See: Huron Pottery

WELDING & BELDING, Brantford, On (1867 - 1872)

WILLIAM E. WELDING, Brantford, On (1873 - 1894)
marks:
- WELDING & BELDING / BRANTFORD, ONT.
- W.E. WELDING / BRANTFORD, ONT.

WHITE & HANDLEY, Brockville, On (1884 - 1890)
mark:
- WHITE & HANDLEY / BROCKVILLE, ONT.

JAMES WOODYATT & CO., Brantford, On (1857 - 1859)
marks:
- WOODYATT & CO.
- JAMES WOODYATT & CO. / BRANTFORD, C.W.

ECANADA ART WARE, Hamilton, On, (ca. 1926 - ca. 1952)
Well designed and colourful Canadian made art pottery in the "Jasper Ware" style with moulded decoration applied in relief to the body of the ware.

George Emery who apprenticed and trained at Wedgwood, in England, emigrated to Canada in 1912. In 1926 Emery began making his pottery at his home in Hamilton and taking it to be fired at the Canadian Porceiain Co. where he was employed until 1945 when he established his own factory, Ecanada Art Pottery. Production ceased 1952 - 53.

marks:
- ECANADA/ART/WARE/HAMILTON
- ECANADA/ART POTTERY/MADE IN CANADA/ EMERY 1296
- AUCANADA
- ECANADA
- ECANADA/ART POTTERY
- EMERY/HAMILTON/CANADA

American Potters

BENNINGTON, VERMONT, POTTERY

Unfortunately for the collector, Bennington potteries left unmarked a large proportion of their wares. Pieces which are marked can be dated since the various combinations of markings have been recorded and are shown here with the years during which they were in use.

The first pottery was started by Captain John Norton in 1793 and continued to be a family concern until 1894.

In 1847 a second pottery was started by Christopher Webber Fenton, a relative of the Nortons by marriage. In 1848 he was in partnership with Calvin Park and Alanson P. Lyman. Many changes of name followed and in 1870 the pottery was demolished.

1845 - 1847

1849 - 1858

1849 - 1858

1849 - 1858

1849 - 1858

1852 - 1858

1852 - 1858

A list of various Bennington Pottery Marks

L. NORTON & CO. BENNINGTON, VT. (1823 - 1828)

L. NORTON & SON East Bennington, Vt. (1833 - 1840)

J. NORTON East Bennington, Vt. (1841 - 1845)

JULIUS FENTON Bennington, Vt. (1847 - 1850)

J. NORTON & CO. Bennington, Vt. (1859 - 1861)

E. NORTON Bennington, Vt. (1881 - 1883)

EDWARD NORTON & COMPANY Bennington, Vt. (1883 - 1894)

LYMAN, FENTON & CO. Bennington, Vt. (1849 - 1858)

L. NORTON Bennington, Vt. (1828 - 1833)

JULIUS NORTON Bennington, Vt. (1841 - 1845)

NORTON & FENTON Bennington, Vt. (1845 - 1847)

J. NORTON Bennington, Vt. (1847 - 1850)

J. & E. NORTON & CO. Bennington, Vt. (1859 - 1861)

EDWARD NORTON Bennington, Vt. (1883 - 1894)

E. NORTON & CO. Bennington, Vt. (1883 - 1894)

UNITED STATES POTTERY CO. Bennington, Vt. (1852 - 1858)

L. NORTON & SON Bennington, Vt. (1833 - 1840)

JULIUS NORTON East Bennington, Vt. (1841 - 1845)

NORTON & FENTON East Bennington, Vt. (1845 - 1847)

J. & E. NORTON Bennington, Vt. (1850 - 1859)

E. & L. P. NORTON Bennington, Vt. (1861 - 1881)

EDWARD NORTON & CO. Bennington, Vt. (1883 - 1894)

EDWARD NORTON COMPANY Bennington, Vt. (1886 - 1894)

A.A. GILBERT CO. Bennington, Vt. (1859 - 1861)

NOTE:

Many types of ceramics were made in the United States – pottery, ironstone, porcelain and semi-porcelain etc.

Because there were so many manufacturers of ceramics who made a large variety of goods, such as utilitarian crocks and jugs etc.; dinner ware and decorative pieces we can only list a few American manufacturers and their marks in this book.

BUFFALO POTTERY CO., Buffalo, NY USA (1901 - present)

1905+

1906+

1907 - 1940s

Deldare Ware Underglaze
1909 - 1925

1911 - 1925

ca. 1930

GLADDING McBEAN & CO., Los Angeles, CA USA (1875 - present)

Tropico Pottery California
1923+

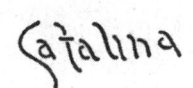

Catalina
1930 - 1937

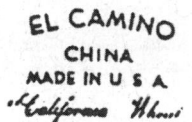

El Camino China Made in U S A
ca. 1934

Oven Nasco Proof
1934 - 1940

GMcB
1934 - 1960

Catalina Made in U.S.A. Pottery
1937 - 1942

F Made in U.S.A.
1938 - 1939

Franciscan Ware Made in U.S.A.
1938 - 1939

Franciscan Made in California U.S.A. Ware
1939 - 1947

Pueblo Made in U.S.A. Pottery
1940+

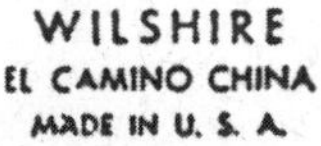

Wilshire El Camino China Made in U. S. A.
1942+

Franciscan China
1947 - 1953

Franciscan Masterpiece China
1963 - 1964

305

HALL CHINA CO., East Liverpool, Ohio, USA (1903 - present)

1903 - 1911

1903 - 1911

1916 - 1930

1930 - 1972

1932 - 1963

1933 - 1976

1933 - 1976

1936 - Ca. 1970

1937 - present

1939 - Ca. 1953

Ca. 1945

Ca. 1945

1950+

Ca. 1950 - Ca. 1955

1960 - present

1973 - present

1969 - 1980+

1981+

HARKER POTTERY CO., East Liverpool, Ohio, USA (1890 - 1972)

Mark	Date
Semi Porcelain	Ca. 1890
Stone China H.P. Co	1890 - 1900
H C (with arrow)	1890 - 1930
Established 1873 Columbia Chinaware (Statue of Liberty)	Ca. 1930 - 1935
Sun-Glow Oven-Tested	Ca. 1935
Cameo ware by Harker Pottery Co. Patented USA	1935 - 1948
Hotoven Harker The Oldest Pottery in America Cookingware	1935 - 1950
Bakerite Oven-Tested Made in U.S.A. Warranted 22 K. Gold	1935 - 1950
Modern Age	1939 - 1947
Cameo Ware by Harker USA Pat. Pending	1940 - 1948
Harker Engobe Ware Bermuda Blue U.S.A.	Ca. 1944
Harker Pate sur Pate Ware Pottery Est. 1840 Resists Acid-Detergents-Craze	1948 - 1955
Harker Oldest Pottery in America Est. 1840 Royal Gadroon	1948 - 1963
White Rose carv-kraft by Harker	Ca. 1950
The Harker Pottery Co. Quality Since 1840	Ca. 1950
Country Style USA 1840 Harker Stoneware Ovenproof	Ca. 1950
Harkerware	Ca. 1954 - 1964
Harkerware Since 1840 U.S.A.	1955 - 1960
Harker China Co. East Liverpool, Ohio	Ca. 1959
Harker China Company U.S.A.	1960 - 1977
Harkerware	1960 - 1972
Genuine Quaker Maid Cook Ware Harker China Co. East Liverpool, Ohio USA Trademark	Ca. 1965

307

HOMER LAUGHLIN CHINA CO.,
East Liverpool, Ohio, USA (1877 - present)

1886+	Ca. 1900	Ca. 1900	1901 - 1915
1901 - 1915	Ca. 1907	Ca. 1914	1926 - present
Ca. 1934	Ca. 1935	1935 - 1941	1935 - 1950
1935 - 1955	Ca. 1936	1936 - 1973	Ca. 1939
Ca. 1939	Ca. 1940	1940 - 1946	1940 - 1965
1941 - 1945	Ca. 1943	1946 - 1960	Ca. 1949

308

Skytone by Homer Laughlin USA
1950 - 1960

Washington Family
Ca. 1953

Dura-Print
Ca. 1953

Bountiful Harvest by Homer Laughlin
Ca. 1955

HL Made in U.S.A.
Ca. 1955

Big Pay-Off Dinnerware / Designed by Bess Myerson
Ca. 1957

Triumph
Ca. 1960

Golden Wheat
Ca. 1960

Homer Laughlin China Co. Color Harmony Dinnerware
Ca. 1965

Alvarado Ironstone by Homer Laughlin
Ca. 1965

Hand Painted Homer Laughlin Made in U.S.A.
Ca. 1965

USA
Ca. 1970

Homer Laughlin
1970 - 1980

A.E. HULL POTTERY CO.,
Crooksville, Ohio, USA (1905 - present)

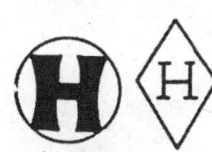

H
1910 - 1935

H (diamond)

Hull Pottery Crooksville Ohio
1930s

A.E. HULL
1930s

Early American All Spice Made in USA
1937 - 1944

Hull U.S.A.
Ca. 1950

Marcrest Oven Proof Quality Made in USA
1950s

Regal
1952 - 1960

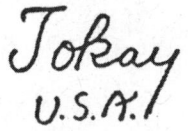

Tokay U.S.A.
1958+

Coronet U.S.A.
1960+

Imperial U.S.A.
1960+

309

EDWIN M. KNOWLES
East Liverpool, Ohio, USA (1900 - 1963)

1900 - 1948

Ca. 1905

1910 - 1948

1925 - 1931

1929+

1929+

1934+

1934+

Ca. 1935

1953+

1955 - 1957

Ca. 1956

1957 - 1963

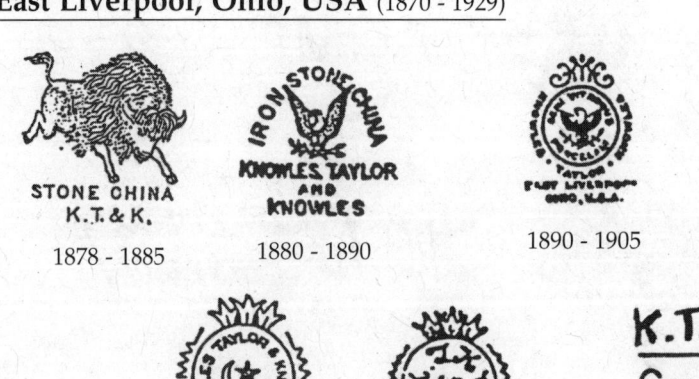

1959+

KNOWLES, TAYLOR & KNOWLES
East Liverpool, Ohio, USA (1870 - 1929)

1878 - 1885

1880 - 1890

1890 - 1905

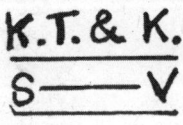

1890 - 1907

1891 - 1898

1891 - 1898

Ca. 1925

LENNOX INC.
Trenton, New Jersey, USA (1906 - present)

| 1906 - present | 1970+ | current | current | current |

NEWCOMB POTTERY
New Orleans, Louisiana, USA (1896 - 1945)

1895 - 1910   1896 - 1945

REDWING POTTERY
Redwing, Minnesota, USA (1878 - 1967)

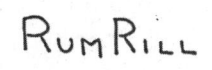

1930+   1933 - 1938   1935+   1935+   Ca. 1967

ROOKWOOD POTTERY
Cincinnati, Ohio, USA (1880 - 1967)

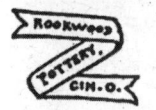

1880 - 1882   Ca. 1881

Rookwood began using the "RP" mark in 1886 adding a flame a year beginning in 1887 until 1900.

Beginning in 1901 the year was indicated in Roman numerals below the mark.

1881 - 1882   ROOKWOOD 1882   1882+

1880 - 1934   Ca. 1883   Ca. 1883

311

ROSEVILLE POTTERY CO.,
Zanesville, Ohio, USA (1892 - 1954)

AZUREAN
1900+

RPCo
1900+

ROZANE WARE
Ca. 1904

ROZANE RPCo
Ca. 1904

ROZANE WARE
Ca. 1905

Fujiyama
Ca. 1906

PAULEO POTTERY
1914+

RV
1914 - 1930

DONATELLO R.P.Co.
1915+

Roseville
Ca. 1930

R U.S.A.
1935 - 1954

ROSEVILLE ROZANE WARE POTTERY
1939 - 1953

Raymor by Roseville U.S.A. OVENPROOF PAT. PEND.
1950s

Lotus
1950s

ROYAL CHINA CO.,
Sebring, Ohio, USA (1933 - present)

ROYAL CHINA INC. SEBRING. OHIO
1933 - present

UNION MADE SEBRING OHIO U.S.A. 22 K. GOLD
1934 - 1935

ROYAL CHINA INC. SEBRING OHIO U.S.A.
1934 - 1960

ROYAL TRADE MARK COPYRIGHTED WARRANTED 22-K GOLD GOLD CREST
1934 - 1960

ROYAL SEBRING CHINA OHIO WARRANTED 22-K GOLD
1934 - 1960

"Royal" OvenServe Guaranteed 100% ovenproof
1938 - 1951

ROYAL CHINA WARRANTED 22 KT. GOLD
Ca. 1940

SHELL PINK by ROYAL CHINA G. SEBRING, OHIO
Ca. 1940 - Ca. 1950

1940 - 1955    1940 - 1955    1940 - 1960    1950 - 1960

1951 - 1960    Ca. 1968    Ca. 1970

SALEM CHINA CO.,
Salem, Ohio, USA (1898 - 1967)

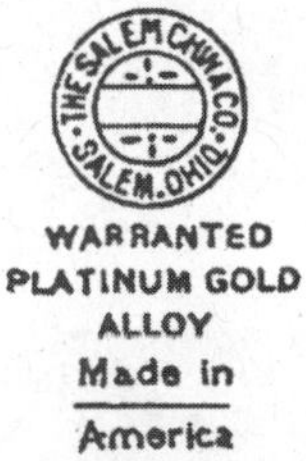

1918+    1918+    Ca. 1940    1940s

1940s    1940+ 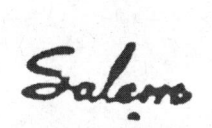   Ca. 1960    Ca. 1970

SEBRING POTTERY
East Liverpool, Ohio, USA (1887 - 1948)

Ca. 1895    Ca. 1895    1890 - 1905    Ca. 1900

313

Ca. 1905

1900 - 1935

Ca. 1920 - 1935

Ca. 1925

Ca. 1925 - 1940

Ca. 1925 - 1942

Ca. 1925 - 1943

STANGLE POTTERY
Trenton, New Jersey, USA (1929 - 1978)

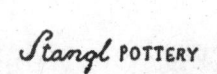

Ca. 1930

Ca. 1941

Ca. 1972

STERLING CHINA CO.,
East Liverpool, USA (1917 - present)

STERLING CHINA
Ca. 1920 - 1972

Ca. 1940

Ca. 1945 - Ca. 1955

Ca. 1946 - present

1947 - 1948

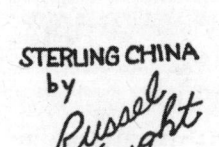

Ca. 1949

Ca. 1949

1951 - 1976

1951 - 1976

1951 - 1976

Ca. 1972

STEUBENVILLE POTTERY CO.,
Steubenville, Ohio, USA (1879 - 1960)
Trenton, New Jersey, USA (1929 - 1978)

Ca. 1879 - Ca. 1904

Ca. 1900+

Ca. 1900

Ca. 1904

1904+

Ca. 1904

Ca. 1904

Ca. 1905

1920s - 1930s

1939+

Ca. 1960

Ca. 1960 - 1978

SYRACUSE CHINA CORP.
Syracuse, New York, USA (1871 - present)

1886 - 1898

1893 - 1898

1930+

1935+

1966+

Ca. 1972

1972+

315

TAYLOR, SMITH & TAYLOR
East Liverpool, Ohio, USA (1901 - present)

1901 - 1935

1908 - 1915

Ca. 1920

Ca. 1925

Ca. 1928 - 1945

Ca. 1935

1935 - 1981

1937 - 1950

1938 - 1945

Ca. 1957

Ca. 1960

Ca. 1960

1963 - 1968

Ca. 1965

Ca. 1970

Ca. 1970

Ca. 1970

Ca. 1972

Ca. 1972

VERNON KILNS
Vernon, California, USA (1912 - 1958)

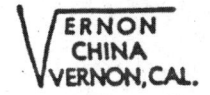

1912+

1912 - 1931

1930s

1930s

1930s

1930s

1931+

1935 - 1939

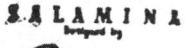

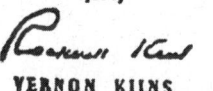

1938 - 1940

1942 - 1947

1945 - 1958

1947+

1947+

1947 - 1956

Ca. 1950

Ca. 1950

1950 - 1954

Ca. 1953/54

1955

1955 - 1958

1956+

1956 - 1960

317

WELLER POTTERY
Zanesville, Ohio, USA (1882 - 1948)

aurelian WELLER
1895 - 1915

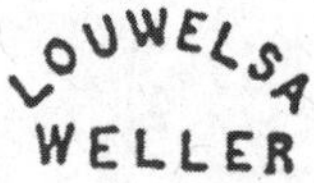

LOUWELSA WELLER
1895 - 1918

TURADA WELLER
1897 - 1898

DICKENS WARE WELLER
1897 - 1910

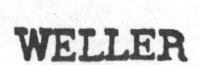

WELLER
1900 - 1925

SICARDO WELLER.
1902 - 1907

Weller Rhead Faience
Ca. 1903

FLORETTA WELLER
Ca. 1904

WELLER
Ca. 1910

ART NOUVEAU WELLER
Ca. 1910

LOUWELSA WELLER — WELLER POTTERY — WELLER WARE
1920s

WELLER WARE
1920+

WELLER POTTERY
Ca. 1925

Weller Pottery
Ca. 1928

Weller Pottery Since 1872
1935+

318

British Designed Art and Studio Pottery

Examples of ceramics by Clarice Cliff

Art Critic and writer John Ruskin, and poet and artist William Morris helped to evolve the thinking that it was time for craftsmen to create individual pieces instead of remaining in what they considered had become a monotonous production style. With their encouragement, what is known as **Art Pottery** began to be produced in England around 1865 in the manner of the Arts and Crafts movement.

Mostly created from small potteries with often only one or two workers, the larger potteries like Spode and Doulton became influenced by the new styles and designs and started creating their own in-house art departments.

In the 1920s the name **Studio Pottery** came into being to differentiate those pieces made and decorated by the same person, as opposed to those designed by one person and decorated by another.

Among the marks shown, Charlotte Rhead, Bernard Leach and Lucie Rie are acknowledged to be among the highest regarded studio potters.

C.J.C. BAILEY & CO., Fulham, London (1864 - 1889)

ALAN CAIGER-SMITH, (born in Argentina)
London (1932 - 1955); **Berkshire** (1955 - 1993)

From 1959 the Aldermaston Pottery, Berkshire included a year mark. After 1993 he worked on his own.

Aldermaston Pottery mark with 1959 year mark.

MICHAEL AMBROSE CARDEW (1901 - 1983)
Winchombe Pottery, Gloucestershire 1926 - 1944.

CARTER & CO. (1873 - 1962)
Name changed to Poole Potteries Ltd., Dorset, 1962 -

HANS COPER
Born in Germany, he fled the country in 1939. Worked with Lucie Rie in London, 1946 - 1959. Worked on his own at Frome, Somerset 1963 - 1979, then ceased production.

1946 - 1959. London with Lucie Rie.

1967 - 1979. Frome, Somerset.

KENSINGTON FINE ART POTTERY, Hanley, Staffordshire (1892 - 1899)

BERNARD LEACH (1887 - 1979)

Leach Pottery, St. Ives, Cornwall. 1920 - 1972. Also worked at Shinners Bridge, Dartington, Devon.

Impressed seal mark. A circular version also occurs, ca. 1921+.

Personal marks of Bernard Leach, 1921 - .

Painted mark, 1940 - .

MINTON'S ART POTTERY, Kensington Gore, London (1871 - 1875)

Printed mark on wares decorated at Minton's short-lived London Art Pottery Studio, ca. 1871-5.

BERNARD MOORE (1850 - 1935)

St. Mary's Works, Stoke-on-Trent, Staffordshire 1867 - 1905. Made earthenware and porcelain. Wolfe Street, Stoke-on-Trent, Staffordshire 1905 - 1915. After 1905 was only a decorator.

Painted mark, 1905 - 1915.

Painted or printed mark, 1905 - 1915. The year may be added to these marks.

WILLIAM STAITE MURRAY (1881 - 1962)

Worked at several English potteries 1912 - 1939. Made studio-type earthenware an stoneware pottery.

Impressed mark, 1919 - 1940. Also has incised or painted signature mark in writing letters, with year added 1919+.

321

CHARLOTTE RHEAD (1885 - 1947)

Designer and outstanding exponent of tube lined wares. Worked at several potteries including Wardle & Co., Hanley 1901 - 1905; Keeling & Co., Dale Hall Works, Burslem 1905 - ?; Wood & Sons, Burslem 1912 - (including a subsidiary); Ellgreave Pottery Co. Ltd., - 1926; Burgess & Leigh 1926 - 1931; A.G. Richardson, Gordon Pottery 1931 - 1942.

Ellgreave Pottery Co. Ltd.
Lottie Rhead ware c.1923

Among the many marks to be found.

LUCIE RIE (1902 - 1995)

Born in Vienna, moved to England in 1938. Albion Mews, London 1939 - 1995. Made simple, distinctly feminine vases and tableware in porcelain and stoneware. Also some jewelry.

Incised or impressed mark, 1938 -

DELLA ROBBIA POTTERY, Birkenhead, Cheshire (1893 - 1906)

Started by Harold Rathbone who made earthenware tiles and plaques in Art Nouveau style.

1894 - 1901. Also could include an initial above which would relate to the decorator.

DELLA ROBBIA *Impressed or incised mark 1894 - 1901*

SPODE, Stoke-on-Trent, Staffordshire (1784 -)

Copeland & Garrett, 1833 - 1847; W.T. Copeland (sons), 1847 - 1976; Royal Worcester Spode Ltd., 1976 - .

For further marks please refer to the Ceramics section.

COPELAND

TORQUAY TERRA-COTTA Co., Hele Cross, Devon (1875 - 1909)

WARDLE AND Co. LTD., Hanley, Staffordshire (1871 - 1935)*

Printed mark, ca. 1890 - 1935.

Printed mark, ca. 1902 - 1909.

* Retitled Wardle Art Pottery Co., Ltd. in 1910 and continued at Stoke as a branch of A.J. Robinson, 1910 - 1924; and to 1935 as a branch of Cauldon Potteries Ltd. at Shelton.

The Potter's Art in China

Ming Dynasty, Xuande period, 1426-1435.

In the early stages of all civilizations, in order to supply some practical need or to convey a messge, the craftsman is called on to exercise his skill and ingenuity. His successors learn by experience to render their work more fit for its purpose, and, in addition, the more sensitive individuals among them naturally seek to please the eye. At some periods of development the perfect fitness of the object is achieved, and it is fortunate if such a period is a prolonged one, for all too frequently the craftsman, having obtained mastery of his material, is tempted to satisfy himself by the liberal use of all his media with the attendant danger of over elaboration and extravagance which eventually leads to decline and decadence. The development of the potter's art in China has followed the normal course of the rise and decline of aesthetic achievement.

In the case of Chinese ceramics, fortunately, there is no need for unanimity of opinion as to the period of "perfect fitness;" some will find it in the excellence of material and delicacy of design of the 17th and 18th century porcelain whilst others will prefer the inventiveness and vigour of the Ming artist or the austerities of the classic periods of Sung, T'ang, and Han.

PRINCIPAL PERIODS OF CHINESE ART

with brief notes on the development of ceramics.

B.C. 1122-255 - Chou Dynasty
Unglazed pottery of archaic form.

B.C. 206-A.D. 220 - Han Dynasty
Pottery usually of bronze form and covered with a deep green glaze.

A.D. 368-557 - Wei Dynasty
Unglazed pottery, usually decorated with pigment and tomb figures of individual form.

A.D. 618-907 - T'ang Dynasty
Glazed pottery in great variety of form and colour. Tomb figures of men, women, horses, camels, and other animals. True porcelain was first made in this period.

A.D. 960-1280 - Sung Dynasty
Many fresh centres for the manufacture of porcelain appear to be active in this period. The chief productions were Ting yao, Ju yao, Lung Ch'uan yao, Chün yao, and Tz'u Chou yao. Stoneware decorated with overglaze enamels was first made at Tz'u Chou.

A.D. 1280-1368 - Yüan Dynasty
A period of comparative inactivity; decoration in underglaze cobalt blue probably commenced.

A.D. 1368-1644 - Ming Dynasty
Underglaze copper red introduced. Polychrome, "san t'sai" (three colour) and "wu t'sai" (five colour) decoration "sur biscuit" or on glazed porcelain. Porcelain and stoneware also decorated in coloured glazes in the "cloisonne" style. New monochrome glazes were invented. Underglaze blue decoration developed with occasional use of "Mohammedan blue." Celadon was made at Chu-Chou.

A.D. 1644-1912 - Ch'ing Dynasty
The inventions of the Ming period developed to "famille vert," "famille juane," and "famille noire."

K'ang Hsi, 1662-1722. Blue and white porcelain brought to perfection. Fine monochrome glazed porcelain produced. Lang yao "sang de boeuf," apple green, "claire de lune," mirror black, etc.

Yung Cheng, 1723-1736. Famous for egg-shell porcelain. "famille rose" decoration commenced. Fine monochromes made. Earlier styles copied.

Ch'ien Lung, 1736-1796. "famille rose" the prevailing style. Range of monochromes and transmutation glazes considerably extended.

Chia Ch'ing Tao Kuang, 1796-1851, Graviata ware and a few fine monochromes made. Polychrome decoration became over elaborated.

PERIOD MARKS

In the six-character period marks the first two characters, reading downward from right to left, name the dynasty, the second two, the Emperor's reign title, and the third two, which are constant to all, mean "period made." With the four-character mark the dynasty is omitted.

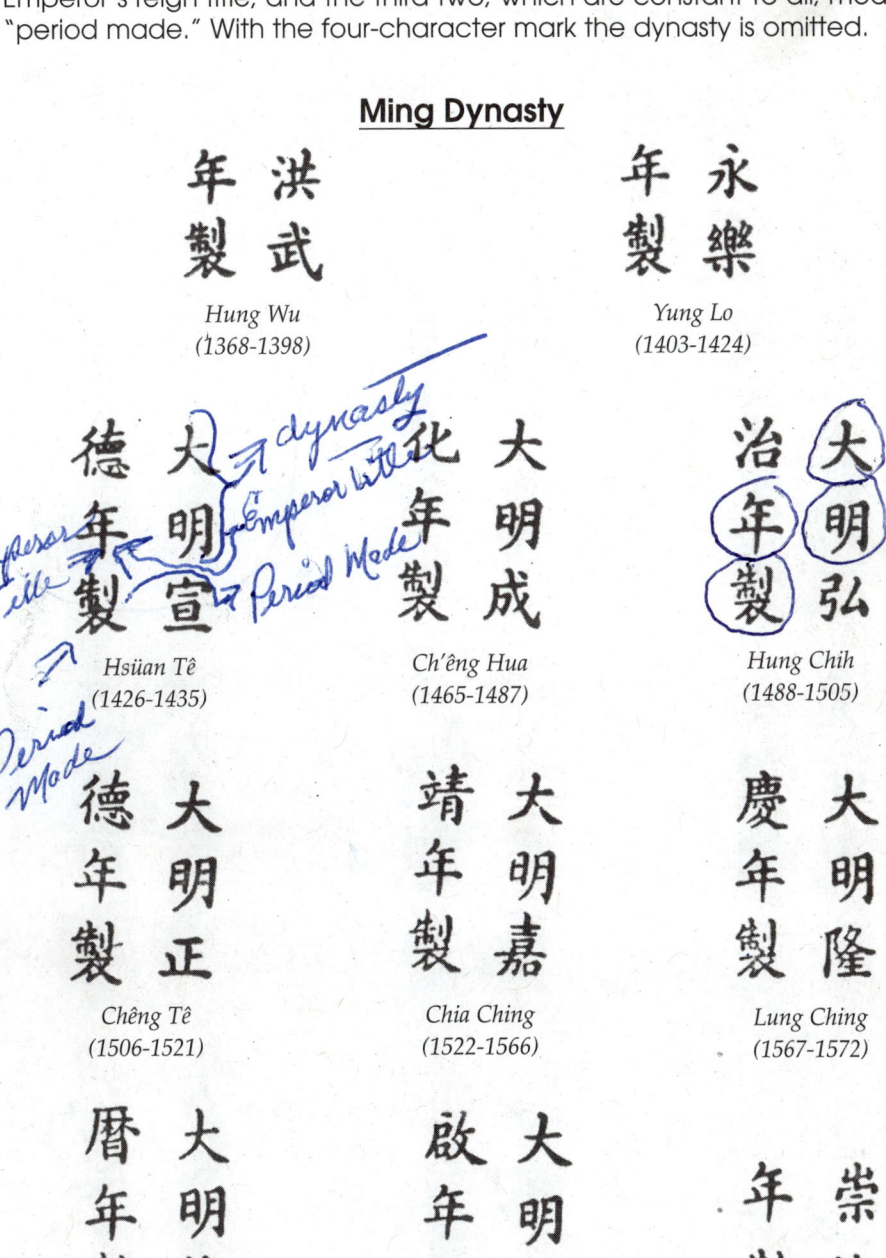

Ming Dynasty

Hung Wu
(1368-1398)

Yung Lo
(1403-1424)

Hsüan Tê
(1426-1435)

Ch'êng Hua
(1465-1487)

Hung Chih
(1488-1505)

Chêng Tê
(1506-1521)

Chia Ching
(1522-1566)

Lung Ching
(1567-1572)

Wan Li
(1573-1619)

T'ien Ch'i
(1621-1627)

Ch'ung Chên
(1628-1643)

Ch'ing Dynasty

Shun Chih
(1644-1661)

K'ang Hsi
(1662-1722)

Yung Chêng
(1723-1735)

Ch'ien Lung
(1736-1795)

Chia Ch'ing
(1796-1820)

Tao Kung
(1821-1850)

Hsien Hêng
(1851-1861)

T'ung Chih
(1862-1873)

Kuang Hsii
(1874-1907)

Hsüan T'ung
(1908-1912)

Hung Hsien
Name adopted by Yüan
Shih Kai in 1916.

PERIODS CLASSIFIED BY DYNASTIES AND EMPERORS

Earlier Periods

Chou Dynasty . . . . 1122-255 B.C.
Ch'in Dynasty 255-206
Han Dynasty . . . . .206 B.C.-220 A.D.
Wei Dynasty 386-557
Sui Dynasty .589-618
T'ang Dynasty 618-907
Sung Dynasty 960-1280
Yuan Dynasty 1280-1368

Ming Dynasty

Hung Wu .1368-1398
Yung Lo 1403-1424
Hsüan Tê .1426-1435
Ch'êng Hua 1465-1487
Hung Chih 1488-1505
Chêng Tê .1506-1521
Chia Ching 1522-1566
Lung Ch'ing 1567-1572
Wan Li 1573-1619
T'ien Ch'i 1621-1627
Ch'ung Chên 1628-1643

Ch'ing Dynasty

Shun Chih .1644-1661
K'ang Hsi .1662-1722
Yung Chêng 1723-1735
Ch'ien Lung 1736-1795
Chia Ch'ing 1796-1820
Tao Kuang 1821-1850
Hsien Fêng 1851-1861
T'ung Chih 1862-1873
Kuang Hsü 1874-1907
Hsüan T'ung 1908-1912
Hung Hsien (Yüan Shih Kai) 1916

SEAL CHARACTERS

Yung-Chêng
(1723-1735)

Ch'ien Lung
(1736-1795)

Chia Ch'ing
(1796-1820)

Tao-Kuang
(1821-1850)

Hsien Fêng
(1851-1861)

T'ung Chih
(1862-1873)

Kuang Hsü
(1874-1907)

The British Registry Mark

Beginning in 1842 decorative art designs were registered at the patent office in Britain. The British Registry Mark is a method for dating decorated metal, wood, glass and ceramic items.

A diamond shaped mark was used from 1842 until 1883, with the aid of several tables the date of registry is determined.

In 1884 a simpler method of marking the registry date was introduced. Design registry numbers preceded by the letters "Rd. No." were marked on a decorative piece, the year of registry is determined by referring to one chart.

Other countries are known to have used the British Registry Mark. Japanese makers used a red painted design representing the mark. Haviland & Co. registered some of their porcelain designs and shapes in England and Limoges wares were exported by them to the United States and Canada. The mark "H & Co." or the full name are found with the registration mark. The date cypher does not indicate the exact year the wares were made as the registration protected the maker's design for three years and was renewable.

1842-1867

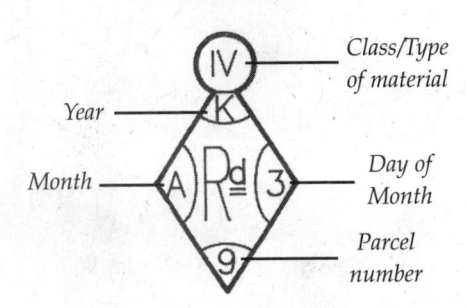

Diagram labels:
- Year
- Month
- Class/Type of material
- Day of Month
- Parcel number

Year of Manufacture

X - 1842		E - 1855	
H - 1843		L - 1856	
C - 1844		K - 1857	
A - 1845		B - 1858	
I - 1846		M - 1859	
F - 1847		Z - 1860	
U - 1848		R - 1861	
S - 1849		O - 1862	
V - 1850		G - 1863	
P - 1851		N - 1864	
D - 1852		W - 1865	
Y - 1853		Q - 1866	
J - 1854		T - 1867	

Month of Manufacture

C - January
G - February
W - March
H - April
E - May
M - June
I - July
R - August
D - September
B - October
K - November
A - December

Type of Material or Class

I - metal
II - wood
III - glass
IV - ceramics

PARCEL NUMBER: Indicates person or company who registered the design.

1868-1883

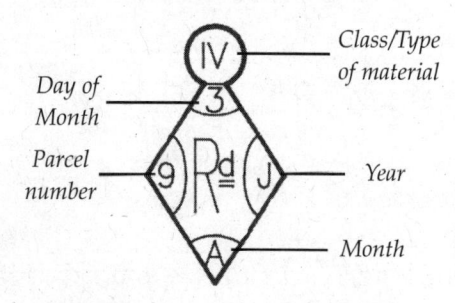

- Day of Month
- Parcel number
- Class/Type of material
- Year
- Month

Type of Material or Class
I - metal
II - wood
III - glass
IV - cermaics

Year of Manufacture
X - 1868   V - 1876
H - 1869   P - 1877
C - 1870   D - 1878
A - 1871   Y - 1879
I - 1872   J - 1880
F - 1873   E - 1881
U - 1874   L - 1882
S - 1875   K - 1883

Month of Manufacture
C - January   I - July
G - February   R - August
W - March   D - September
H - April   B - October
E - May   K - November
M - June   A - December

PARCEL NUMBER: Indicates person or company who registered the design.
NOTE: From March 1, to 6, 1868 the registration letter for the month was G – for the year W.

Registry numbers came into use after 1883.

Jan-01	Regd No.	Jan-01	Regd No.	Jan-01	Regd No.
1884	1	1926	718057	1968	934515
1885	19754	1927	726330	1969	939875
1886	40480	1928	734370	1970	944932
1887	64520	1929	742725	1971	950046
1888	90483	1930	751160	1972	955342
1889	116648	1931	760583	1973	960708
1890	141273	1932	769670	1974	965185
1891	163767	1933	779292	1975	969249
1892	185713	1934	789019	1976	973838
1893	205240	1935	799097	1977	978426
1894	224720	1936	808794	1978	982815
1895	246975	1937	817293	1979	987910
1896	268392	1938	825231	1980	993012
1897	291241	1939	832610	1981	998302
1898	311658	1940	837520	1982	1004456
1899	331707	1941	838500	1983	1010583
1900	351202	1942	839230	1984	1017131
1901	368154	1943	839980	1985	1024174
1902	385180	1944	841040	1986	1031358
1903	403200	1945	842670	1987	1039055
1904	424400	1946	845550	1988	1047478
1905	447800	1947	849730	1989	1056076
1906	471860	1948	853260	Jul-1989	1061406
1907	493900	1949	856999	Aug-1989	2000000
1908	518640	1950	860854	1990	2003720
1909	535170	1951	863970	1991	2012047
1910	552000	1952	866280	1992	2019933
1911	574817	1953	869300	1993	2028110
1912	594195	1954	872531	1994	2036116
1913	612431	1955	876067	1995	2044229
1914	630190	1956	879282	1996	2053113
1915	644935	1957	882949	1997	2062102
1916	653521	1958	887079	1998	2071420
1917	658988	1959	891665	1999	2080159
1918	662872	1960	895000	2000	2089190
1919	666128	1961	899914	2001	2098476
1920	673750	1962	904638	Dec-2001	2106868
1921	680147	1963	909364	Dec-2001	3000001
1922	687144	1964	914536	2002	3000396
1923	694999	1965	919607	2003	3009769

BRITISH MONARCHY ACCESSION and CORONATION DATES

CROWNED

William I (Ca. 1027 - 1087) . . . . December 25, 1066
William II (Ca. 1056 - 1100) . . . . December 26, 1087
Henry I (1068 - 1135) . . . . August 5, 1100
Stephen (Ca. 1097 - 1154) . . . . December 26, 1135
Henry II (1133 - 1189) . . . . December 19, 1154
Richard I (1157 - 1199) . . . . September 3, 1189
. . . . and April 17, 1194
John (1167 - 1216) . . . . May 27, 1199
Henry III (1207 - 1272) . . . . October 28, 1216
Edward I (1239 - 1307) . . . . August 19, 1274
Edward II (1284 - 1327) . . . . February 25, 1308
Edward III (1312 - 1377) . . . . February 1, 1327
Richard II (1367 - 1400) . . . . July 16, 1377
Henry IV (1366 - 1413) . . . . October 13, 1399
Henry V (1387 - 1422) . . . . April 9, 1413
Henry VI (1421 - 1471) . . . . November 6, 1429
Edward IV (1442 - 1483) . . . . June 28, 1461
Edward V (1470 - 1483) . . . . Never Crowned
Richard III (1452 - 1485) . . . . July 6, 1483
Henry VII (1457 - 1509) . . . . October 30, 1485
Henry VIII (1491 - 1547) . . . . June 24, 1509
Edward VI (1537 - 1553) . . . . February 20, 1547
Mary 1 (1516 - 1558) . . . . October 1, 1553
Elizabeth I (1533 - 1603) . . . . January 15, 1559
James I (1566 - 1625) . . . . July 25, 1603
Charles I (1600 - 1649) . . . . February 2, 1626
Charles II (1630 - 1685) . . . . April 23, 1661
James II (1633 - 1701) . . . . April 23, 1685
William III (1650 - 1702) . . . . April 11, 1689
    & Mary II (1662 - 1694) . . . . April 11, 1689
Anne (1665 - 1714) . . . . April 23, 1702
George I (1660 - 1727) . . . . October 20, 1714
George II (1689 - 1760) . . . . October 11, 1727
George III (1738 - 1820) . . . . September 22, 1761

	ACCESSION	CROWNED

George IV (1762 - 1830) . . . . January 29, 1820 . . . . . . July 19, 1821
William IV (1765 - 1837) . . . . June 26, 1830 . . . Septemebr 8, 1831
Victoria (1819 - 1901) . . . . June 20, 1837 . . . . . . June 28, 1838
Edward VII (1841 - 1910) . . . . . . January 22, 1901 . . . . . . August 9, 1902
George V (1865 - 1936) . . . . May 6, 1910 . . . . . . June 22, 1911
Edward VIII (1894 - 1972) . . . . . . January 20, 1936 . . . . Abdicated
. . . . December 11, 1936
. . . . Never crowned
George Vi (1895 - 1952) . . . . . December 11, 1936 . . . . May 12, 1937
Elizabeth II (1926 -   . . . . February 6, 1952 . . . . June 2, 1953

U.S. Patent Number Reference Table

Year	Invention#	Design#	Year	Invention#	Design#	Year	Invention#	Design#
1836	1		1888	374,720	17,995	1940	2,185,170	118,358
1837	110		1889	395,305	18,830	1941	2,227,418	124,503
1838	546		1890	418,665	19,553	1942	2,268,540	130,989
1839	1,061		1891	443,987	20,439	1943	2,307,007	134,717
1840	1,465		1892	466,315	21,275	1944	2,338,081	136,949
1841	1,923		1893	488,976	22,092	1945	2,366,154	139,862
1842	2,413		1894	511,744	22,494	1946	2,391,856	143,386
1843	2,901	1	1895	531,619	23,922	1947	2,413,675	146,165
1844	3,395	15	1896	552,502	25,037	1948	2,433,824	148,267
1845	3,873	27	1897	574,369	26,482	1949	2,457,797	152,235
1846	4,348	44	1898	596,467	28,113	1950	2,492,944	156,686
1847	4,914	103	1899	616,871	29,916	1951	2,536,016	161,404
1848	5,409	163	1900	640,167	32,055	1952	2,580,379	165,568
1849	5,993	209	1901	664,827	33,813	1953	2,624,046	168,527
1850	6,981	258	1902	690,385	35,547	1954	2,664,562	171,241
1851	7,865	341	1903	717,521	36,187	1955	2,698,434	173,777
1852	8,622	431	1904	748,567	36,723	1956	2,728,913	176,490
1853	9,512	540	1905	778,834	37,280	1957	2,775,762	179,467
1854	10,358	628	1906	808,618	37,766	1958	2,818,567	181,829
1855	12,117	683	1907	839,799	38,391	1959	2,866,973	184,204
1856	14,009	753	1908	875,679	38,980	1960	2,919,443	186,973
1857	16,324	860	1909	908,436	39,737	1961	2,966,681	189,516
1858	19,010	973	1910	945,010	40,424	1962	3,015,103	192,004
1859	22,477	1,075	1911	980,178	41,063	1963	3,070,801	194,304
1860	26,642	1,183	1912	1,013,095	42,073	1964	3,116,487	197,269
1861	31,005	1,366	1913	1,049,326	43,415	1965	3,163,865	199,955
1862	34,045	1,508	1914	1,083,267	45,098	1966	3,226,729	203,379
1863	37,266	1,703	1915	1,123,212	46,813	1967	3,295,143	206,567
1864	41,047	1,879	1916	1,166,419	48,358	1968	3,360,800	209,732
1865	45,685	2,018	1917	1,210,389	50,117	1969	3,419,907	213,084
1866	51,784	2,239	1918	1,251,458	51,629	1970	3,487,470	216,419
1867	60,658	2,533	1919	1,290,027	52,836	1971	3,551,909	219,637
1868	72,959	2,858	1920	1,326,899	54,359	1972	3,631,539	222,793
1869	85,503	3,304	1921	1,364,063	56,844	1973	3,707,729	225,695
1870	98,460	3,810	1922	1,401,948	60,121	1974	3,781,914	229,729
1871	110,617	4,547	1923	1,440,362	61,748	1975	3,858,241	234,032
1872	122,304	5,452	1924	1,478,996	63,675	1976	3,930,271	238,315
1873	134,504	6,336	1925	1,521,590	66,346	1977	4,000,520	242,881
1874	146,120	7,083	1926	1,568,040	69,170	1978	4,065,812	246,811
1875	158,350	7,969	1927	1,612,700	71,772	1979	4,131,952	250,676
1876	171,641	8,884	1928	1,654,521	74,159	1980	4,180,867	253,796
1877	185,813	9,686	1929	1,696,897	77,347	1981	4,242,757	257,746
1878	198,733	10,385	1930	1,742,181	80,254			
1879	211,078	10,975	1931	1,787,424	82,966			
1880	223,211	11,567	1932	1,839,190	85,903			
1881	236,137	12,082	1933	1,892,663	88,847			
1882	251,685	12,647	1934	1,941,449	91,258			
1883	269,820	13,508	1935	1,985,878	94,179			
1884	291,016	14,528	1936	2,026,516	98,045			
1885	310,163	15,678	1937	2,066,309	102,604			
1886	333,494	16,451	1938	2,104,004	107,738			
1887	355,291	17,046	1939	2,142,080	112,765			

Invention Patent: Granted for something not previously known and or/existing.

Design Patent: Granted for a new appearance to a manufctured article which enhances its saleability.

Index

CERAMICS

A & S 182
A B J & S 219
A B J & Sons 219
A Bros 183
A P 246-248
A R 205
Acadia Pottery 294
Adams 181
Adderley Floral China Works 250
Adderleys 181
Admiral Line 265
Ahrens, J. H. 294
Albion Pottery 294
Alcock - *See Majolica* 290
Alexander Pottery 237
Allerton 182
Aluminia 255
American Limoges China Co 223
Arcadian 182
Arcadian China 182
Arkinstall & Sons 182
Ashworth, G L & Bros
  - *see also Mason's and Morley* .. 183
Atlas 214
Aucanada 302
Aynsley 184
Azurean 312
B & G 188
B F B 282
B P 305
B P & Co 294
B S Mfg Co Ltd 295
Bailey, C.J.C. & Co. 320
Bailey, F. 294
Bakerite 307
Ballard, Orrin L 294
Baltimore Steam Packet Co. 265
Barr Flight Barr 282
Bedford 250
Beech, G 294
Belding 295
Belleek 184-186
Belleville Pottery Co 294
Belleville Stoneware Co 294
Bennett - *see Majolica* 290
Bennington 303
Bertrand & Lavoie 294
Beswick 187
Bierenstihl, Adam 294
Bing & Grondahl 188
Bloor 203
Blue Mountain 189

Bock, Jacob 294
Boehler & Weber 294
Boehler, Joseph 294
Bohemian Porcelain 189
Boote, T & R 190
Booths 190
Brantford 295
Brantford Pottery 295
Brantford Stoneware Works 295
Britannia - *see Cochrane* 196
Britannia Pottery Co Ltd 196
Brown, J, J & W.O. 295
Brown, T 295
Brownscombe & Goodfellow 295
Brownscombe, S 295
Brownscombe, W 295
Brown-Westhead Moore
  - *see also Majolica* 191, 290
Buffalo Pottery Co 305
Burgard, F 298
Burns & Campbell 295
Burns, D 295
Burns, J R 295
Burns, S 296
C & F 196
C & F G 196
C & G 267
C B D 193
C D 192
C E P 300
C F 206
C F H 222
C F M 222
C J M & Co 225
C M 228
C M & S 228
C M S P & S 228
C R A 193
C S N 193
C T M 224
C T M & Sons 224
Caiger-Smith, Alan 320
California Navigation
  and Improvement Co. 265
Calypso China 315
Campbell & Sons 296
Canada Potteries Ltd 296
Canton China 315
Cap Rouge 296
Cardew, Michael Ambrose 320
Carefree 315
Caribe 314
Carlton China 280

Carlton Ware Ltd	
- see Wiltshaw & Robinson	280
Carter & Co.	320
Catalina	305
Caughley - see also Coalport	192
Cauldon Ware	191
Cauldon Potteries Ltd.	194
Cauldon Ltd	193
Ceramic Art Co	185
CetemWare	224
Chamberlain & Co	282
Chelsea	194
Chesapeake Pottery Co.	290
Clarice Cliff - see also Wilkinson	195
Classic	310
Classic Heritage	316
Clementson	195
Clews	196
Clio	315
Coalbrookdale	193
Coalport - see Caughley	192
Cochrane	196
Colclough	197
Columbia Chinaware	307
Columbian Art Pottery Co	186
Cook Pottery Co	187
Cooper - see Susie Cooper	269
Copeland	
- see Spode, Copeland, Garrett	267-268
Hans Coper	320
Cornwall Pottery	296
Coronado Pottery	317
Coronet	308
Courtney	203
Coxon Pottery	186
Craftsman	308
Crescent China Co	314
Crescent Pottery	291
Crown Brick & Pottery Works	296
Crown Devon	197
Crown Ducal	198
Crown Staffordshire	198
Cunard White Star Line	266
D S P	258
Dale, C	192
Dartmouth	199
Davenport	199
Davis, John & Son	296
Davis, Joseph	296
Delft	201
Della Robbia Pottery	322
Denby	202
Derby	203, 204
Derby Pottery	296
Detroit & Cleveland Navigation Co.	265
Distel Goedenaagen	211
Dolphin Cruise Line	266
Don	315
Don, Edward & Co	306
Donatello	312
Donath	205
Doulton - see Royal Doulton	257-259
Dresden	205
Dupoma	260
Dux Porcalain Manufactory	189
E L F	246
E M K	310
E S	248
Eberhardt & Halm	296
Eberhardt, Nicholas	296
Eby, William	296
Ecanada	302
Egmondville	298
El Camino	305
Elmsdale Pottery	296
Emery	302
Etruria Pottery	186
Farrar	297
Farrar & Deneau	297
Fenton Stone Works	225
Fenton's Works	303
Fermangh Pottery	184
Ferrybridge Pottery	278
Fielding - see Crown Devon	
- see also Majolica	197, 290
Fiesta	308
Fischer & Meig - see Bohemian	190
Flack & Vanarsdale	297
Fleming	196
Flight	282
Flight & Barr	282
Flight Barr & Barr	282
Foley - see Wileman, Shelley	279
Ford	206
Ford, A B	224
Ford, Charles	206
Ford, Thomas	206
Ford, T C	206
Foreign Backstamps	207
Franciscan Ware	305
Furnival	208
G & C J M	190
G & Co W.	212, 282
G B	214
G B & Co.	297
G Bros.	214
G D A	221
G G & Co	212
G G W	212
G J	90
G McB	305
G T M	237
G W	212
Garrett - see Copeland, Spade	267, 268

Gilbert	303
Gilbert, Eban T	297
Gillespie & Mace	297
GLA Bros	183
Gladding McBean & Co	305
Glass Bros	297
Glough - see Grindley	215
Goebel	209
Goedewaagen	211
Golden Wheat	308
Goold, F P	297
Goss	210
Gouda	211
Grafton - see Jones	219
Grainger	212
Grand Trunk Pacific Steamship Co.	266
Gray A E	212
Gray & Betts	297
Gray & Glass	297
Green	213
Griffen, Smith & Hill - see Majolica	290
Grimwades - see also Royal Winton	214
Grindley	215
Groh, John	297
H & Co	221
H & K	216
H B	246
H B & L	298
H L	308
H P	300
H P Co	307
H R	247
Haas & Czjzek - see Bohemian	190
Hadley's	283
Hallcraft	306
Hall China Co	306
Hall's	306
Hamilton Potteries	298
Hamman	205
Hammersley	215
Hancock & Sons	262
Hancock, Sampson & Sons	262
Handley Bros	298
Harker Pottery Co	307
Harkerware	307
Harlequin	306
Hart Bros & Lazier	298
Hart, W	298
Haviland	221
Haynes - see Majolica	290
Henriot	247
Herculaneum	216
Hewitt & Leadbeater	216
Hiawatha	196
Hirsch	205
Holdcroft - see Majolica	290
Holkirk	216
Hollingshead & Kirkham	216
Homer Laughlin China Co	308
Hull Pottery	217, 309
Humberstone, S T	298
Hummel	210
Huron Pottery	298
Imperial	308
Importers Marks	218
Indian Stone China	228
Ironstone China	225, 300
J & T F	208
J C	195
J F & Co	208
J H	223
J M & S	228
J M S	228
J R & Co	192
Jackson & Gosling	218
Jensen, Georg	89, 90
John, Ernest Creations	306
Johnson Bros	219
Jones, A B & Sons Ltd	219
Jones, George - see Majolica	291
K P M	229
K T & K	310
Keeling	220
Kennedy, J A	298
Kensington Fine Art Pottery	321
Klemm, Richard	205
Knoll - see Bohemian	189
Knowles, Edwin M	310
Knowles, Taylor & Knowles	186, 310
Kokus	313
Kulp, J	299
Lamm	205
Late Spode	267
Laughlin China	308
Lazier, A J	299
Lazier, G I	299
Leach, Bernard	321
Lennox - see Belleek (American)	185
Lenox Inc	311
Lent, B	299
Lessore	275
Limoges	221-223
London Crockery Mfg Co	299
London Pottery	299
Looker&Co	203
Losolware - see Keeling	220
Lotus	312
Lucie Rie	322
Lyman Fenton & Co	303
M 231	
M & B	231
M & Co	231
M & H	232
M & S	229

M S & Co	237
MacIntyre, James & Co	236
Magnet	262
Majestic	308
Majolica	387
Malcom, R	296
Maling	224
Malvern	252
Marcrest	308
Marlatt, J M	299
Mason's - see also Morley	225
McBirney, David & Co	184
McGlade & Schuler	299
Meakin	226, 227
Medalta	299
Meigh	228
Meissen	229, 230
Melba	252
Meyers & Son	205
Minton - see also Majolica	231-234, 291
Minton's Art Pottery	321
Miyao/Miyawo	235
Mooney, J	299
Moorcroft	236
Moore, Bernard	321
Morgan Belleek	186
Morgan Line	266
Morley, Francis & Co	237
Morley, George - see Majolica	291
Morton & Bennet	299
Morton & Co	295, 299
Morton Goold & Co	300
Mountford, George T	237
Murray, William Staite	321
Myott	237
N	205, 264
N C	311
N S	267
N S Pottery Co Ltd	252
N W	276
Nasco	305
Newcomb Pottery	311
Nippon	238
North Staffordshire Pottery	251
Norton	303
Norton & Fenton	303
O H E C	229
O P Co	271
O S	248
Old Bay Line	265
Old Curiosity Shop	312
Old Hall - See Meigh	228
Old Rose	310
Opaque Porcelain	228
Orangeville Pottery	300
Orth D	300
Ott & Brewer	185
Owen Sound Pottery Co	300
P	246
P B	246
P C	246
P E I Pottery	300
Pacific Steamship Co.	265
Palissy	244
Paragon	244
Pauleo Pottery	312
Pearl	276
Charles E Pearson	300
Plant	245
Plazuid	211
Podmore, Walker & Co	278
Poland, Tillowitz	248
Poole	245
Portland Pottery	250
Portmeirion - see Gray	212
Potter's Co-operative Co	205
Prescott, Henry	300
Prescott, James	300
Priscilla	308
Pueblo Pottery	305
Quebec Importers	246
Quimper	246-248
R	253
R & B	282
R & C	253
R & L	252
R C	253
R C & Co	312
R F	264
R H	222
R K	205
R P	311
R P Co	311
R S	248
R S Germany	248
R S Poland	248
R S Prussia	248
R S R	251
R S Tillowitz	248
R V	312
Ram	211
Rathbone, Harold - See Della Robbia	322
Redwing Pottery	311
Regal	309
Regina	211
Rhead, Charlotte	322
Richard - see Crown Ducal	198
Richardsons	300
Ridgway	250-252
Riviera	314
Robinson & Leadbeater	252
Roma	310
Romantic England	227
Rookwood Pottery	311

Rosenthal	253
Roseville Pottery Co	312
Roxon China	316
Royal	312
Royal Bayreuth	254
Royal Cauldon	193
Royal China Co	312
Royal China Works	212
Royal Copenhagen	
- see also Bing & Grondahl	255
Royal Coronaware	262
Royal Crown Derby	203, 204
Royal Doulton	256-259
Royal Dux	260
Royal Grafton	219
Royal Porcelain Manufactory	229
Royal Staffordshire Pottery	279
Royal Tettau	254
Royal Tunstall	278
Royal Vale	252
Royal Winton - see also Grimwades	260
Royal Worcester	282-284
Rozane	311
Rum Rill	311
S	192, 263
S & T	248
S A	255
S H	262
S H & Sons	262
S P	315
S P Co	313, 315
S S	262
Saint-Jean	261
Salem China Co	313
Salopian	192
Sampson Hancock & Sons	262
Sampson Smith	262
Schegelmilch, Erdman	248
Schegelmilch, Oscar	248
Schegelmilch, Reinhold	248
Schoonhoven	211
Schuler, H	300
Schwab, W	300
Sebring Pottery	313
Select	308
Sevres	263, 264
Shelley	265
Ship's China	265
Silhouette	271
Simcoe Street Pottery	300
Skinner, S	301
Smith, William & Co	275
Soho	266
Spode, Copeland, Garrett	267, 268, 323
St Johns Pottery	297
St Johns Stone Chinaware Co	300
St Johns Stoneware	297

Stangl Pottery	314
Star Pottery	301
Sterling China Co	314
Steubenville Pottery Co	315
Stevenson & Hancock - see Derby	203
Stevenson Sharp & Co	203
Stone Chinaware Co	300
Sturdi Ware	313
Sumida	269
Sun-Glow	307
Susan Cooper	269, 270
Sutherland Pottery	290
Swan and Soho - see Booths	190
Swan China	206
Swinnertons	270
Syracuse	271
Syracuse China Corp	315
T & C F	206
T & R B	190
T B & S	190
T F	206
T F & Co	208
T F Sons	208
T H	221
T S & T	316
T S T	316
Tara Pottery	301
Taylor, J W	301
Taylor, Smith & Taylor	316
Taylorstone	316
Taylorton	316
Tettau Porcelain Factory	254
Thieme, Carl	205
Thompson - see Majolica	291
Thun - see Bohemian	189
Tillsonburg Pottery Co	301
Tilson, F B	301
Tokay	309
Toronto Pottery Co	272, 273
Torquay	272, 273
Torquay Terra Cotta Co	323
Trent Pottery	291
Triumph	308
Tropico Pottery	305
Tudor Rose	308
Tujiyam	312
Turner	192
Tuscan - see Plant	245
U S P	303
Ultra Dine	314
Ulysses Cruise Line	266
United States Pottery Co	303
Vale	252
Vernon China	317
Vernon Kilns	317
Vernon's	317
Vernonware	317

Vitrilain	278
W & B	275
W & C	279
W & Co	274
W & R	275
W G	209
W H G	210
W M	236
Wacolware	278
Wade	274
Wagner, Joseph	301
Wardle - see Majolica	291
Wardle and Co. Ltd.	323
Warner & Co	301
Weber, J B	301
Wedge Wood, John	278
Wedgwood - see also Majolica	275-278, 291
Welding	295
Welding & Belding	301
Welding, W E	301
Weller	318
Weller Pottery	318
Wells	308
White & Handley	301
White Star Line	266
Wild Rose	308
Wileman - see Foley, Shelley	279
Wilkinson, Arthur J	279
Willets Mfg Co	186
Wilson, Norman	276
Wiltshaw & Robinson	280
Wolfsohn	205
Wood	281
Woodyatt & Co	301
Woodyatt, James	295
Wright, Russel	310, 314
Zdekauer - see Bohemian	190
Zenith Gouda	211
Zsolnay	285
Zuid Gouda	211

DOLLS

Alt, Beck & Gottschalck	95
Amberg - see Fulper Pottery Co.	100
Amusement Novelty Supply Co.	95
Armand Marseille	104
Max Oscar Arnold - see Welsch & Co	95
Barbie - see Mattel	104
Bähr & Pröschild	95
Beaver Doll & Toy Co.	95
Beck - see Alt, Beck & Gottschalck	95
Richard Beck & Co.	96
Bisco Doll Company	96
George Borgfeldt & Company	
- see Rose O'Neill's Kewpie	96
Brand Toys & Dolls	
- see Dominion Toy Manufacturing	97
Brophy Doll Company Ltd.	96
Bruyere Toy Mfg. Co. Ltd.	96
Cameo Doll Company	
- see Noma Toys Ltd.	105
C&W Dolls & Pottery Ltd.	96
C.L.S.	96
Canadian Toy & Novelty Co.	96
Celluloid-Fabrik	
- see Rheinische Gummi-Und	106
Cheerio Toy Company	97
Commercial Toy Company	97
Cuno & Otto Dressel	97
Dee an Cee Toy Company Ltd.	97
Dominion Toy	
Manufacturing Company Ltd.	97
Dressel - see Cuno Otto & Dressel	97
The T. Eaton Co. Limited	98
Eaton's Beauty Dolls - see Cuno Otto	
& Dressel, and Jointed Dolls	98
Effanbee Doll Company	98
E.I.H. Co. Inc. - see E.I. Horsman & Co.	101
The Florentine Statuary Company	98
Floradora Dolls	99
Freeman Toy Company	99
The French Art Doll Mfg. Co.	99
Fulper Pottery Co. - see Kewpie Dolls	100
Francois Gaultier	100
Otto Gans	100
Gans & Seyfarth - see Otto Gans	100
Giltoy Company	100
Ginny Dolls - see Vogue Dolls Inc.	110
Goodtime Toys	100
Gottschalck - see Alt, Beck & Gottschalck	95
Hancock & Son	100
S. Hancock & Sons	100
H.B. Co. - see Standard Quality Dolls	100
Hesli	107
Hertwig & Co.	101
Ernst Heubach	101
High-Grade Doll Mfg. Co.	101
Hoffmeister	
- see Schoenau & Hoffmeister.	107
E.I. Horsman & Co.	
- see Fulper Pottery Co.	101
Ideal Dolls	101
Jointed Doll - see Eaton's	102
Jumeau - also see S.F.B.J.	103
Kämmer & Reinhardt	103
Kewpie Dolls - see George Borgfeldt	
& Company, Fulper Pottery Co.,	
Rose O'Neill Tip Top Toy Co.	96, 100, 105
Lloyd-Harlam Toy Co. Ltd.	104
Lloyd Toy Co. - see Lloyd Harlam	104
A. Luge & Co.	104
Mattel - see Dee and Cee	
Toy Company Ltd.	104
Armand Marseille - also see Floradora.	104

My Playmate - see Floradora..........................99
Mighty Star Company Limited
 - see Goodtime Toys. 105
Noma Toys Ltd. 105
NTIBOY..107
Rose O'Neill - see Kewpie Dolls. 105
Cuno Otto & Dressel....................................97
Perfect Doll Company 106
Dr. Dora Petzold...106
Earle Pullan Company 106
Pröschild - see Bähr & Pröschild. 95
Regal Toy Company 106
Reinhardt - see Kämmer & Reinhardt........103
Reliable Toy Company Limited
 - see Dominion Toy Manufacturing. 106
Rheinische Gummi-Und Celluloid-Fabrik ..106
Schildkröt-Puppen
 - see Rheinische Gummi-und. 106
Schmitt & Fils...106
Heinrich Schmuckler 107
Schultz-Marke - see Rheinische
 Gummi-Und Celluloid-Fabrik....................106
Schoenau & Hoffmeister............................107
Schützmeister & Quendt............................107
Scootles 105
S.F.B.J. - also see Francis Gaultier,
 and Jumeau...107
Simon & Halbig
 - also see Welsch & Co...................93, 107
Smith Doll & Toy Co. Ltd. 108
Standard Toys Ltd. (Bowmanville). 108
Standard Toys Ltd. (Hamilton). 108
Standard Quality Dolls 108
Star Doll Manufacturing Company
 - see Goodtime Toys. 108
St. Maurice and Charenton
 - see Francols Gaultier. 100
Margaret Steiff 109
Sunn Rubber Co. - see Viceroy. 109
Thuringia..104
Tilco International Incorp. 109
Tip Top Toy Co. - see Kewpie Dolls. 109
Valentine Doll Company.............................109
Viceroy Manufacturing Company Limited ..109
Victoria Doll & Toy Mfg. Co. Ltd. 109
Vogue Dolls Co...110
Herman Von Berg..110
F. Welsch 110
Welsch & Co. - also see Max Oscar
 Arnold, Simon & Halbig. 110

Glass

A,H, Heisey & Co. 157
Acmelite...148
Acorn 153
Adams & Co..145
Adna 130

Aerators Ltd. 170
Air-O-Lite 147
Akro-Agate 145
Alart & McGuire 167
Alford 131
Almy & Thomas 131
Altaglass 141
Amberina 113
American Arts Products Corp 145
Anchor Glass Co 145
Anchor Hocking Glass................................145
Argy-Rousseau 118
Arkansas Glass Container Corp 145
Armstrong Cork Co. 145
Art Glass 117
Atlas 145
Aurora 146
Averbeck Cut Glass 131
B...144
B F G Co. 142
B G Co 142
B G W 142
B.C. Co. 146
Baccarat 113
Ball Brothers Co. 146
Baltimore Bargain House 131, 146
Banner 146
Bartlett-Collins Co......................................146
B-C 146
Beaumiroir...147
Beaver..147
Beaver Flint Glass Co 138, 142
Beckert, Adolf 120
Belle Vernon Mapes 147
Belleville Cut Glass....................................135
Bergen J D 131
Best Light Co. 146
Bibi & Co. 146
Birks, Henry 135
Blenco Glass Co. 146
Blue Ribbon 146, 147
Bohemian Glass 120
Borgfeldt, Geo & Co. 131, 146, 165
Bottlers Protective Assn.............................147
Bryce Bros. Co. 149
Bryden, Robert 128
Buckley-Newhall Co. 146
Burgun, Schverer & Co 122
Burlington Glass Works 138, 142
Burmese 119
Burr M.S. & Co. 163
C...142
Caledonia Glass Works 138
Cambridge Glass Company 125, 149, 164
Cameo Glass 122
Canada Glass Works 137
Canadian Factories 136

Canadian Glass Mfg. Co	0.14
CanJade	151
Canton Glass	150
Carnival Glass	124
Centennial	150
Centradrink Filters Co.	165
Century Inkstand Co.	151
Chandler Specialty Mfg. Co.	151
Charles Boldt Glass Co.	168
Chatanooga Glass Co.	150
Chicago Heights Bottle Co.	167
Clapperton & Sons	135
Clark T B	131
Clark's Pyramid &	170
Cline, Stanley C.	163
Clover Leaf	151
Cohansey Glass Mfg. Co.	150
Colonial	152
Colony Crystal	149
Community	152
Concord Glass Mfg. Co.	149
Consumers Glass Co	137, 142
Cook & Bernheimer Co.	162
Corning Glass Works	150, 165
Corona Cut Glass Co.	131
Corona Cut Glass Co.	151
Coronet	148
Cricklite	170
Cristallerie d'E	119
Crown Milano	113
Crystal Glass Company	139
Crysto	152
Cut Glass	131
Cyclone	151
D	143
D G Co	142
D'Argental	118
Dault Glass & Crockery Co.	151
Daum	118, 122
DaumNancy	118
Davidson, George & Co.	117
De Goey, C.R.	152
Decker, William M.	157
DeLatte, Andre	118, 122
Derbyshire, John & Co.	117
Deutsche Gasgluhlicht	171
DeVez	119
Diamond Flint Glass Co.	138, 140
Diamond Glass Co	140, 142, 143, 151
Dithridge & Co.	149
Domglas Inc	136
Dominion (Early)	137, 142, 143
Dominion Glass Co.	137, 139, 140
Dorflinger	131, 152
Douglas, Richard & Co.	154
Drysdale, Thomas & Co.	152
Dunbar Glass Corp.	151
Duncan & Miller Glass Co.	151
Dunfee, Hod. C.	158
Duryea & Potter	145
E.	143, 152
E G Co	143
E. & J.	152
E. De La Chapelle & A.M. Paturle	159
E. Gerard, Dufraisseix & Morel	171
Eagle C.E. & Cut Glass Works	154
Ebenezer Cut Glass Co., Inc.	155
Eggington O.F. Co.	152
Egginton	131
Ehrich & Graetz	171
Eisell, Paul	120
Elite	135
Emerald Glass Co.	152
Empire State Glass Co.	152
Emunds & Jones Mfg. Co.	152
Erie Glass Works	138, 143
Excelsior Glass Co	135, 143
Fairmount Glass Works	153
Fairy Light Co. Ltd.	170
Favrile	113
Federal Glass Co.	152
Fenton Art Glass	125, 153
Fine Anco Flint	148
Flögl, Mathilde	120
Foster Bros	137
Foster Glass Works	138
Fostoria Glass	153, 154
Fr. Steuben & Co.	172
Franklin	155
Frederick W. Buning	146
Fredrop	152
Friedlaender, Oscar O.	161
Fry H C	132
G C Co.	135
G. Union Seal W.	162
Galle, Emile	119, 123
Gayner, John William	161
Gebr, Putzler Glass Works	172
General	154
General Automotive Supply Co.	154
General Electric Co.	168
Gill Brothers Co.	148
Gillinder & Sons	155, 156
Gillinder Bros., Inc.	155
Glasbake	154
Gleason-Tiéout Glass Co.	166
Glenshaw Glass Co.	153
Glenshaw Glass Co.	156
Globe	147
Globe	155
Gloria	148
Gotham	149
Gowans & Kent	135
Granite	148

Gravic	156
Greener & Co.	117
Gregory, Mary	126
Grozart Glass Co.	155
Gruder, Blank & Co.	171
Gulfport Glass Corprn	155
Gundersen	128
Gundy - Clapperton	135
H G	143
H G Co	143
H G W	143
Haley Pressware Dir.	155
Hallmark	156
Hamilton Glass Works	139, 143
Hammer	148
Hawkes	132, 156
Hawthorn Mfg. Co.	165
Hazel-Atlas Glass Co.	145, 156
Heckert, Fritz	120
Heisey A H & Co., Inc.	132
Hemingray Glass Co.	147
Hemsley, Alexander	169
Hoare, J & Co.	132, 158
Hobbs	132
Ho-Hi	159
Hope Glass Works	132
Hope Glass Works	158
Houze Glass Corpn.	155
Humphreys Glass Co	137
Hunt	132, 158
Hydro Carbon Co.	147
I X L	143
Ideal	158
Illinios Glass Co.	158
Illinios Pacific Glass Co.	147
Imperial	125, 149, 157, 159
Indiana Glass Co.	158
Iroquois Glass Ltd	144
Irving	132
Japana	158
Jeanette Glass Co.	158
Jefferson Glass Co	140, 161
John Agnew & Sons	145
Josephinenhütte, Gräflinch	120
Justrite	158
Kavalier, Edward	170
Kemple John E. Glass Works	158
Kerr Glass Mfg. Corp.	159
Kimble Glass Products	159
Kirchberger, Moritz	163
Klepa Arts	147
Knox Glass Assocs., Inc.	155
Knox Glass Inc.	160
Koch, Andrew	159
Koehler & Hinrichs	159
Koh-i-noor	159
Kruth China Co.	160
L	132
L C T	130
L C T & Co	130
L G Co	144
L. Rose & Co. Ltd.,	170
L.A. Becker Co.	147
La Bastie	159
La Bastie Glass Co.	153
La Compagne de Cristalleries Baccarat	171
Lackawana Cut Glass	132
Lakefield Cut Glass	136
Lalique, Rene	127
Lamb Glass Co.	160
Lamont Glass Co.	137, 140, 144
Laurel	132
Laurens Glass Works	159
Legrand, Albert	161
LeGras & Cie	119
Leotric	161
Libbey	132, 140, 160
Libbey-St Clair Inc	140
Liberty Glass Co.	159
Lighting Studios Co.	169
Lightning	161
Litch, Wilbur F.	151
Livermore & Knight Co.	168
Lobmeyr, J & L	121
Loetz, Klostermuhle	119
Lornita Glass Corp.	159
Lorraine	152
Lotus	133, 160
Luceo	161
Lucky Cross	148
Lustre	160
Lyons	133
M	144, 161
M T W G Co	119, 133
M.B.W.	161
M.V. Garnsey	158
Macbeth-Evans	146, 149, 157, 159
Majestic Cut Glass	133
Mallorytown Glass Works	139
Manitoba Glass Mfg Co	139, 144
Manitoba Glass Works	139, 140
Maple City Glass Co	133
Mariani & Co.	162
Marion Flint Glass Co.	162
Marion Glass Mfg. Co.	162
Martin, Henry	162
Mckee Glass Co.	154
Mckee-Jeanette Glass Works	166
Mcpike Drug Co.	152
Medallion	163
Mehlem, Franz A.	172
Meriden Cut Glass	133
Merritt Glass Co.	162
Metro Glass	161

344

Metro Glass & China Dec. Co.	162	Pairpoint	128, 133
Meyr's Neffe	121	Palmer, Austin D.	164
Michel	123	Pantin (E S Monot)	119
Mid-West Glass Co	139	Parche, P X & Son	133
Miller, Edward & Co.	162	Parian	148
Modoc	148	Passow & Sons	164
Monarch	148	Pennsylvania Glass Products Co.	164
Monart Glass	117	Perilstein, H	166
Moncrieff, John Ltd.	117	Philadelphia Vacuum	165
Monogram Glass Co. Inc.	161	Phillips, George & Co	136
Moonlight Patent Lamp Co.	170	Phoenix Glass Co.	165
Morganstown Glassware Guild	164	Pierce Glass Co.	165
Moser, Ludwig & Sohne	119	Pilgrim Glass Corp.	165
Moser, Ludwig & Sons	121	Pilkington Bros. Ltd.	170
Mosser	125	Pitkin & Brooks	133
Mount Vernon	162	Pittman-Drietzer & Co.	149
Mountainee Glass Co.	162	Power, Edward A. & Co.	168
Mt Washington Glass Co	113, 119, 133	Price's Patent Candle Co.	170
Mueller, Freres	119	Protective "Freflo" Stopple Co.	152
Mult-Flex	163	Putnam, Henry W.	161
Murr, Richard	159	Quaker City Cut Glass Co	133
Mygatt, Otis A.	165	Queen	147
Napanee Glass Works	139	Queen's Burmese	118
Nash, A Douglas	129	Quezal	113
National Glass Mfg. Co.	163	Quicksilver Mining Co.	164
National Stamping	164	R	135, 166
Nearcut	164	R G Co T	144
New Brunswick Glass Co	137	Reid, Bros.	166
New England Glassworkers	113	Resistal Ultra	150
Newark	133	Richards Glass Co.	144
Noblac	154	Richardson's of Wordsley	117
Norec	153	Rigo	144
North American Glass Co	138	Roberts & Matthews	164
Northwestern Glass Co.	164	Rock	148
Northwood	117, 125	Roden Bros	135
Northwood, Harry	125	Rose Amber	113
Nova Scotia Glass Co	140	Royal Brierly Crystal	118
Novil Nultra	150	Royal Glass Co.	166
NS	170	Rumpp C F & Sons Inc	166
Nulite	164	Rutherford & Co	143
Obear-Nester Glass Co.	163	S	134
Oertel, Johann & Co.	121	S & W	117
Oil City Glass Co.	164	S T L	144
OK	148	S W	117
Old Sol	165	S. Maw, Son & Sons	170
Oneida Community Ltd.	152	Samson	148
Ontario Glass Works	139	Sandwich & Boston Glass Co	126
Ottawa Cut Glass	136	Schaffgotsch'sche	120
Ottawa Glass Works	137	Schloss Crockery Co.	166
O-U-Kid	164	Schmidt & Co.	167
Our Darling	156	Schneider	119, 123
Ovington Bros. Co.	165	Schott & Gen	121
Owen-Illinios Glass Co.	155	Schott & Gen.	172
Owens-Illinois Glass Co.	161	Schverer, Burgun & Co	122
P	133, 165	Seneca Glass Co.	167
P & B	133	Signet	134
Pacific Coast Glass Works	165	Signet	167

Silex Co.	168
Silver City Glass	154
Silver City Glass Co., Inc.	168
Sinclaire, H P & Co	134
Sloan Glass Co.	167
Smalley, Kilan & Onthank	147
Socony	149
Solar Prism Co.	167
Sowerby John	117
Specialty Co.	165
St John's Glass Co.	138
St Lawrence Glass Company	136, 138
St. Gobain	171
Standard Glass Co.	147
Standard Oil Co.	149
Steam Guage & Lantern Co.	151
Sterling	134
Steuben	119, 134, 145, 150
Stevens & Williams	117, 124
Straus	134
Strauss L. & Sons	167
Stuart Glass Works	170
Sudan	168
Sun Vapor Street Light Co.	169
Sun-Flash	169
Susquehanna Glass Co.	156
Sydenham Glass Co	139
Syl-Fau Art Glass Co.	168
T B	134
T G Co	144
T G D Co.	129
T. DeForest, Charles	147
T. G. Hawkes & Co.	156
T.B. Clark & Co.	151
T.G. Cook & Co.	150
Taylor	134
Taylor, Smith & Taylor Co.	167
Tharaud, Justin	166
Thatcher Glass Mfg. Co.	167
The Best	149
The McBride Glass Co.	161
Theresienthal	121
Thomas Wightman	168
Tiffany, Louis Comfort	129
Tiffin Art Glass Corp.	167
Tobin, J.W.	169
Tongue R.E. & Bros.	160
Tonneau	167
Toronto Glass Co.	139
Tuthill	134
Tweed, Douglas J.	155
Unger Bros.	134
Unicorn	148
United Grocers Co.	168
United Jewellers Inc	156
United States Glass Co.	154, 166
Universal Glass Products Co.	169
Val St Lambert	119
Van Heusen, Charles	134
Van Houten, Erskine B.	169
Vancleave, Robert A.	164
Veluria	154
Victoria Glass & Bottle Co	139
Viking Glass Co.	169
W & W	118
W.H. Hamilton Co.	156
Wallaceburg Cut Glass Co	136
Walter, Almaric	118
Warren Fruit Jar Co.	165
Washington Co.	168
Webb	118, 124
Webb-Corbett	118
Weiss & Biheller Ltd.	171
Welsbach Co.	163
Westbrook, Florence Talbot	169
Westmoreland Specialty Co.	169
Wheaton Glass Co.	168
Wheaton, T.C. Co.	161
Wheelcock C.E. & Co.	168
Whichway	169
Whitall, Tatum & Co.	161
White Star	148
Wiener Werkstätte	122
Woodhall	124
Wright Rich Cut Glass	134
Wright, L G	125
Zenith	149

Silver

A & E	63
A & J HAY	8
A B	61
A C J & B	61
A H	65
A J R	62
A K & S	61
A M	9
A P	10
A PAGE	10
A R	20
A S H	8
A S HAY	8
A T	21
Acme Plate Company	45
Acme Silver Co., The	37
Addison, Charles	36
Agnew, James	6
Allan, Thomas	49
Allen, Josiah	6, 11
Amiot, Jean Nicolas	64
Amiot, Laurent	64
Anderson, Robert	23
Arms & Quigley	37
Arnoldi, Charles	49

Arnoldi, John Peter	49
Arnoldi, Michael	49
B B E	15
B E	15
B ETTER	15
B H	16
B HURD	16
B M CO	48
B P & B	12
B P M CO	48
B W	6
Baker, T. H	33
Barlow, Edouard	50
Barry, John	6, 7
Baume, Gustave La	11
Bean, John	50
Beaudry, Narcisse	50
BEAVER	32
Becker & Cornelius	11
Beemer & Newbury	31
Begnay, Jean Baptiste	64
Bell, Wm	37
Benedict Ptoctor Mfg. Co	48
Bennett, John B	11
Bessonett, J. S. B	11
Bewes, Daniel	64
BILSKY & SON	60
Birks, Henry & Sons	50, 55
Bishop, Henry	23
Black & Parker	11
Black, Parker & Black	12
Black, Wm. A & S	11
Bohle, David	50
Bohle, Francis	50
Bohle, Peter	50
Boivin, Louis Phillipe	51
Bolton, Thomas	12
Booth, John	6
Boure, Narcisse	64
Braun, F B	12
Breadner Manufacturing Co	48
Breadner, S	31, 48
BREMNER	53
Brothers, Wm	6
Brown & Co., M S	13, 61
Brown, George Stairs	12
Brown, Michael Septimus	12, 13, 60
Brown, T B	13
Brown, Thomas	12, 13
Bruff, Charles Oliver	23
BULL DOG BRAND	29
Burns, James	6, 7
Butler, James	13
C & J A	49
A & J ALLEN	11
C A	49
C A O	37, 62
C E R	62
C O B	23
Camirand J D & Co	51
Campbell, A	31
CANADA MFG. CO	38
Canadian Jewellers Ltd	51
Canadian Wm. A Rogers Limited	38
Caron Bros	51
CARON FRERES	51
Carter, J F	31
Christmas, D S	64
Claringbowl, Fred	32
COMMUNITY PLATE	35
Cornelius & Co	14
Cornelius Becker & Co	24
Cornelius, Julius	14
Couture, Pierre	64
Crawford, William	14
CROWN SILVER PLATE CO.	38
Cruickshank, Robert	51
D & S	52
D B	50, 64
D G	23
D H W	22
D L	8
D M M	62
D MILLER	62
D S CO	30
D SAVAGE	31
D W	10, 22
Darling, George	37
Davis, Henry	33
Denman & Bohle	51
DERBY SILVER CO	30, 38
Desroche, Alfred	51
Dewey, William	33
Dingman, James F	31
DUCHESS PLATE	43
Dwight & Savage	52
Dwight, James Adams	52, 53
E & T S	20
E G W & S	28
E M M	42
E S	20
EAGLE BRAND	38
Eastwood, James	22
ED BARLOW	50
1847 Rogers Bros	24
Ellis, James	64
Ellis, James E	39
Ellis, P. W. & Company	39
Etter, B B	15
Etter, Benjamin	15
EUREKA SILVER CO	25
F B	50
F M	18
F R	67

347

F S	67
F W S	32, 62
F W S & B	62
Fairbanks, Whitcombe	6
Fletcher, W S	23
FORBES PLATE	24
G B	61
G G R & CO	62
G H	8
G L DARLING	37
G RODGERS	43
GS	44
G S & S	54
G S B	12
G SEIFERT	62
G W	22
G WARREN	62
Gano, David	23
Gard, Thomas Dapleton	6
Gatien, M	64
Geddie, John	23
Gendron, P	64
Goldsmith's Stock Co. of Canada	40
Grigg, William	15
Grothe, Z	65
H & A S	62
H & E	40
H & L	58
H & P	16
H B & CO	60
H C	52
H G B	23
H J	40
H M	19
H R S & CO	53
H S M	62
Hall, George A	15
Hamman, Thomas	15
Hanna & Delagrave	65
Hanna, James	65
Hanna, James Godfrey	65
Hardy, Anselm	65
Harris, E B	65
Harwood, Arthur	6
Hay, A & J	8
HEIRLOOM	35
Hemming Mfg. Co	52
HENDERY & LESLIE	61
Hendery, Robert	58
HENRY ROGERS SONS & CO	53
Herbin, John Frederic	23
Hersey, John A	8
Hill & Houghton	40
HOLMES & EDWARDS	28, 40
Hosterman & Parker	16
Hosterman, Thomas	16
Hull, E Mrs	65
Hulsman, Louis	16
Hunt, William	16
Hunter, William	65
Hurd, Benjamin	16
Hurd, Nathaniel	16
Hutchinson, Georg G	8
I A	64
l A D	52
l B	13
I F L	66
I M	9
I O	66
I S	27
I S CO	28
Inlaid Silver Co	40
INLAID SILVER PATD	40
Innes, William	65
INSICO	27
INTERNATIONAL SILVER CO	28
Internation Silver Co. of Canada Ltd	45
INTERNATIONAL SILVER COMPANY	27
INTERNATIONAL STERLING	27
J & B	7
J A	6
J A D	52
J A H	8
J B	6, 11
J B W	63
J C	14
J C C	61
J CORNELIUS	14
J D CAMIRAND & CO	51
J E	22
J E E	39
J ELLIS	64
J F	61
J F C	31
J F D	31
J G J & CO	40
J H	65
J H J & CO	61
J HURD	16
J L	36
J LESLEY	36
J LESLIE	36
J M	8
J MC	18
J MUNRO	9
J R	42
J R & CO	63
J R H & CO	61
J RAMAGE	32
J W	47
J W M & CO	61
J ZIMMERMAN	63
J FROLAND	61
Jackson, Henry	40

348

Jeanneret, Robert J	33
JOHN WANLESS & CO	47
Johnson, Thomas Charles	17
Joseph, J G & Co	40
Judge, Michael	31
K & T	62
K T	8
KENT BROS	41
Kent, Ambrose & Sons Ltd	41
KERR & THORNE	8
L & A	41
L & C	41
L A	64
L H	16
L P B	51
Labaume, Gustave	11
Lafrance, Ambroise	66
Lambert, Paul	66
Lamontagne, Michael	66
Landron, Jean Francois	66
Langford, Jas. I	17
LASH & CO	41
Lash, J B	41
Learmont, William	52
Lee & Chillas	41
Lees, George H	32
Leslie, John	36, 61
Lesperance, Pierre	66
Lido Jewellers Co	52
Lord, Daniel	8
Lowe & Anderson	41
LOWE & CO	61
Lowe, Wm. G H	41
Lucas, Joseph	66
M & B	61
M A	49
M B CO	25
M C	61
M C D	18
M COCHENTHALER	61
M G	64
M GAGE	61
M L GURD	61
M S B	13
M S B & CO	61
M S BROWN & CO LTD	13, 61
Malone, William	31
Marks, N M	36
Marsters, R U	18
Martyn, John, Mrs	66
McCullock, John	18
McDonald, Daniel	18
McLaughlin, Samuel	66
McNaught & Lowe	41
Melick, James Godfrey	8
Melrose, George	18
MERIDEN B CO	26

Meriden Britannia Co. Ltd	24
MERIDEN S P CO	26
Meriden Silver Plate Co	42
Meves, Otto	52
Meyer & Bolton	12
Meyer, Franz F	18
Mignowitz, Henry	19
MILLER	53
Miller & Bremner	53
MONARCH SILVER CO	28, 45
MONARCH SILVER PLATE CO	42
Morgan, C P	23
Morin, Paul	66
Morphy, Edward M	42
Munro, Alex	9
Munro, John	9
N B	10, 64
N BEAUDRY	50
N F NICKEL SILVER 1877	33
N F SILVER CO 1877	34
N M MARKS	36
N MARKS	61
Newman, William Herman	19
NIAGARA FALLS CO 1877	33
Niagara Falls Silver Co	33
Niagara Silver Co	33
Nordbeck, Peter	12, 19
NORMAN PLATE	46
NOVA SCOTIA SILVER C B & CO	24
O & H	37
O L	22
O MEVES	52
Oliver, Richard Kestell	42
Olmstead, C A	37, 62
ONEIDA	34
ONEIDA COMMUNITY	35
ONEIDA LTD	35
Oneida Ltd	34
Oneida Silversmiths	35
ONEIDACRAFT	35
Orkney, James	66
Osborne, Robert	32
P A	49
P B	50
P E P	62, 67
P L	66
P M	66
P N	12, 19
P W ELLIS	39
Page Bros	9
PAGE SMALLEY & FERGUSON	9
Page, Amos	10, 23
Page, David	10, 23
Page, Jacques	66
Page, Smalley & Ferguson	9
Page, Thomas	10, 11
Paradis, Roland	67

349

Peacock, Henry	53
PELTON	62
PIECES OF 8	30
PINETREE	30
POST	42
Post, Jordan	42
Poulin, P E & Co	62, 67
Powis, Thomas	67
R & B	30
R C	51
R H	58
R H TWEEDELL	24
R HENDERY	58
R K O	42
R O	32
R OSBORNE	32
R P	67
R S	54
R SHARPLEY	54, 62
R SHARPLEY & SONS	55, 62
R T	9
R U MARSTERS	18
R W & CO	63
R W & S	32
Ramage, John	32
Ranvooyze, Ignace Francois	67
RELIANCE	35
REXPLATE	35
RIDEAU PLATE	56
Robinson, Joseph & Co.	42
Roden Bros., Ltd.	43
Rodgers, G	43
Rogers, Henry, Sons & Co.	53
Rogers, William & Son	24
Rogers, Wm. A	33, 34
Rosenthal, A J	37, 62
Rosenthal, Abraham	44
Ross, Adam	20
Ross, J	20
Round, John & Co	63
Russell, Richard	32
Ryrie Birks	44
RYRIE BROS	44, 60, 62
Ryrie, James	44, 60
S & S	55
S A S	62
S B	31
S B S	61
S B W	63
S C	46
S H M & CO	55
S L & CO	54
S W S	31
Sargent, S J	44
Sasseville & Orkney	67
Sasseville, Francois	67
Sasseville, Joseph	67
Saunders, Lorie & Co	44
Saunders, S & A	44
SAVAGE	54
SAVAGE & LYMAN	54, 62
SAVAGE LYMAN & CO	54, 62
Savage, David	31
Savage, George	44, 53
Saxton, John	44
Schindler, Jonas	67
SEIFERT	62
Seifert, Gustavus	60, 68
Sharpley, Rice	54, 62
Sharpley, Rice & Sons	55, 62
SHEFFIELD HOUSE	45, 68
SILVER METAL	35
Simeon L & George H Rogers Company	34
Simpson, Hall, Miller & Co	26, 55
Smith, S. W.	31
Sovereign Plate	45
Spahn, Justin	6
Spanenberg, Frederick W	32
Spanenberg, George	32
Spanenberg, S A	32
Spike, Edmun Lloyd	20
Spike, Thomas Daniel	20
STANDARD "S" CO	26
STANDARD SILVER CO LTD	45
Standard Silver Co	45
Stanley & Aylward Ltd	45
Stennet, Wm	32
Stephanis, Gothelf	20
Sterling Craft Ltd	46
Stern, Samuel	46
Sterns, Edwin	20
T A	49
T A & CO	49
T B	21
T B BROWN	13
T B STEACY	62
T C J	17
T C J & S	17
T C JOHNSON & SONS	17
T H	16
T HAMMAN	15
T S P	63
Taggart, Frank	46
TASKER & SONS	62
THE ACME SILVER CO	37
THE HIGHLAND BRAND	26
THE TORONTO SILVER PLATE COMPANY	46, 63
Thompson, Richard	9
Toler, Joseph	21
Toronto Silver Plate Company	46, 63
TORSIL	46
Tracy, William H	37
Troop, Alexander	21

TUDOR PLATE	35
Tully, Henry Wentworth	21
Tweedell, Richard Henry	24
V & W	21
Veith & Witham	17, 21
Veith, William James	17, 21
VENNING	10
Venning, J H	10
Venning, William Norris	10
VIANDE	27
VICTOR SILVER COMPANY	30
VIKING PLATE	47
W & P M	62
W A & S B	11
W B	7
W BRAMLEY	60
W C	14
W C M	61
W F	7
W G YOUNG	63
W H	65
W H K	61
W H KEARNEY	61
W H N	21
W H NEWMAN	21
W H S	62
W H TRACY	37, 62
W I	65
W L	52
W LEARMONT	52
W R	35
W S P CO	29
W S W	63
W V	21
W W	63
WALKER	63
Wallace & Balcom	21
Wanless, John	47, 63
Ware, D T & Co	33
Ware, T P & Co	32
Warlock, Daniel O L	10
WATROUS MFG CO	26
WATSON	62
WELCH & TROWERN	47
Whiston, David Hudson	22
White, T & Son	47
WILCOX	27
Witham, George	22
WM A & S BLACK	11
WM A ROGERS	33
Wolhaupter, Benjamin	6
Y S & CO	6
Z G	65
Z MCN & CO	62
Zimmerman & McNaught & Co	63
SILVER, HALLMARKED	72
Birmingham	76, 77
Chester	78
Dublin	87
Exeter	79
Glasgow	88
Jubilee Mark 1934/45	74
London	80-82
Newcastle	83
Sheffield	84, 85
York	86